DEALING WITH DRINK

DEALING WITH DRINK

ALCOHOL AND SOCIAL POLICY:
FROM TREATMENT TO MANAGEMENT

Betsy Thom

FREE ASSOCIATION BOOKS / LONDON / NEW YORK

First published in 1999 by
Free Association Books
57 Warren Street, London W1P 5PA

A catalogue record for this book is available from
the British Library

ISBN 1 85343 449 3 hbk; 1 85343 450 7 pbk

Designed, typeset and produced for Free Association Books by
Chase Production Service, Chadlington OX7 3LN
Printed in the EC by TJ International, Padstow

TO BILL AND ELLIE

Contents

Preface

In 1998 the Department of Health announced that it was preparing a new strategy on alcohol to set out a practical framework for a positive response to the recognised health and social harms associated with alcohol misuse (DoH 1998a). The announcement came at a time when policy statements on wider public health, social welfare and community safety issues regularly included alcohol misuse as an important factor contributing to personal and community harms and national costs (DoH 1998b; Acheson 1998; Mental Health Foundation 1996; All Party Group on Alcohol Misuse 1995).

Consumption of alcohol has risen over the past fifty years from around 4.9 litres per capita absolute alcohol in the early 1950s to around 7.6 litres in the 1990s (Royal College of Psychiatrists 1979; Brewers and Licensed Retailers Association 1997). Over the same period, many other changes have taken place – in perceptions of the alcohol problem, in the nature and size of the target groups for intervention and in the structure and delivery of services, in lay and professional approaches to prevention and treatment, and in government responses to pressures for action. Rising consumption and perceptions of alcohol-related harm alone are insufficient to explain the changes which have occurred or the ways in which governments and government departments have responded. Current policy statements and approaches to dealing with the unwanted effects of alcohol use have emerged from a long process of interaction between many stakeholders and the drive to formulate and implement policy based on consultation and consensus is likely to encounter many of the same tensions and barriers which have attended earlier efforts.

My interest in alcohol policy arose initially from my own observations and experience as a sociologist in alcohol research and from an interest in debates and issues highlighted in the alcohol literature. With the exception of work by Baggott (1990; 1986; undated) and Heather and Robertson (1985) there had been few attempts to document the history of contemporary (post 1950) alcohol policy in the UK or to examine alcohol policy within the wider framework of social and political change. Almost ten years have passed since I began research for the PhD on which this book is based and the last decade has witnessed a growing interest in alcohol policy and increasing pressure on government to develop a national strategy (Alcohol Concern 1999; Society for the Study of Addiction 1999). This book starts from the premise that, however great the changes which have taken place, alcohol policy today is embedded in the past. In examining evolution and change in policy formation and implementation in the alcohol field, the intention is to enhance understanding of current approaches to dealing with the adverse effects of alcohol consumption.

At the same time, this account of alcohol policy provides a case study which will be useful to those who have an interest in how social policies emerge, change and develop. How do issues move on and off policy agendas? Why do some policy statements fail to be implemented? What is the role of civil servants, professional leaders, or pressure groups in policy formation? How do inter-departmental tensions or the conflicting interests of different social groups influence policy objectives and policy outcomes? To what extent is policy 'evidence based'? These are some of the questions which are raised and illustrated through an examination of alcohol policy over the past fifty years.

Certain limitations and boundaries must be acknowledged at the outset. The study focuses on tracing changes in treatment policy in England. In this respect it complements Baggott's work which analyses shifts in the wider alcohol policy arena prior to the 1980s. A number of important trends and influences have been recognised but warrant more detailed examination. These include the inter-relationship between the development of drugs and alcohol policy, the role of the World Health Organization, the influence of international policy networks in the cross-national transfer of models of policy and practice, and consideration of the role of the alcohol industry on policy formation in recent years. Hopefully, the present study sets the scene and provides a framework for future analyses.

The study uses information drawn from a range of sources including public records, files of information on alcohol from the Ministry of Health, and documentary material from a number of archival collections and collections of private papers. These sources are listed with the references. Interviews and correspondence with individuals active in the alcohol field during the period covered by the research, informal 'chats' and chance discussions at meetings provided invaluable accounts of the course of events and a diversity of perceptions and interpretations of the factors influencing policy development. The voices heard in the resulting history belong to those with some influence within their own spheres of activity – as hospital consultants or professional leaders, as directors of services, as researchers and writers and as civil servants. However, the interpretation of events and any conclusions drawn are entirely the responsibility of the author.

I am indebted to a great many people for their assistance. Special thanks are due to those who gave generously of their time and thoughts and to those who offered access to personal papers: Sir Donald Acheson, Mr Larry Ackroyd, Dr Peter Anderson, Ms Sue Baker, Dr Alan Cartwright, Mr Timothy Cook, Mr John Duffy, Professor Griffith Edwards, Ms Maggie Findlay, Ms Victoria Fitch, Professor Hugh Freeman, Dr Max Glatt, Sir George Godber, Ms Judy Graham, Mr Larry Harrison, Professor Nick Heather, Ms Celia Hensman, Dr Brian Hore, Dr Norman Imlah, Dr Dilys Jones, Ms Sue Kenton, Professor Neil Kessel, Mr David Kitchen, Ms Elspeth Kyle, Mrs Penny Lee, Dr Gloria Litman, Ms Ann MacIntyre, Dr Stephen MacKeith, Dr P. Madden, Mrs Maryse Metcalf, Dr Marsha Morgan, Dr Jim Orford, Ms Shirley Otto, Dr Denis Parr, Dr Richard Phillipson, Dr Benno Pollak, Dr Raj Rathod, Ms Fiona Richmond, Professor David Robinson, Dr Robin Room, Mr Derek Rutherford, Dr Terry Spratley, Dr Anthony Thorley, Dr Ron Wawman, and interviewees who preferred to remain anonymous. Professor Ilana Crome provided moral support and advice and Professor Gerry Stimson facilitated a period of study leave. I was able to work full-time on the research as a PhD student between January 1991 and June 1992 thanks to a grant from the Economic and Social Research Council (Grant number R000232736), and I benefited from the continuing support and friendship of my PhD supervisor, Professor Virginia Berridge. The staff of Alcohol Concern library, The Institute of Alcohol library, The Joseph Rowntree Foundation library and the Wellcome Institute for the History of Medicine, Contemporary Archives Centre, were especially helpful in locating information. Finally, I would like to thank Bill Thom and Eleanor Thom for letting me believe it was all worthwhile.

1 Dealing With Drink:
From Alcoholism Treatment to the
Management of Alcohol Problems

Alcohol Treatment Prior to the National Health Service

The concept of alcoholism as a disease amenable to treatment dates back only to the nineteenth century. Prior to that time, heavy drinking and habitual drunkenness were simply facts of life. Symptoms and experiences which became known as 'alcoholism' or 'addiction', were known and recorded in earlier periods, but the conceptualisation of the problem as a criminal or moral offence led to a response centred on the punishment or moral reform of the wrongdoer (MacAndrews 1969; Levine 1978). The concept of 'treatment' became relevant around the beginning of the nineteenth century when the emerging medical profession formulated existing medical and common-sense wisdom into a distinctly new paradigm which explained habitual drunkenness or inebriety as a 'disease of the mind' to be managed by 'the discerning physician' (Trotter 1804 cited in Porter 1985).

This new way of interpreting the experience and behaviour of drunkards was closely linked with broader developments in eighteenth- and nineteenth-century thinking, especially in the understanding of deviance and mental illness. The mid-eighteenth century had witnessed the beginning of a differentiation in the 'needy' and 'deviant' members of society who began to be separated out and placed into various categories of institutional restraint – prisons, workhouses and asylums, each under the supervision of 'expert' groups of professionals. Habitual drunkards were more commonly found among the inmates of these institutions than in any facility able to respond to their specific treatment needs. The problems they caused made their incorporation increasingly difficult and contributed to attempts to separate them into special 'inebriate asylums', where, it was thought, they might be cured by methods being pioneered by the emerging psychiatric profession (Radzinowicz and Hood 1986; McLaughlin 1991). But it was not until the passing of the Habitual Drunkards Act of 1879 that state-funded residential treatment was made available. Under the Act, certified inebriate reformatories were set up to provide treatment for non-criminal inebriates. In addition, state inebriate reformatories were established as institutions of 'last resort' for difficult, violent or unresponsive inmates of the certified reformatories. The regime practised in the reformatories was based on hard work, structured leisure, good diet and firm authority with the aim of rehabilitation to an abstinent lifestyle. Attempts were made to secure compulsory treatment of habitual drunkards – a proposal which was to recur in the post-war period – but met with little success. The reformatories, for reasons which have been discussed elsewhere, were a resounding failure; they ceased to function by the beginning of the First World War having housed only 4590 inmates (the majority of them women – 81 per cent according to one source) in twelve reformatories over the entire period of their existence (Hunt *et al.* 1987; Berridge 1990).

Both in the US and in England, views had differed from the start on the nature of the new disease and on the goals of treatment. One view held that habitual drunkenness was amenable to 'temperate living' which permitted the drinking of some liquors in moderation. Pioneered by Benjamin Rush in the US, this was the approach favoured by the early temperance movement. But the dominant model, which emerged in the course of the century and was adopted in the reformatories, drew its inspiration both from Rush and from the British physician, Thomas Trotter; it stressed 'loss of control', 'compulsive activity' and an abstinence goal as central concepts in the treatment response (Harrison 1971; Porter 1985). By the end of the nineteenth century, the conception of inebriety as a disease, with recognisable physical symptoms, had come to include the element of heredity and was linked to degeneration theory. Belief in abstinence as the cure was strengthened and the temperance movement shifted towards total abstinence as a lifestyle. There were still advocates of moderate drinking within the temperance movement and the medical profession, but they lacked the powerful public image and political connections which were being fostered by the abstinence lobby (Bynum 1984; Rutherford 1991). Nearly a century later, this early divergence of opinion was to be rekindled in the 'controlled drinking' debate which, in the 1970s, came to challenge the prevailing disease concept of alcoholism and the abstinence goal of treatment.

The nineteenth century also witnessed the emergence of different perspectives on the role of state intervention in responding to excessive alcohol consumption. One strand of thought, associated with the temperance movement and with public health physicians, linked inebriety with deprivation and poverty and stressed the importance of legislative and environmental reform as a national priority – although, as Williams and Brake (1980, pp. 8–11) point out, there was considerable divergence of opinion even within the temperance movement regarding the pursuit of prohibition as a legislative objective. A second strand of thought was associated with doctors organised in the Society for the Study of Inebriety, which had been formally established in 1884. This stressed the notion of inebriety as an individually focused, physiological disease to be cured. Advocates of the approach espoused an institutional solution to treatment, limiting the role of government intervention to the legislation and funding of treatment facilities (MacLeod 1967). These two perspectives on responses at national level to excessive alcohol consumption – preventive and curative – and the tensions between them are themes which become particularly important again in the period following the Second World War.

At the same time, although nineteenth-century perspectives on the problem and its solution differed, the individuals concerned with eliciting a public and policy response to inebriety moved in overlapping networks, linking the institutional and organisational bases from which pressures for change developed. This, too, was to be a feature of the post-war alcohol arena although the professional and social backgrounds of individuals involved in the policy community and policy networks around alcohol and the organisational bases from which they came were to broaden and change during the latter half of the twentieth century.

By the beginning of the twentieth century, the visibility of drinking problems and public drunkenness, which had provided much of the impetus behind medical and temperance campaigns, was on the wane. Legislation passed at the turn of the century to control the worst excesses, reforms to tackle problems of environmental and social deprivation associated with inebriety, moves to nationalise the drink trade, the social upheaval of the First World War, and the economic depression of the 1930s, all contributed to a continuing decline in alcohol consumption (Turner 1980; Williams and Brake 1980). In the inter-war years, interest in alcohol treatment both at policy and professional levels was at a low ebb. At the national level, led by the activities of the temperance movement with its strong parliamentary links, attention had shifted towards a public health approach with an interest in alcohol control and in prevention – but there was little policy action (Williams and Brake 1980; Rutherford 1991).

At the professional level, few medical practitioners worked in the field. Physicalist approaches to treatment were dominant although psychological insights were beginning to emerge and the seeds of later psychological input can be traced back to the early years of the twentieth century. Around 1914 psychologists had begun to arouse an interest in the neuroses and in the role of the unconscious. With the development of the psychological treatment of shellshock during the First World War, prevailing physicalist approaches to psychiatric treatment were called into question. In the alcohol field, the impact of psychology on conceptions of alcoholism and alcohol treatment was evident in discussions of 'the psychic treatment of inebriety' and the possibility of out-patient care. The establishment of 'anti-alcoholic dispensaries' was recommended at a meeting of the Society for the Study of Inebriety and it was proposed that, for inebriates, treatment should be an alternative to imprisonment (Berridge 1990). These trends also offered opportunities for the expanding psychiatric profession to cultivate a middle-class clientele outside the asylums. Again, the seeds of later debates and tensions on treatment modalities, service structures and professional ownership of alcohol treatment are visible in these early discussions. It was not, however, until the 1970s that psychology would acquire the distinctive theoretical base it needed to present a coherent alternative to the dominant disease models of addiction and dependency.

Other causal explanations of inebriety, latent in nineteenth-century public health, had placed the emphasis on the environmental and structural influences on health and health behaviour; explanations of this type did not reappear until the late 1960s when concern with skid row drinkers triggered a new awareness of the importance of the social context on drinking behaviour and on rehabilitation (Archard 1975). But the new social theories emerging in the following decade differed from the public health explanations of the nineteenth century in that they focused on the relationship between the individual and the immediate community, family and peer group networks, and on individual 'lifestyles' and 'risk behaviour' rather than on the links between alcoholism and major socio-economic structures. It was this individualist perspective which was to form the focus of the new public health approach to alcohol problems from around the mid-1970s (Lewis 1991).

1950 to the 1990s: An Overview

By the time the National Health Service (NHS) was set up in 1948, alcohol issues, in general, had a low policy profile. The World Health Organization (WHO) featured alcoholism as a major policy issue on its agenda, but consumption and alcohol-related harm appeared to be low in the UK, especially if compared with other European countries, and the British government was slow to respond to demands for action. Pressures to introduce alcohol issues on the policy agenda or develop a national response to alcohol consumption and harmful drinking were impeded also by the division of responsibility for alcohol matters between different government departments (Tether and Harrison 1988) and the fragmented nature of the many different types of groups pressing for reforms. The temperance movement, while maintaining political links, had less influence than in the nineteenth century and this was to decline still further in the post-war period. The voluntary services were in a state of flux as they reassessed their role within the new Welfare State (Finlayson 1994). As yet, there was no 'medical lobby' around alcohol. Doctors, as a profession, did not become a policy force until the late 1950s when they activated the resurgence of a new 'alcoholism treatment arena' and helped to form a policy community at national level.

Beginning with the 1950s, a time when policy interest in alcohol was at a low ebb, Chapter 2 examines in detail the pressures and personalities active in placing alcohol issues back on the policy agenda and in influencing the formulation of the first policy statement on alcoholism treatment to be issued within the new National Health Service. In the course of the 1950s, the disease concept of alcoholism was 'rediscovered' and, clothed respectably in the new 'scientific' treatments available within psychiatry, was adopted by many professionals, policy makers and the public. It dominated alcohol treatment approaches at least until the 1970s and provided a focus around which the emerging alcohol arena could press for action. Together with the development of new treatment approaches and techniques, the promotion of the disease concept had a significant influence on professional activity and involvement in alcohol issues. By the end of the 1950s, alcohol treatment had found its way on to the policy agenda, resulting in a memorandum issued by the Ministry of Health (MoH) in 1962 which introduced a new form of state-funded institutional provision for alcoholism treatment – specialist alcoholism treatment units attached mainly to psychiatric hospitals (MoH 1962).

From the start there was a lack of consensus among the small group of doctors and activists in the field; not everyone wholeheartedly espoused the disease concept with its associated abstinence goal; nor was there agreement on the need for specialist in-patient units. Research findings, neglected in the drive to activate policy, began to be re-evaluated and new research was initiated to assess the need for in-patient care of alcoholics. Within a few years of the first Memorandum, official policy, as set down in a second Memorandum (MoH 1968), was already moving away from an institutional treatment approach towards out-patient care and, by the early 1970s, towards community care provided by generalist health and welfare workers.

The trends and influences which determined the fate of the alcoholism treatment units (ATUs) from the 1960s to the 1980s are examined in Chapter 3.

Chapter 4 looks back to the 1950s and examines the emerging role of the voluntary sector in responding to alcoholism. In the immediate post-war period, the voluntary sector as a whole was engaged in a reassessment of its role within the new welfare state. Two traditions in voluntary care in the alcohol field can be traced back to the nineteenth century. One tradition, epitomised by the Salvation Army, was concerned with 'saving' the inebriate or down-and-out drinker and with the direct provision of care for individuals (Booth 1890; Trench 1969); the second tradition, taken up by temperance groups among others, was concerned with controlling consumption of alcohol by both supply and demand reduction strategies (Rutherford 1991). Both strands of activity had been reactivated, although only to a modest extent, by the end of the 1950s although the emphasis was on the provision of a treatment response to alcoholism rather than on prevention. In the early 1960s, an alliance between psychiatrists and philanthropic leaders in the voluntary sector became particularly significant in the development of the new voluntary movement in the alcohol field. Interaction between professional and voluntary workers, resulting in increasing consolidation and growth of the alcohol treatment arena, is illustrated in Chapter 4 in an examination of the origins and development of two organisations, the Camberwell Council on Alcoholism (CCA) and the National Council on Alcoholism (NCA), both of which became leading organisational players in the policy community. As the policy focus turned in the 1970s to non-specialist, community approaches to alcohol treatment, the size and influence of the voluntary sector increased; by 1990, organisations and services evolving from voluntary effort had become major players in the policy arena, and the non-statutory sector, as it was usually called by then, had become the dominant provider of treatment and advisory services.

One of the issues which drew together individuals from the statutory and voluntary sectors was concern over the response to habitual drunken offenders, an issue which had aroused debate since the nineteenth century and which drew attention to the unresolved tension between penal and medical approaches to habitual drunkenness (Out of Court 1988). In the post-war period, responsibility for habitual drunken offenders still lay with the Home Office although the appropriateness of a penal response to the problem continued to be criticised as ineffective. The alliance between policy sponsors in the voluntary and statutory sectors was an important element in directing policy proposals regarding habitual drunken offenders and in initiating a government working party to consider the appropriateness of existing penal and health service responses. Chapter 5 traces the events leading up to the Home Office working party and the issue of the report *Habitual Drunken Offenders* in 1971. At a time when the disease concept of alcoholism was the dominant influence on treatment responses, the division of responsibility for drunken offenders between the Home Office and the Department of Health and Social Security (DHSS) seemed more than ever open to question. The analysis reveals ways in which policy was influenced by the policy community using research to build a case in a situation where inter-departmental responsibilities and boundaries interacted with alternative definitions of the problem of alcoholism to create a 'grey' area of responsibility. The chapter also examines the fate of the report's recommendations and considers why one major treatment initiative recommended by the working party, the establishment of detoxification units, never passed the experimental stage.

By the 1970s, rising alcohol consumption, the perceived economic costs of alcohol misuse, and the interplay of competing interests brought to the fore in a new public health and prevention paradigm, began to raise the policy salience of alcohol issues and alcohol policy gained increasing attention on the policy agenda. Chapters 6 to 9 focus on the 1970s and 1980s and discuss a number of parallel trends which radically altered alcoholism treatment policy and provision. It was during these years that the shift from 'treatment' to 'problem management' began to take place. Former tensions between curative and preventive approaches re-emerged in the 1970s with the pendulum swinging towards the latter; policy concern focused on per capita consumption of alcohol and on alcohol-related harm rather than on 'alcoholism'; policy statements and official reports emphasised primary prevention, early intervention and the increased involvement of primary care workers to reach groups 'at risk' from harmful alcohol consumption. New ways of measuring harmful drinking helped to identify 'at risk' drinkers, swelling the potential treatment population and creating new areas of professional activity within statutory and non-statutory services. The result of these trends was an increase in the target groups for intervention, in the range of professionals involved in alcohol treatment, and in the pool of available theories and treatment approaches, in short, an expansion of the alcohol treatment arena. The policy community around alcohol also broadened and diversified, although psychiatry, partly through its close professional links with the medical stream of the civil service, retained the dominant policy position it had established in the 1960s.

The first of the parallel trends mentioned above, conceptual change and the factors influencing the adoption of an epidemiological rather than a medical definition of the alcohol problem, is examined in Chapter 6. At the conceptual level, the post-war period witnessed more than one change in the understanding and construction of the problem of alcohol. Soon after the rediscovery of the disease concept of alcoholism, the scientific validity of the 'popularised' version of the concept – which had provided a useful rallying call in the early years of the 1950s – was being challenged by research findings. A second major influence was the shift away from 'alcoholism' – a 'disease' affecting a small minority of the population – towards a concern with the consumption patterns of the population as a whole and with the rates of individual and social harms associated with per capita consumption of alcohol. Again alternative perspectives were available which challenged the evidence for the 'consumption–harm' theories. But the policy community was changing; the new paradigm helped to legitimate changing alliances and, at the same time, consolidate a more diffuse policy community growing around the new understanding of the alcohol problem. Research findings to support the 'consumption–harm' theory were gathered over subsequent years and policy 'outsiders' were unable to counter the increasing international accumulation of evidence. Finally, Chapter 6 discusses the steps taken in the 1970s and 1980s to obtain a clearer picture of national consumption patterns and to develop more appropriate ways of measuring harmful drinking.

By 1990, the acceptance of a standardised method of measuring individual consumption was being used in national surveys to provide epidemiological data on the extent of harmful drinking in the population and to legitimate policy and service responses. The new approach to the problem of alcohol which emerged in the 1970s was epitomised in three reports (issued in 1978–79) from an Advisory Committee on Alcoholism. The Kessel Committee, as it became known after its chairman, strengthened the move towards a prevention and early intervention response to alcohol problems and encouraged a community-based approach to the delivery of alcohol services. The findings of this committee are widely quoted as the foundations for subsequent developments in alcohol treatment policy and service provision. At the same time, it must be recognised that strongest support for state intervention in alcohol consumption per se came from outside ministerial circles. Official policy statements – although using research evidence on the problems associated with rising consumption – concentrated on strategy to reduce harmful levels of drinking and alcohol-related problems. As a result of these trends, alcohol treatment policy from the 1970s has to be examined within the increasingly important public health and prevention paradigm with its emphasis on individual lifestyles as a determinant of aggregate population health and its focus on 'risk' groups and 'risk' behaviours. This, too, opened the doors to new theoretical approaches to the management of alcohol problems, new policy networks and new sources of influence on official responses to tackle alcohol-related harms.

Chapters 7 and 8 use case studies to illustrate the interactive nature of factors resulting in the expansion of the alcohol treatment arena. Chapter 7 presents a case study of the emergence of clinical psychologists and considers the impact of psychological theories and approaches on policy and intervention. Clinical psychologists were not the only group of professionals to become more involved in the expanding alcohol arena; but they were, possibly, the most influential. They contributed to the conceptual development of the field, especially by their use of 'learning theory' as a base for understanding the development of alcohol problems and for designing appropriate intervention responses. As Gusfield (1982) and Room (1980) have noted in the US situation, there is a complex interaction between the activities of interest groups committed to mobilising support for a social problem, the theories offered to explain the problem, and the policies recommended for its alleviation. In the process of gaining attention for a cause and in defining a problem as policy relevant, interest groups generate 'needs' as much as respond to them. The new conceptualisation of the alcohol problem to emerge in the 1970s and the expansion of professional and voluntary groups within the alcohol arena could be seen as the product of just such an interactive process.

The second case study, in Chapter 8, takes up this theme in an examination of responses to women's problem drinking. The social and political contexts within which interest groups in the nineteenth and twentieth centuries defined women's drinking as a policy relevant issue are discussed and the chapter traces the activities of a small 'policy advocacy group' emerging in the mid-1970s to campaign for greater policy prominence for women with alcohol problems. The entry of issues of women's drinking on to the policy agenda is indicative of the wider policy shift towards addressing 'risk' groups and 'risk' behaviour within a prevention framework.

While the analyses in Chapters 6 to 8 highlight conceptual change and the expansion of the alcohol arena, Chapter 9 is concerned with policy implementation and with tracing the effects of policy change on the structure and delivery of treatment services. The shift from hospital-based psychiatric care provided by specialists to community-based care provided by a much wider group of professionals and voluntary workers is, possibly, the major policy trend in service delivery in the post-war period. This trend, visible long before the 1970s, was confirmed with the publication of the report by the Advisory Committee on Alcoholism in 1978, *The Pattern and Range of Services for Problem Drinkers*, and has continued into the 1990s. Chapter 9 examines changing expectations of the role of general practitioners in identifying and responding to alcohol problems and traces moves by the DHSS to encourage the development of a co-ordinated network of services provided by primary health and social care workers in alliance with voluntary organisations.

The 'consumption–harm' perspective of the alcohol problem was refined over the course of the 1970s and 1980s but was not radically altered until the 1990s when new research evidence and a shift in policy objectives began to broaden the emphasis on achieving a reduction in harmful drinking at national level to include concern over changing harmful drinking patterns especially problems associated with intoxication and binge drinking. The final chapter considers ongoing shifts in the conceptualisation of the problem of alcohol and the influence of current perceptions – many drawing on criminal justice perspectives and lessons from the drugs field – on policy and practice to 'manage' alcohol-related harms.

For many people working in the alcohol field, the 1970s represents a watershed. Government finally began to take an interest in alcoholism and money was made available for service development (DHSS 1973). Although ministerial interest and financial support were short-lived, the alcohol arena began to expand and to incorporate a wider network of alcohol workers within the policy community than had previously been the case. For some people, the post-1970s expansion of the alcohol field was seen as 'fragmentation', the loss of an earlier cohesive vision which had provided unity and direction in the field. For others, growth and diversification was the inevitable result of 'professionalisation' and marked the maturity of the alcohol treatment arena. To some extent, this account of policy development follows the established 'folk history' in accepting that the 1970s witnessed an important paradigmatic shift in alcohol policy which affected treatment approaches and services. But breaks between time periods are somewhat arbitrary. Elements of continuity as well as change can be traced back to the nineteenth century and throughout the post-NHS era; and the seeds of changes taking place in the 1970s or 1990s can be distinguished in debates and conflicts of the 1950s and 1960s. In telling the story of the development of alcohol treatment policy since 1950 the intention is to examine the shifting contexts from which present constructs and structures have emerged, and in which they are embedded. An examination of policy change is a central concern of this book. Cutting across the historical narrative, subsequent chapters trace three main areas of influence on policy development: the role of research and new knowledge, the importance of people, and the influence of changing conceptions and beliefs about alcohol consumption and alcohol-related harm.

The evidence base of alcohol policy

First of all, to what extent has policy development been evidence based? What part has been played by concern over rising alcohol consumption, or by new knowledge and evidence from the increasing volume of research on the individual and social costs of harmful drinking?

The potential for scientific research to guide and inform public policy has, at various times, been greeted with enthusiastic optimism and cynical pessimism (Berridge and Thom 1996). In the latter half of the twentieth century, early hopes that 'research' and 'science' were objective, value-free processes capable of directing policy making were soon dashed by critics who pointed out that the construction of scientific 'fact' and its translation into the policy process were the result of complex social processes and the interplay of diverse interests (Higgins 1980). Early debates on the relationship between 'science' and policy soon led to the more realistic view that, 'policy research, or any other kind of research, is not going to determine the major direction of policy' (Weiss 1991, p. 308). Nevertheless, interest in the research – policy connection and, more broadly, the generation and use of knowledge in the policy process, has remained a matter of theoretical and practical concern. Studies in this field have yielded a number of 'ideal type' models suggesting ways in which research may have an effect on policy.

'Rational' models, for instance, conveying the notion of research as the scientific, value-free basis of the policy-making procedure are used in presenting research evidence in policy debates, government papers and professional publications. 'Advocacy' models, which describe how information use is determined by group or individual interests, are illustrated in the alcohol field by the relatively minor part research and 'scientific' data played in the 1950s adoption of the disease concept of alcoholism, by the frailty of the research findings which lent support to arguments for specialist alcohol treatment units, by the use of a scanty mixture of research to build the initial case for policy responses to women alcoholics, and other examples which emerge in later chapters. But research has not been without influence in the alcohol field and, at the very least, it has often helped to shape the environment in which discussion and policy making takes place (Edwards 1993). The 'enlightenment' model, where knowledge and concepts are seen to infiltrate gradually into policy discourse over a period of time, perhaps best describes the way in which research has influenced alcohol policy over the past fifty years. At the same time, the history of the post-war relationship between research and alcohol treatment policy reveals the symbiotic nature of the relationship, the one helping to frame and alter the other over time. The generation of research, itself, has been subject to economic, social and political influences; change has occurred in the institutional and professional structures within which research is commissioned and produced; and there have been important shifts in the balance of power in the relationship between policy and research. The recent appearance of the 'economising' model, which views policy and research as bound in a mutually useful relationship based on economic principles (Fox 1990), is indicative of the changing balance of power between researchers and the commissioners of research and draws attention to the increasing importance of the use of commissioned research in the policy process. The 1971 report of the Central Policy Review Staff (the Rothschild Report) set the scene for this 'customer–contractor' relationship throughout government departments by encouraging greater government influence over the research it funded (Bulmer 1987). More recently, the purchaser–provider structure of service administration has added to the utilitarian approach to research and brought increasing pressure (and financial incentives) to bear on service providers to produce research in the shape of monitoring and service evaluation data (Culyer 1994).

The role of policy networks and the policy community

A second set of questions concerns the role of individuals, professions, organisations and interest groups in steering the course of policy. What role has the policy community played and how have changes in the policy community influenced the policy process? How have charismatic individuals or professional rivalries influenced events; and how powerful have civil servants been in setting the policy agenda?

The term 'policy community', developed in the UK by Richardson and Jordan (1979), characterises the central policy-making machinery as divided into sub-systems organised around central departments. These sub-systems, and the close relationship that exists with outside lay or professional groups or institutions are 'policy communities'. In this account of alcohol policy, the Department (or Ministry) of Health lies at the core of the policy community. But, just as the concept of 'community' is ill-defined when applied to the social world (witness the difficulty of finding a definition that can be operationalised in social research), the term 'policy community' introduces problems when studying the interactions that surround policy making. It has connotations of consensus and permanence which seldom apply in relation to policy. Some critics of the concept prefer the term 'policy networks' as more measurable (Harrison, personal communication). Studying the way in which organisations are linked in alcohol policy networks makes it clear that there are many separate but overlapping policy communities and policy networks in relation to different issues, such as licensing, road safety, community policing, advertising, taxation and so on, and that these networks are fluid and changing over time. Indeed, in the alcohol field, Tether notes that, 'there is a bewildering array of organisations and groups at the national level ... all involved in debating, making and implementing alcohol-relevant policy of every sort with government departments, with a constantly changing pattern of other organisations or on their own' (Tether 1987, p. 277). The Home Office, the Department of Transport, the Department of Trade and Industry and the Department of Education are also at the heart of important policy communities, and other government departments have a stake in alcohol policy.

The importance of policy communities and policy networks in the policy process is indicated widely in the literature. Through an exchange of ideas or activities, the policy community provides 'a number of different fora in which the early stages of opinion formation and consensus building among experts takes place', some of which reaches government policy makers (Tether 1987, p. 277). Discussing the way in which policy communities operate, Smith (1991) maintains that, 'it is a common observation about British political life that it works through who knows whom'. Relationships may be so close between government policy makers and policy community networks that shared priorities and strategies develop, making it difficult for 'outsiders' to gain a voice in policy formulation. Subsequent chapters trace the emergence and evolution of a policy community around issues of alcohol treatment policy and the ways in which policy consensus was achieved and changed. At the same time, we are also concerned with the policy networks which link professional groups, treatment or prevention organisations, or activist groups, and with the dynamics which result in the inclusion or exclusion of networks and individuals in the policy community at particular historical periods or within particular social contexts.

Only a few individuals in the policy networks will become part of the core policy community and have direct access to government ministers; more usually the link will operate through civil servants who occupy a central position within the policy community. The extent and nature of civil servants' influence over the policy process has been examined in several studies (Walt 1994). Meacher (1980), for instance, has argued that British civil servants are extremely powerful, able to control policy by using a variety of tactics including the manipulation of information. Baggott has observed that the role of the civil servant is greatest where ministers are not committed to a particular policy response:

> technically complex issues, matters currently attracting little attention from the public or from major pressure groups, and issues of little party political significance, are those decisions which tend to be dominated by the civil servants, in view of the low levels of ministerial interest in these matters. (Baggott 1994, p. 101)

In the case of alcohol treatment policy, civil servants in the professional stream of the civil service – doctors, nurses and social workers – may be particularly influential especially when the Minister concerned does not have medical training. However, many other factors determine civil servants' power over policy making, including the structure of the civil service itself and the nature of departmental boundaries of responsibility. As Tether and Harrison's (1988) study has shown, alcohol issues cut across many government departments, and interaction between departments is a necessary part of the policy-making process.

The importance of the structures within which individuals work and act – their 'institutional embedding' – is commented on by Rein and Schon (1991) who draw attention to the significance of institutional embedding on the definition of problems and solutions and on the development of networks of individuals linked by common roots. In the alcohol field, institutional contexts include organisations such as the Department of Health, the Maudsley Hospital and the Institute of Psychiatry which incorporate alcohol activities and interests within a wider remit, and organisations such as Alcoholics Anonymous, the New Directions in Alcohol Group, Alcohol Concern and others concerned solely with alcohol issues. Changes occurring in the institutions and groups with an interest in alcohol treatment are reflected in the changing composition and patterns of interaction of the policy community centred around alcohol treatment, and in its overlap with policy communities and networks less centrally concerned with treatment issues or with alcohol.

Within the concept of policy community, it is also possible to examine the separate impact of charismatic leadership, policy intellectuals, policy 'sponsors' or 'brokers', elite groups and 'disciple networks'. The research reported here, for instance, examines how events in the 1950s gave rise to an alcohol policy community centred around a few prominent psychiatrists mainly working in the London area and how influential and sometimes divergent 'disciple networks' evolved out of this core group. Despite the emergence of new, competing networks of influence or 'advocacy coalitions' in the 1970s and 1980s, psychiatry retained its position as the elite group, its leaders filling the role of 'policy intellectuals' into the 1990s. At least until recently, other disciplinary perspectives and other professional groups entered the heart of the policy community only in alliance with psychiatry. Of course, the key role of the medical profession in health policy making is not confined to alcohol issues but is a feature of the British health policy arena as a whole (Klein 1983; Webster 1988).

Shifts in the conceptualisation of the problem and the response

The third major theme is change in how the problem of alcohol has been conceptualised over the last fifty years. Beliefs about the nature of the alcohol problem and its management have changed more than once in the post-war period. Two major shifts occurred in the period between 1948 and 1990. The first was a shift away from a 'moral' model of alcoholism which tended to see the problem as one of individual deficiency of willpower or moral worth towards a 'disease' model which likened the problem to a medical condition requiring treatment, and attempted to dispel the stigma attached to alcoholism. The second frame shift, towards a public health perspective, removed the pathological, 'disease' label and redefined the problem in epidemiological and public health terms as arising from levels of alcohol consumption in the population as a whole and, at the individual level, as a consequence of lifestyle and 'risk behaviour'. More recently, conceptualisation of the alcohol problem has been moving towards a criminal justice model with the introduction of surveillance, harm reduction and community safety approaches. However, changes in the dominant explanatory models around alcohol use do not mean that one model has replaced another entirely; rather differing perceptions of the nature of the alcohol problem have continued to co-exist and to form the basis for individual and institutional actions depending on the social context and the beliefs of the individuals concerned. At any one time, clinical practice, lay beliefs, and policy discourse might draw on a moral model, the disease model, epidemiological or criminal justice explanations for problem drinking. The self-help group, Alcoholics Anonymous, for example, and the more recently established Minnesota Model approaches to treatment, both continue to adhere to a version of disease theory. A key question is how do such shifts in thinking come about?

One approach to understanding conceptual change is discussed by Rein and Schon (1991) who suggest that participants in the policy process construct ideological frames. These are problematic policy situations in which facts, values, theories and interests are integrated. They define framing as 'a way of selecting, organising, interpreting and making sense of a complex reality so as to provide guideposts for knowing, analysing, persuading and acting' (p. 263). The policy community and the policy networks around alcohol are crucial in the production and reproduction of ideological frames since they are the central actors involved in the process of 'selecting, organising and interpreting'. Policy discourse and policy formation may take place within a consensus frame within which policy disagreements can be settled because participants agree on basic rules and principles. One example is the general acceptance, in the 1950s and 1960s, of the disease concept of alcoholism, of the need for an abstinence goal in treatment, and of the value of specialist treatment approaches – a consensus arising from the desire to activate policy measures and place alcohol on the policy agenda. On the other hand, there are examples of situations where participants hold conflicting frames, and policy decisions cannot be settled by recourse to 'facts' or 'evidence' or by reference to a higher priority. Bitter debates in the US and the UK surrounding the construction and use of knowledge on controlled drinking and abstinence as treatment goals bear witness to ideological clash in the alcohol treatment field. Tensions between advocates of consumption theory who propose the need for national policy to control per capita consumption of alcohol and advocates of approaches to address harmful alcohol consumption have been a constant theme over the second half of the twentieth century. Such conflicts in ideological frames are likely to arise from the diversity of vested interests in the alcohol field or when competing professions, interest groups or individuals attempt to gain a more central position in the policy arena.

Shifting conceptualisations of the alcohol problem and of appropriate policy responses are reflected in changes in the way lay people, professional groups and policy makers talk about alcohol. For example, by the post war period, the nineteenth century terms 'inebriety' and 'habitual drunkenness' had virtually given way, at least within policy and professional discourse, to the use of 'alcoholism'. As 'alcoholism' lost its appeal, we began to talk about 'alcohol dependence', 'alcohol disabilities', 'alcohol misuse' and 'alcohol-related harms', and finally 'alcohol-related problems' and 'problem drinking'. Over the past fifty years, the 'alcoholic' became the 'problem drinker'; the 'skid row' drunk has been replaced by the 'persistent street drinker'.

Changes in language represent more than de-stigmatising devices or the stamp of professional imperialism, although such factors have played a part in the evolution of the discourse on alcohol issues. The changes symbolise shifting conceptualisations of the problem and indicate how, in each era, the language of alcohol has packaged prevailing theories and understandings of the problem for communication and dissemination; language has provided the tool for putting new ideas into practice at both policy and practice level. It is, therefore, an integral part of the shifting frame (or paradigm) through which 'an amorphous, ill-defined problematic situation can be made sense of and acted upon' (Rein and Schon 1991). Changing terminology also symbolised the move towards more 'scientific' (or more standardised) treatment approaches; 'drying out', for instance, became 'detoxification', 'advice' became 'counselling' and 'treatment' became only one element in a range of 'interventions'. From the 1970s, the use of the term 'treatment' itself became questionable as an appropriate descriptor of policy and practice. As the alcohol arena broadened to include a wide range of client groups treated by therapists from a variety of professional backgrounds, and as prevention approaches assumed increasing importance over treatment, 'management' became a more apt term for the multi-faceted responses to problem drinking current by the 1990s.

As far as possible, different terminology is used in the text to reflect such changes over time or between different perspectives of the problem. But, as in the case of changing explanatory models, the emergence of new terminology did not necessarily sweep away prior terminology or existing understanding. The continuing co-existence of terms, indicates the longevity of different ways of conceptualising the problem and different approaches to treatment and intervention. As a result, it is not possible to define a precise time when it became appropriate or inappropriate to use a particular term and this is reflected especially in chapters dealing with events from the 1970s.

Structural and administrative changes are also reflected in changes in terminology. In 1968 the Ministry of Health (MoH) became the Department of Health and Social Security (DHSS). In 1988 responsibility for health and social security was again split and the Department of Health (DoH) became separate. New alcohol organisations occasionally changed their names over time, reflecting changes in their function, size or administration; Helping Hand, and Rathcoole House, for instance, small voluntary agencies set up in the 1960s, became respectively Turning Point and Alcoholics Recovery Project, growing into two of the largest voluntary organisations by the 1990s. Changes such as these are indicated in the text as they occurred.

Alcohol Policy in Perspective:
The Wider Social and Political Framework

Alcohol has rarely attracted the policy spotlight. It has not received the sustained political and media attention accorded to illicit drug use in recent years nor the crisis response which greeted the AIDS epidemic in the 1980s (Berridge 1996). The allocation of resources at national or local level has rarely favoured the implementation of alcohol policies. Most policy makers are not talking about alcohol most of the time. Policies to address problem drinking and alcohol-related harms have emerged from a complex interplay of many competing pressures and demands on policy makers and have to be examined against the wider backdrop of social, economic and political change in the late twentieth century. Changes in public attitudes towards the use of alcohol, the extent to which alcohol-related harm is visible, the 'cosmopolitisation' of drinking habits through travel and the communication explosion, the changing role of women, or changes in the period of transition from childhood to adulthood which affect drinking habits are a few of the wider social factors which impinge on and stimulate policy action. Alcohol policy has to be located also within trends in health and social policy towards a customer–contractor culture, towards administrative and professional partnerships in service delivery, towards community-based intervention and community development approaches to address health and social problems at local level. The focus on alcohol policy in subsequent chapters and examination of the themes outlined above should not detract from the importance and prominence of this wider canvas of policy activity.

2 The 1950s: A New Alcohol Policy Community

Overview

Throughout most of the 1950s, alcohol consumption in England was at a comparatively low level; the Ministry of Health (MoH) maintained that alcoholism was not a problem, and that the provision of services for alcoholics was adequate. This chapter examines the circumstances and pressures which, in the course of the decade, led to a redefinition of alcoholism as a problem which warranted policy attention. The pressures on policy makers included the emergence of a new 'alcohol arena' to replace the temperance movement whose influence had waned in the inter- and post-war periods. Led by psychiatrists, the emerging 'alcohol arena' gained visibility only towards the end of the 1950s by which time links were being forged between psychiatrists working in alcoholism treatment and their medical colleagues in the MoH. The impetus to medical and psychiatric action came from a number of directions. The rediscovery of the 'disease concept' of alcoholism, adopted by the World Health Organization (WHO), provided the conceptual basis for a new understanding of the problem, strengthened the rationale for medical input and played an important role in unifying diverse interests around alcohol issues. WHO activity helped to sensitise interested members of the medical profession to alcohol issues and provided further legitimisation for their involvement in alcoholism treatment. New drugs and new treatment approaches, introduced in the early 1950s, attracted psychiatrists to the field and lent support to the contention that the disease approach was 'scientifically' grounded whereas former treatment methods had depended on 'moral suasion' and were allied with temperance propaganda. Other activists, linked to the churches and the temperance movement, were attempting to organise but remained policy 'outsiders' at this time. By the end of the decade, the disease concept of alcoholism had caught the professional and lay imagination, a new alcohol arena was beginning to take shape, and pressures to place alcoholism treatment on the policy agenda were mounting within the MoH.

Alcohol Consumption and Alcoholism in the 1950s:
Diverse Perspectives

Alcohol consumption in England in the late 1940s was comparatively low. Legislative controls imposed at the beginning of the
century, the economic depression of the 1930s, and restrictions on
the availability of spirits after the Second World War helped to curb
consumption well into the 1950s. Whereas between 1900 and 1904
the average annual per capita consumption was 10.6 litres of
absolute alcohol, between 1930 and 1934 it was 4.2 litres. Although
consumption rose slightly in the 1950s, by 1960 per capita
consumption was still only 4.5 litres. As Table 2.1 indicates, at the
start of the 1950s, the level of alcohol consumption in England
compared favourably with the high levels found in many other
countries and this situation continued throughout the decade
(Williams and Brake 1980). England also appeared to suffer fewer
problems of alcoholism than elsewhere. WHO estimates of the
number of severe alcoholic cases in eleven countries showed
England bottom of the league with 0.28 per cent of the adult
population probably affected by alcoholism compared to Switzerland
at the top of the league with 1.6 per cent (WHO 1952).

The official view within the Ministry of Health throughout the
1950s was that alcohol consumption was not a problem. On occasion,
the WHO estimates of the number of alcoholic cases were quoted as
justification for official opinion;[1] at other times, MoH personnel
evinced some scepticism over WHO estimates since, it was claimed,
the formula on which the figures were based had never been
validated.[2] The lack of interest in alcohol issues was further demonstrated in the failure of the Ministry to send official delegates to
international meetings on the topic, the reason reported on one
occasion being that it had 'not been found possible to find suitable
persons who could conveniently be spared to take part' (*British Journal
of Addiction* 1953, 50, p. 5). Frequently, the results of a questionnaire
sent to 480 General Practitioners in February 1956 were quoted as
evidence of the low level of alcohol problems; GPs in the study had
reported seeing few patients whom they diagnosed as alcoholic and
were unaware of any widespread or unfulfilled demand for treatment
(Parr 1957).

Then, as now, responsibility for questions of alcohol consumption and alcohol problems cuts across several ministries and
government departments including the Ministry of Transport, the

Table 2.1
Per capita consumption of alcohol in some European countries, 1950–52

Country	Per capita consumption in litres absolute alcohol
Austria	5.4
Belgium	6.6
Denmark	4.0
Finland	2.2
France	17.6
Germany (Federal Republic)	3.6
Italy	9.4
Netherlands	1.9
Norway	2.1
United Kingdom	4.9

Source: Royal College of Psychiatrists (1979), p. 95, Table 6.

Home Office and the Department of Education as well as the MoH. At this time, the MoH held a narrowly medical view of its responsibility for alcohol problems, in part because of the association of broader concepts with the temperance approach. Resolutions and circulars from the temperance movement, drawing attention to increasing juvenile drunkenness and the part played by alcohol in road accidents, were seen as dealing with 'a social rather than a mental health question' and forwarded to the Home Office.[3] MoH officials advised that, in responding to drunkenness problems, all they could do was promote health education; but correspondence from the Ministry's files suggests that there was little enthusiasm for the educational role. Although the MoH had indicated a need for educational material to be addressed to the general public, this was regarded as a matter for local health authorities and was not seen to warrant a nationally organised campaign at that time (MoH 1957).[4]

Overall, members of the medical profession – in as far as they thought about the topic at all – shared the official view that England was less affected by alcoholism than its European neighbours. A few doctors felt that total consumption still remained high. One of these was Pullar-Strecker, superintendent of a private mental hospital and a prominent member of the Society for the Study of Addiction (Berridge 1990). He was to play a part in pressurising for action on alcoholism and in disseminating information about the 'new' disease. Nevertheless, in a letter to the *British Medical Journal* in 1951, even he noted that the WHO figure of 1000 alcoholics per 100,000 adults was barely a quarter of the US figure, and he concluded that excessive drinking seemed to be linked to prohibitive societies like Sweden and the US and to countries like Norway and Finland which, unlike England, had 'a bad head for alcohol' (Pullar-Strecker 1951; 1952a). This comforting picture of *comparatively* low levels of alcohol consumption and alcohol-related harm continued to be reflected in articles and commentaries in both the *British Medical Journal* and the *Lancet* until well on into the 1950s, supporting the view held by policy makers that alcohol consumption, in itself, was not a problem. In the nineteenth century, 'temperance doctors' had played a leading role in pressing the state to make an institutional response to alcoholism (Macleod 1967). In the 1950s, the role of the profession was usually muted; but as the decade progressed, medical pressure to improve the policy response to alcoholism and its treatment increased, perceptions of the problem changed and a small number of key individuals emerged as policy leaders.

Criticism of the government came from the temperance movement which held to its traditional view on the necessity for strengthening government control on alcohol consumption and reducing overall consumption levels. The temperance journal, *Alliance News* (March/April 1950, p. 23), attacked government complacency, commenting that in Parliament, 'Usually a debate on this subject is regarded as an appropriate occasion for hilarity and irrelevant humour.' Members of the temperance movement and their parliamentary supporters attempted to keep alcohol use on the political agenda by raising questions in the House on the allocation of barley and honey for alcohol production in the immediate post-war years, by opposing vigorously moves prior to the 1951 election to nationalise the liquor trade, by persistent opposition throughout the decade to extensions to the licensing laws, and by drawing attention to the problems of alcohol-related road accidents, drink driving and increasing juvenile drunkenness (*Alliance News* 1948; throughout 1950s). However, the power of the temperance movement had waned considerably and despite retaining a strong following in the parliamentary Labour Party, it had little real influence on the course of policy at this time (Williams and Brake 1980; Rutherford, interview). Thus, when it came, policy action concentrated on the medical aspects of alcoholism, emphasising special treatment for alcoholics and did not extend to the wider issues of alcohol consumption or prevention measures.

Alcohol Treatment in the Post-war Period

Treatment services

At the beginning of the 1950s, state-supported provision for people with alcohol problems was virtually non-existent. The state inebriate reformatories, established at the end of the nineteenth century to provide specialist care for alcoholics, had long ceased to function (Hunt *et al.* 1987; McLaughlin 1991). Charities and church organisations such as the Salvation Army, the Methodist Church and the Rowntree Trust retained an interest in working with alcoholics and provided some refuge for the most uprooted individuals; but the voluntary movement as a whole was in a state of uncertainty over its role within the new National Health Service (Finlayson 1994) and did not regain its sense of purpose in the alcohol field until the 1960s. General practitioners (GPs) appeared to have little to do with alcoholics, and, despite pronouncements about their potential role, were usually assumed to be incompetent in the treatment of alcoholism.[5] For those who could afford it, alcoholism treatment could be obtained from a few private practitioners; but for most people, there was little alternative to the scanty National Health Service (NHS) hospital care provided in the mental health services. This was regarded by some practitioners as inappropriate. As one critic recalled, throughout the 1950s, it was likely that people with drinking problems would find themselves 'in the terrible back wards of mental hospitals', at a time when mental hospitals were largely 'asylums, custodial institutions ... they weren't the sort of place where someone who had run into a drinking problem would find themselves very much at home' (Edwards, interview). Writing in 1952, Pullar-Strecker roundly condemned the apathy towards alcohol issues in the UK, stating that,

> The fountain-head of our profession, the British Medical Association, unlike the American Medical Association, does not seem to take any interest in the matter ... The National Association for Mental Health is silent on the subject of alcoholism, so is the Board of Control, so is the Royal Medico-Psychological Association ... No research into the cause of alcoholism is being done at our university institutions and no government grants are forthcoming ... Nothing is being done to acquaint the medical profession with the importance and relative hopefulness of treating the alcoholic and no information on the subject is offered to the general public. (Pullar-Strecker 1952b, pp. 21–32)

This view was reiterated in almost identical terms in the 1952/53 report of the Council of the Society for the Study of Addiction, which concluded that, 'when one approaches the powers that be on this matter, one is fobbed off with the stock reply that alcoholism is a more serious problem over there – as if it were not serious enough a problem in this country' (reported in *British Journal of Addiction* 1953, vol. 50).

The difficulties of obtaining help for alcoholism were well illustrated in an enquiry to the Ministry of Health in 1952 from Dr Esher, Regional psychiatrist of the Sheffield Regional Hospital Board. Dr Esher complained to the Ministry that mental hospitals were refusing to take cases of alcoholic addiction and that harassed relatives were unable to obtain appropriate assistance. In the north of the region, it was impossible for urgent cases of any kind to gain admittance to hospital and as Dr Esher noted in his letters to the Ministry, 'When we have to refuse admission for acute and urgent cases, I feel that the quiet alcoholic who would like a retreat and protection, would stand a very thin chance of admission.' Dr Esher's request for information regarding public and private treatment centres for people with drug and alcohol addiction was answered with the following list of private facilities: Wyke House, Isleworth (where Pullar-Strecker was medical superintendent); Heigham Hall, Norwich (the former Heigham Lunatic Asylum which had been owned by Donald Dalrymple, a surgeon and Liberal MP for Bath and a key figure in legislation in the 1870s); and Caldecote Hall, Nuneaton in Warwickshire (where Dr A.E. Carver, a medical psychologist who advocated a psychological approach to alcoholism, was medical superintendent in the 1950s). It was also mentioned that 'a number of licensed houses take addiction cases though not specialising in treatment' but no details were given. The list of public facilities named the Maudsley Hospital, the York Clinic at Guy's Hospital and University College Hospital in London; and added that addictions were looked after, 'in most large hospitals'.[6]

Within the new National Health Service, mental health provision as a whole was very much the Cinderella of the services. Hastily included at the last minute, the mental health sector still retained a large degree of separation from general health services despite the goal of integration. The powerful Board of Control, the regulatory body in the mental health field, which took over the functions of the Commissioners in Lunacy in 1913, retained a semi-autonomous status within the NHS, acting as the mental health division of the Ministry of Health with personnel of the Board responsible for administration in mental health matters. The Board of Control retained this position until it was abolished following the 1959 Mental Health Act. The Board had not been in favour of integration of the mental health sector within the NHS, and war-time surveys of hospital resources had not included mental health services. When a national review was finally undertaken in 1952, the woeful state of the service was incontestable and the inevitable conclusion drawn that more money was needed (Busfield 1986; Webster 1988). Money, however, was in short supply and Ministry officials could only express relief 'that there was a major discrepancy between the size of the problem and the public awareness of it' (cited in Webster 1988, p. 329). In the light of the financial problems which beset the infant NHS and of the general disarray of mental health services in the immediate post-NHS period, it is hardly surprising that it proved difficult to arouse official concern over alcohol problems or the provision of treatment services for alcoholics.

The MoH adviser on mental health issues for most of the 1950s was Dr Walter Symington Maclay who had joined the Board of Control in 1954, having worked for thirteen years prior to that under Dr Mapother at the Maudsley Hospital in London. In 1954 Dr Maclay succeeded Dr Rees Thomas as the senior medical member of the Board of Control and the senior principal medical officer of the MoH, a position he retained until 1961. Dr Maclay appears to have been well informed about current theories and trends in the alcohol field and was familiar with the Society for the Study of Addiction and many of the leading professionals of his day. Described as 'one of the early people with a proper consciousness about alcohol' (Godber, interview), Maclay nevertheless had no particular interest in alcohol problems and appeared to adhere throughout his period of office to departmental perspectives on alcohol consumption and alcohol treatment, believing that consumption was not a major problem and that alcoholism could be treated appropriately within existing services.

By 1958, a similar enquiry to Dr Esher's earlier correspondence about facilities for treating alcoholism was answered with a slightly expanded list of services. In addition to the previous public institutions, the following were listed: Coney Hill Hospital, Gloucester; Warlingham Park Hospital, Somerset; Addenbrooke's Hospital, Cambridge (out-patient only); St George's Hospital, London. To the private facilities were added: St Andrew's Hospital, Northampton; The Hall, Harrow Weald; Chiswick House, Pinner.[7] Until the close of the 1950s, provision for alcoholics and official attitudes towards alcoholism remained virtually unchanged; but the circle of critics was growing and there was mounting pressure towards the establishment of a specialist approach to the treatment of alcoholism.

Treatment approaches

One important factor in the eventual drive towards specialisation was the development of new treatment approaches and new perspectives on the nature of the problem. The discovery of 'antabuse' in 1948 by a Danish doctor, Dr Erik Jacobson, heralded the dawn of a new optimism in treating alcoholism. The discovery had been made quite by chance in the course of an experiment to find a cure for intestinal worms in small animals. Having tried tetramethylthiuram disulphide (antabuse) experimentally, Dr Jacobson took some himself before beginning clinical trials. Shortly after taking the substance, he had a glass of beer with his lunch whereupon he soon began to feel 'queer'. On reflection, he decided it must be the tetramethylthiuram disulphide.[8] The discovery was welcomed as a useful aid in the treatment of alcoholism (*British Journal of Addiction* 1949, 46, p. 466; *British Medical Journal* 1949, 2, p. 1365), and a lecture given by Jacobson in 1950 to the Joint Meeting of the Royal Society of Medicine and the Society for the Study of Addiction, was greeted enthusiastically. Pullar-Strecker had high hopes for the new drug, commenting in the discussion following Dr Jacobson's 1950 paper that, 'whether or not antabuse will keep its therapeutic promise there can be no doubt that it represents an important and exciting medical discovery. In some ways, one could almost liken this discovery to the Philosopher's Stone' (*British Journal of Addiction* 1950, 47, p. 18).

In the 1940s and 1950s, physical methods of treatment were again on the ascendant in psychiatry in general, and antabuse was only one of a number of physical treatments in use for alcoholism. Dr John Yerbury Dent, a Kensington general practitioner interested in the treatment of alcoholism since the 1920s and a long-standing editor of the *British Journal of Addiction*, was well known for his use of apomorphine. He had lectured widely on the subject, his first paper being given in 1934 to the Society for the Study of Addiction (cited in Berridge 1990, pp. 1038–9). It was an interest in physical treatments which led to the recruitment of D.L. Davies, Dean of the Institute of Psychiatry, to the alcohol field. According to Griffith Edwards, who joined Davies' unit as a registrar in 1959, Davies 'had got into alcoholism because he was looking for some territory which could be his ... it was the age of physical treatment and everyone was trying to find a physical treatment for schizophrenia and depression; and antabuse came along and it was antabuse which caught Davies' attention in the first place rather than simply alcoholism' (Edwards, interview; Edwards 1991, pp. 189–205). Within a few years, Davies was to become one of the most important figures in the emerging alcohol field and the 'father' of an influential network of psychiatrists trained at or linked to the Maudsley Hospital and the Institute of Psychiatry. As later chapters will show, members of the network played a significant role in policy formation and service implementation throughout the post-war period.

Despite the interest in physical treatments, psychiatrists at the Maudsley Hospital were never possessed entirely by drugs. Influenced by the work of Adolf Meyer in the US, they adopted a holistic attitude to psychiatry, taking a life history which included an account of psychological problems and social influences. The treatment approach to alcoholism, although it included antabuse for all patients, also emphasised the individual's social situation. This openness to the social-psychological context of alcoholism was to prove important in the coming decades for it allowed for the incorporation and absorption of perspectives, treatment approaches and professionals from different disciplines, and enabled the emerging network of Maudsley psychiatrists to remain in the forefront of policy developments for many years to come. Psychological treatment approaches, however, were not favoured at the Maudsley in the 1950s and Davies appears to have remained particularly contemptuous of psychotherapy which he saw as anti-scientific 'mumbo-jumbo' (Edwards, interview). Others in the field were also hostile to psychological and psychotherapeutic approaches; Dent, for example, remained throughout his career a confirmed advocate of biochemical methods of treatment (Berridge 1990, pp. 1043–4).

While psychological and biochemical approaches jostled for supremacy in the early years of the 1950s, as the decade progressed, they appeared to reach a synthesis with an increasing number of professionals arguing for mixed approaches tailored to suit the individual drinker and to take account of the particularity of the person's psychological state, personality and social situation. One of the most persuasive voices in favour of eclectic treatment methods was that of Lincoln Williams who, like Dent, was a private practitioner. Williams was, reputedly, a man of great enthusiasm who achieved considerable success in his work with alcoholics. His interest in alcoholism had been kindled by a chance meeting just after the war with Aubrey Lewis, Professor of Psychiatry at the Institute of Psychiatry. Lewis suggested that Williams use his nursing home for the treatment of alcoholism since there were interesting new developments coming on the scene. This – so the tale goes – acted like a religious revelation. Williams went to America to learn what was happening there and on his return opened his nursing home to care exclusively for alcoholics (Edwards, interview). Williams' books and articles, an important and

useful contribution to the scanty British literature on the treatment of
alcoholism, advocated the 'new' humanitarian approach to alcoholism
and proposed that all available techniques be used to combat the
'disease' (Williams 1951; 1952; 1956). As Berridge suggests, shorn of
the language of progress, Williams' argument presented a realistic
assessment of what practitioners active in alcoholism treatment
needed to do in order to establish special status and retain control over
the burgeoning number of alternative approaches (Berridge 1990,
p. 1046).

Support for a more eclectic approach to treatment also came
from the World Health Organization which, in the first half of the
decade, played a decisive role in influencing medical perspectives on
alcohol consumption and in legitimating the status of alcoholism as
a medical problem. The work of the WHO, strongly influenced by
developments in the US, laid the foundations for a new disease
'ideology' which was to provide the rallying point for the emerging
policy community, dominate the alcohol field until the 1970s, and
survive as a major influence on treatment approaches to the present
day. It is to an examination of the emergence of this new
conceptualisation of the alcohol problem and its impact on
alcoholism treatment in England that we now turn.

The Problem of Alcoholism: Changing Perspectives

While the Ministry of Health held to the view that alcohol consumption in England was relatively low, it was difficult to ignore mounting
pressure from international sources to face the problem of alcoholism
and its treatment. In particular, the work of the WHO was to prove an
important, if indirect, influence on policy developments. The WHO,
established in 1948 to assist Member States in improving public
health as a whole, included alcoholism in the terms of reference of the
Expert Committee on Mental Health which first met in 1949 (Moser
1975). A report in 1951 from the WHO Expert Committee stressed
the importance of alcoholism as a disease and a serious social
problem. It emphasised the role of the medical profession and of
public health workers in the prevention and treatment of alcoholism,
urged governments to develop methods of gathering national statistics
on the incidence of alcoholism, and proposed the establishment of
'outpatient dispensary services' to treat cases of alcoholism at an early
stage before institutional care became necessary. Perhaps unsurprisingly, since the Committee was composed largely of psychiatrists, it
was suggested that out-patient dispensaries – although preferably sited
in general hospitals – should be in the charge of an interested
psychiatrist. Furthermore, it was recommended that staff in the

voluntary sector should receive training in alcoholism and should work under medical supervision (WHO 1951). Further reports between 1952 and 1955 along with a WHO-organised European Seminar and Lecture Course on Alcoholism in 1952 and a European Seminar on Prevention and Treatment in 1954, continued the international pressure on national governments, strengthened the legitimisation of alcoholism as a medical concern, and were crucial in stimulating and focusing medical interest (WHO 1952; 1954; 1955). The WHO reports thus confirmed both the medical nature of alcoholism and the medical 'ownership' of the alcohol field although the importance of recruiting the support and involvement of other voluntary and social welfare professionals was acknowledged and encouraged.

The period of WHO interest and activity in alcohol coincided with the period of collaboration between the head of the WHO Mental Health Unit, G.M. Hargreaves, a British psychiatrist, and E.M. Jellinek, a scientist and scholar, who had established his reputation in the alcohol field at Yale University in the US and became a consultant to the WHO from 1950 to 1957. Looking back on that period, Joy Moser, who joined the WHO in 1951, explained that Jellinek was employed because Dr Hargreaves 'was very keen that some sensible things should be done about alcohol problems .... He believed that alcoholism was tremendously widespread, very much misunderstood and that there were possibilities of diminishing the extent of the problem' (Moser 1975). Jellinek came to the WHO with ideas derived from the 'new scientific approach' to understanding alcohol and alcoholism emerging in post-prohibitionist America (Page 1988; Roizen 1993). He had entered the alcohol field to undertake a review of the literature on the biological effects of alcohol on humans and had continued, on the invitation of Howard W. Haggard, Director of the Laboratory of Applied Physiology at Yale University, to head a multi-disciplinary research centre on alcohol. Through the influence of Jellinek, his Yale colleagues, the *Quarterly Journal of Studies on Alcohol* which they established, and the summer schools which began in 1943, American influence filtered into the UK. Griffith Edwards, working at the Maudsley hospital in the 1950s as a registrar under D.L. Davies, later recalled the importance of the American connection, 'It was wonderful for a young man interested in the subject to find himself in touch with a community of scholars who were interested – because there was no community of scholars here.' Jellinek, along with other American scholars, largely social scientists such as Seldon Bacon, Robert Straus and David Pittman (Edwards 1991, pp. 57–141), led the way in the theoretical development of ideas on alcohol and alcoholism, ideas which undoubtedly influenced WHO thinking. With the departure of Hargreaves in 1955, Jellinek seems to have fallen out of favour and WHO interest in the alcohol programme virtually ceased until the late 1960s (Room 1984). By this time, British psychiatrists had assumed greater prominence on the international circuit and were in a position to play a more influential role at that level.

Concurrent with the development in the US of professional interest in the 'new alcohol movement' – as it later came to be called, was the emergence of a lay fellowship, Alcoholics Anonymous (AA), a group established in the mid-1930s by two recovering alcoholics to provide mutual support in achieving sobriety. The history of AA in the United States and its growth internationally has been well documented (Leach and Norris 1977; Kurtz 1979; Robinson 1979). Heather and Robertson (1985, p. 51) attribute its success in part to its 'ability to convey an essentially moral and religious message in an ostensibly scientific package'. The message conveyed was that alcoholism is a disease with a physiological component which separates the 'alcoholic' from the rest of the drinking population; the disease is characterised by 'loss of control' over alcohol consumption and by the experience of a specific withdrawal syndrome in the absence of alcohol; total, lifelong abstinence from alcohol is a requirement for recovery. The fellowship of AA offered a treatment philosophy, a treatment plan – the Twelve Steps – and a new lifestyle supported by a network of abstinent members. Its methods, based on group interaction, were later to merge with, and influence, group therapy approaches to recovery. AA was closely associated with the Yale Centre and other leading American authorities and there is no doubt that the 'disease concept' and its promotion emerged from the interaction between these organisations (Roizen 1993; 1994). Alcoholics Anonymous reached the UK in the late 1940s and, although quickly accepted by some leading medical professionals in the alcohol field, initially made as few inroads into official policy-making circles as had Jellinek and the WHO message (Edwards 1991, p. 189).

European perspectives, although apparently much less important than American thinking, were available to British practitioners through publications in the journal of the Society for the Study of Addiction which in the first half of the decade carried items on treatment and research in Europe, especially in Switzerland and Scandinavia. The International Council on Alcohol and Alcoholism (ICAA), an organisation which had existed since 1907, held annual international meetings open to a broad spectrum of professionals and attempted to generate inter-disciplinary discussion on alcohol issues

(Edwards 1991, pp. 37–48). The meetings and activities of the Council were reported in the medical press but, as in the case of the WHO, UK representation during the 1950s was very low.

Within the MoH, international activity was not without some effect. In his annual report for 1951, the Chief Medical Officer, Sir John Charles, drew attention to the fact that:

> The section on mental health statistics includes in addition to general information about admissions and discharges to mental hospitals and other institutions in 1949 and 1950, some factual details about admissions attributable to addiction of various kinds. These are particularly apposite at this time when increasing attention is being given to such matters internationally. (MoH 1951, p. 3)

Despite such pronouncements in 1951 and again in 1957 (MoH 1957), WHO activity and a visit by Jellinek to officials at the Ministry of Health had little direct impact on alcohol policy. At the same time, the seeds of future policy directions in England were visible in the WHO reports issued in the 1950s, both in the shorter-term development towards establishing specialist treatment services for alcoholics and in the longer-term move towards out-patient and community-based care. It took, however, the emergence of a new perspective on the nature of the problem – the disease concept of alcoholism – and its acceptance by influential figures within the nascent alcohol policy community to put pressure on official opinion and obtain policy action on alcohol issues. In essence, the importance of the new vision lay in its usefulness as a practical device to stimulate action and cohesion in the alcohol field rather than in its validity as a scientifically sound construct.

The Disease Concept of Alcoholism

Much has been written about the 're-emergence' of the disease concept of alcoholism and of its effect on treatment approaches (Wiener 1981; Room 1983; Heather and Robertson 1985). But the literature is replete with confusion and contradiction regarding the precise nature of the concept and of its mutations over the years and between one social context and another. Wiener (1981, p. 91), for instance, notes how the disease concept of alcoholism has 'hopped from the temperance world to the worlds of law and of volunteer action, to the worlds of medicine, psychiatry, psychology and related health services, to its current movement into a world which is attempting to replace the disease concept with a "social model" of alcoholism'. Wiener's discussion of the redefinition of the alcohol problem in post-prohibitionist America illustrates the social and intellectual climate which generated conditions leading to the adoption of the disease concept of alcoholism at the same time as parallel trends undermined that movement and planted the seeds of a competing paradigm, the 'drinking problems' perspective which was to flower at a later period. What emerges from the literature is that the 'career' of the disease concept since the nineteenth century has reflected the symbolic use of the concept as a marker of change in perceptions of the alcohol problem and its value as an organising concept around which to rally support for action in the alcohol field. At least in the early post-prohibition years, the rediscovered disease concept was left deliberately vague (Heather and Robertson 1985, p. 46) and the scientific validity of the concept or the evidence on which treatment of the 'disease' was based, was of lesser importance than its propagandist role. The conclusion, that the statement 'alcoholism is a disease' indicated a recommendation for public policy rather than a scientific discovery (Seeley 1962), aptly conveys the primary importance of the disease concept as a vehicle for the dissemination of a new wisdom. This was as important in the UK as in the US.

In the UK, the Ministry of Health adhered, throughout the 1950s, to a view of alcoholism which emphasised the mental health aspects of the problem and the appropriateness of existing treatment provision. Government policy was based on the view that alcoholism was a *symptom* of underlying disease, not a disease in itself. This was the basis of the argument advanced by Dr Maclay at a meeting with Alcoholics Anonymous in 1954, when AA's recommendation for the establishment of special hospitals or units for alcoholics was rejected. Maclay stated the official view that, since alcoholism was a symptom rather than a disease it was better treated where various medical specialisms were available.[9] The answers to enquiries on the treatment of alcoholism changed very little between 1952 and 1958 when the following letter was suggested by Maclay as a reply to a Dr Casson, who was hoping to write a newspaper article on the extent of alcohol problems in the UK and the counter-measures being taken by the Ministry of Health:

Alcoholism is commonly regarded by the medical profession as an illness which may have many causes. The alcoholism is therefore often a symptom of an underlying condition, e.g. depression, anxiety, psychopathy, the culture in which the patient lives and it is this underlying condition to which attention should be paid. It has therefore been the policy of the Ministry to expect doctors and particularly psychiatrists to deal with alcoholics according to their needs, making use of the facilities of the NHS as they would for any other type of illness. Some may need OP clinics, some neurosis centres of mental hospitals. This has meant that no special separate provision has been specifically allotted for the treatment of alcoholics but at some existing clinics and hospitals special attention is given to the treatment of persons suffering from this form of addiction.[10]

This viewpoint was stated publicly in the report of the Chief Medical Officer in 1957; it was repeated by Maclay in 1961, when he attended a committee meeting where the issues surrounding the treatment of alcoholics were being discussed, and it appeared in internal memos in 1960 (MoH 1957).[11]

Thus MoH spokesmen held to a psychodynamic explanation for 'deviant' drinking, while professional and lay opinion was careering rapidly towards an addiction model which defined alcoholism as a discrete illness requiring specialist (medical) attention. That the disease concept was quickly adopted and vigorously promoted in the UK is evident in the literature of the time. Lincoln Williams, for example, by 1951 was describing alcoholism as 'an illness every bit as real and compelling as any of the maladies generally recognised as such' (Williams 1951). The influence of AA in defining the nature of the illness was considerable and the role of AA in relation to the medical profession was established early on. An article published in the Lancet in 1948 by a member of AA described the 'disease' and its manifestations, and provided a personal account of recovery through the AA fellowship (Lancet 1948, 2, p. 231). Commenting on the article, Pullar-Strecker (1948) concluded that, although he was favourably disposed to the AA approach to rehabilitation, 'few addicts are capable of performing such a feat unless medicine has paved the way'. It was on the strength of its role in after-care that AA built collaboration with the medical profession, becoming particularly influential in developing a relationship with Max Glatt, a psychiatrist working with alcoholics at Warlingham Park Hospital in Surrey. By 1958, lay dissemination of the disease concept was aiming at a wider general public through the medium of programmes such as the BBC television documentary Rock Bottom which had reported on, 'The serious problem of providing adequate inpatient treatment for all patients' (Lancet 1957, 2, p. 854). Why did the disease concept appeal so quickly and so widely? Three aspects of the change in perceptions of the problem were especially significant.

First, medical allegiance was underpinned by the legitimisation of alcoholism as a medical problem, on scientific grounds and on the grounds that medicine now had the means to provide an effective response. The work of the WHO, discussed earlier, was important in this respect. The first report from the WHO Expert Committee emphasised 'the importance of alcoholism as a disease and a social problem', and continued: 'it is only within comparatively recent years that a medical and scientific outlook on the problem has developed which makes public health action possible'. The report provided a rationale for separating contemporary medical involvement from its old alliance with the temperance movement by noting that lack of 'medical and scientific knowledge' had previously resulted in 'no differentiation between a medical and scientific outlook on the one hand and the approach of lay reform groups on the other. Action against alcoholism was confused with political and social action against alcohol' (WHO 1951, p. 4). Subsequent reports concentrated on the pharmacology of alcoholism and the features of alcoholism such as 'craving' and 'loss of control' (WHO 1954; 1955). The intention was, at least partly, to show that alcoholism was per se a medical disorder. The medical profession was free, therefore, to take up the cause of 'alcoholism' as a separate problem from the old temperance concern with alcohol consumption.

A second important reason was the humanitarian vision embodied in the view that alcoholism was a disease and not a moral failing or a sin. This made it easier to attack negative public attitudes towards the alcoholic and further legitimated professional, especially medical, intervention which could prevent loss to the community of 'valuable or even outstanding members' (Williams 1952).

Third, the disease concept provided a bridge between different interest groups, facilitating interaction between lay and professional discourse with a common core of 'taken-for-granted' knowledge. While professionals at national and international levels attempted to construct more precise definitions of 'alcoholism' and were engaged in debates on the nature of 'disease', lay discourse could ignore such niceties finding common ground in the term 'disease' to communicate the message through different social groups. The penetration of the disease concept into political, professional and lay discourse thus provided the emerging alcohol field with a focus – on the treatment of alcoholism – and with a coherence of perspective on the nature of the problem which was important in pressing for government action and service provision.

Establishing Psychiatric 'Ownership'

Establishing a specialist status for alcoholism did not necessarily mean control of the field by psychiatry. The treatment of alcoholism within the new NHS came under the mental health umbrella but nineteenth-century temperance doctors had been drawn from a wider range of medical specialisms and this was still so in the 1950s. Dent, for one, was not a psychiatrist and was said to have loathed psychiatrists – 'If there's anything wrong with alcoholism, it's too many psychiatrists', was his famous phrase (Edwards, interview). The Society for the Study of Addiction included many non-psychiatrists – McAdam Eccles for example, a temperance surgeon active in the society since the early 1900s; Professor Golla, a former pathologist at the Maudsley Hospital, who became Director of the Burden Neurological Institute at Bristol and President of the Society from 1949–51 (Berridge 1990, p. 1042); and Francis Camps, a forensic pathologist, who became President of the Society for the Study of Addiction in 1966, and was recorded by a contemporary of the 1960s as being 'highly sceptical about treatment in general and psychiatrists in particular'.[12]

But over the course of the 1950s, a number of concurrent trends resulted in psychiatric dominance within the emerging policy community as individual psychiatrists began to play an increasing role in promoting the expansion of the new specialism. The Institute of Psychiatry provided the institutional base from which emerged an academic 'wing' of the new field. Within the Institute, there was already some tradition of research and interest in alcohol issues. Most notably, Mapother, formerly Professor of Psychiatry and Superintendent of the Maudsley Hospital, had written quite extensively on alcoholism in the 1930s (Edwards 1991, p. 199); as mentioned earlier, Maclay, the government adviser on alcoholism throughout the 1950s, had worked under Mapother and, not surprisingly, was seen to hold 'a Maudsley point of view' (interview, anonymous). Aubrey Lewis, Professor of Psychiatry in Davies' time, had written on alcoholic psychotic states and, reputedly, made a notable contribution to the literature in the 1920s (Edwards 1991, pp. 198–9). Lewis was instrumental in developing the Institute into the premier centre of psychiatric training at a time when there were far fewer undergraduate departments of psychiatry with professorial ranking (Edwards, interview). Within this institutional setting, D.L. Davies, as Dean of the Institute of Psychiatry and consultant at the Maudsley Hospital, was in a powerful position to place alcoholism within an academic framework and provide it with a window into academic psychiatry.

Davies was the first of a network of Institute psychiatrists and, later, clinical psychologists who were to assume leading positions in the alcohol field.

With regard to the development of treatment services, the psychiatric lead in the 1950s came from a different direction. As mentioned earlier, WHO recommendations placed alcoholism ideally under the supervision of an interested psychiatrist. When, in 1962, the government opted for hospital treatment of alcoholism in specialist units, their model was the unit established by Max Glatt, a psychiatrist working in Warlingham Park, a mental hospital in Surrey. Glatt, a refugee who had fled from Germany in 1937, came to Warlingham Park Hospital in Surrey in 1951, having worked for several years previously in psychiatric hospitals. He had been attracted to Warlingham by its reputation as a progressive mental hospital. Under T.P. Rees, the medical superintendent, Glatt found Warlingham Park 'a liberal, pulsating, active community' where Rees encouraged 'initiative and experimentation by his staff' (Glatt, interview; Edwards 1991, pp. 207–25). For most of his career, Glatt was to remain on the margins of the policy community with little direct contact with policy makers. Nevertheless, during the 1950s, he became an important figure in the development of the specialist approach to alcoholism treatment.

The Glatt Model of Treatment

Given the dearth of facilities for alcoholics, and the virtual inexperience of most doctors in treating alcoholism, Max Glatt's descriptions – published in the mid-1950s – of a treatment programme 'evolved by trial and error' at a public mental hospital, aroused considerable interest. Most importantly, perhaps, it created a model which could be adopted elsewhere. An interest in group therapy and the observation that alcoholics in the groups run for neurotic patients were interesting people who somehow 'didn't fit in with what was happening', led Glatt to experiment with a separate group for alcoholic patients. The first group in August 1952 consisted of four men and in Glatt's own words, 'they didn't really think what was offered by me was other than a waste of time, but compared to the even more boring occupational therapy, there was no harm in wasting another hour'. Soon, however, 'it was clear that something was happening', although Glatt confesses that at the time he had no clue about alcoholism and could not explain why the group seemed to be working. Contact with Alcoholics Anonymous was established and the four patients became the nucleus of the first AA group in Croydon in November 1952 (Glatt, interview; Glatt 1955a; 1955b). As interest grew within the hospital and contacts with AA strengthened, the alcoholic group became a 'unit' lodged in one ward where they formed at least half of the ward population. Gradually, the treatment programme developed to include AA meetings in the hospital as well as outside, a group for relatives and, starting in February 1954, a meeting of ex-patients at the Crypt of St Martin-in-the-Fields Church at Trafalgar Square. Group discussions, held within and outside the hospital, were the central part of the treatment programme although some use was made of drugs, namely disulfiram (antabuse) and apomorphine in individual cases. The reading of a 'life story' by a patient in the group was a focus of discussion and psychodramatic techniques were used to act out emotionally highly charged life experiences. While acknowledging that there was no single form of therapy appropriate to all individuals, Glatt came to feel that the group method was particularly suitable in the case of alcoholism, 'as the patient himself is a very active participant in the group method ... Group psychotherapy is thus a form of treatment carried out *with* and to a large extent *by* the patient rather than therapy meted out to him' (Glatt 1955b).

Faith in the group approach to treatment, a belief in the importance of after-care and in the efficacy of AA, prompted Glatt to press for special centres for the treatment of alcoholism:

> If instead of admitting alcoholics in a haphazard way to *any* hospital, care were to be taken to designate in each region in the country certain hospitals only for this purpose, each of these hospitals would contain not as hitherto one or two, but a certain number of alcoholics, who would assist each other (and the doctor) whilst in hospital, constitute a group there, and help each other after discharge in their newly formed AA groups. It should be possible to form quite a number of new AA groups all over the country in this way. Spread of AA will gradually dispel the notion that the alcoholic is a hopeless person, and will ultimately lead to the identification in the mind of the general public of the alcoholic with the recovered AA man instead of with the tragic comic figure depicted in the Music Hall. (Glatt 1955b, p. 64)

Interim results of a follow-up of 150 patients treated at Warlingham Park between 1952 and 1955 seemed to indicate that the treatment programme could be successful, although Glatt was cautious and realistic about claiming success from short-term follow-up. He found that over 40 per cent of patients who had left hospital six or more months previously had remained 'dry' and approximately another 25 per cent had no more than one relapse. In both these

categories, the majority of people also showed improvement in other
spheres of adjustment (Glatt 1955b, p. 71). Four years later, Glatt
summarised subsequent follow-up of his patients and concluded that
two-thirds had shown, over the years, clear evidence of having
benefited from their stay in hospital. Again he reiterated his belief
that, 'regional alcoholic units working in close collaboration with local
AA groups, should replace the present unplanned and haphazard
scattering of alcoholics to places where they feel they do not belong.
The units could also become centres for research, education and
teaching' (Glatt 1959). Glatt's pioneering efforts were well received
when he spoke in 1955 to the Medical Society of London. Pullar-
Strecker hoped that 'other mental hospitals will follow in the steps of
Warlingham', and Lincoln Williams appreciated the feeling of optimism given by Glatt's talk, 'an impression of progress and sustained
progress achieved' (discussion in *British Journal of Addiction* 1955, 52,
pp. 89–92).

Although Glatt, according to his own testimony, did not have close
personal contact with the Ministry of Health and did not campaign
politically for the establishment of special alcohol units – other than
writing about his work in the medical press – it was the Warlingham
Park experiment which provided the blueprint for future government
action resulting eventually in the move towards alcoholism treatment
units (MoH 1962). Thus, while Davies has been assessed as the
academic leader in the newly emerging alcohol world, Glatt has been
credited as the clinical leader (Pollak, interview). Yet Davies, too, was
a prominent clinician although his approach to treating alcoholism
differed from that of his colleagues at Warlingham Park. Davies
considered that he had started 'a sort of alcoholism unit' in 1950 when
he began to admit four or five alcoholics at any one time to his
twenty-two-bed male ward where they were offered 'a comprehensive
treatment approach'. Alcohol patients were deliberately not segregated
from other psychiatric patients although Davies knew that they often
expected something different and felt that they did not belong; Davies
himself thought 'it was good for them to be with other patients'. A
visit to Warlingham Park in 1952 did not change his mind about the
advantages of treating alcoholics in a general psychiatric unit because
'It didn't require any special expertise' and, although not opposed to
the use of group therapy, he did not see any particular need for it
(Edwards 1991, pp. 198–200). With a leaning towards the use of
physical treatments – which he later appeared to lose[13] – and an open-
mindedness towards the new orthodoxies of the 'disease concept',
Davies was never fully convinced by Glatt's approach and it was
illustrative of the differences between the two men that Glatt was

never invited to lecture at the Maudsley (Edwards, interview). As far as can be judged from official correspondence, Davies' approach to alcohol treatment was much more closely in tune with government policy than was Glatt's. As Dean of the Institute of Psychiatry and a member of influential professional committees, Davies was in a strong position to influence opinion within the Ministry of Health. Glatt, on the other hand, was more of an 'outsider'. The mechanism through which Glatt's influence filtered into policy-making circles was, initially, through T.P. Rees, the medical superintendent of Warlingham Park. Rees was in touch with MoH officials; like Davies, he was a member of the Standing Mental Health Advisory Committee, set up as part of the committee structure which informed and advised the Ministry. As we shall see in the next chapter, it was through Rees that Glatt was co-opted on to the British Medical Association and the Magistrates' Committee, the body whose report is generally credited with nudging the Ministry of Health into action in 1962, and it was Glatt's treatment approach which – for a number of reasons – provided the model for policy implementation (Glatt, interview).[14]

'Alcoholism': A Medical and Social Problem

For the most part, events in the UK in the 1950s have been passed over on the basis that little was happening – there was no 'alcohol field', no alcohol 'movement' (Edwards 1991, p. 198). Such may be true, but the seeds of later policy decisions can be traced to changing technologies, new philosophies and networks of influence, and a policy community which emerged at that time. With the temperance movement at a low ebb, the 1950s witnessed a renewal of medical interest in the problem of alcoholism and the emergence of individual psychiatrists as leaders in both the academic and clinical branches of the alcohol arena. The rebirth of the disease concept of alcoholism under the cloak of 'science' was enormously important in promoting the cause of the new campaigners for it legitimised alcoholism as a medical problem and provided a campaigning slogan with the optimistic message that – as with other diseases – help and cure were possible. In the rhetoric of the time, the concentration on *alcoholism* separated the new campaigners as professional men of science who had effective treatments at their disposal from the 'old' campaigners who were now seen as laymen dependent on moral suasion and propagandist techniques and who, moreover, attacked the drinking habits of the nation rather than the disease of the unfortunate minority. International influences had a more immediate impact on medical thinking than on government policy, but there is no doubt that international patronage of alcohol issues in the early 1950s lent credibility to the new concern and was a valuable tool with which to prod the political consciousness. As we shall see in Chapter 4, a different network, evolving from voluntary, church and temperance alliances, was also emerging in the 1950s; but it took longer for this network to establish itself within the policy arena. In the early 1960s, when the medical-psychiatric link with policy makers was strengthening, the voluntary network was still outside decision-making circles.

By 1960, then, the scene was set for increasing activity in both the statutory and voluntary sectors of treatment provision; important leading figures had emerged who were to dominate the growing alcohol field over the next decade and there was pressure on the Ministry of Health to place alcoholism treatment on the policy agenda. The next chapter examines the events leading up to the first policy statement on alcoholism treatment to be issued in the post-NHS years, a statement which, initially, reaffirmed the nineteenth-century role of the state as the provider of an institutional approach to treatment. Chapter 4 then continues the story of the 1960s by examining the parallel development of voluntary, and community-based approaches to alcoholism.

3 The Specialist Option

Overview

In 1962, the government issued the first official statement regarding alcoholism treatment within the NHS. It recommended the establishment of Regional Alcoholism Treatment Units (ATUs). This chapter traces the events, personalities and pressures which led up to the issue of the government's Memorandum and helped to shape the recommendations. Following the Memorandum, the development of ATUs was slow and patchy; within the decade treatment policy was again changing towards community-based approaches to the provision of care. In 1980, it was decided that no new units would be funded. The factors which influenced the development of specialist treatment units over the twenty years from 1960–80 are discussed.

Towards Specialist Provision

Throughout the 1950s, the Ministry of Health received enquiries and criticisms concerning the availability of treatment facilities for alcoholics. Correspondence with medical and lay critics revealed problems because mental hospitals were refusing to take alcoholic patients; because when patients did not wish to go into mental hospitals there were no alternatives; and because the voluntary nature of treatment meant that there was no way to deal with the patient who refused care. Correspondents pointed out that there was general ignorance of the extent of the problem and little public awareness that free treatment was available under the NHS. Only a small number of alcoholics actually came for treatment and there was a need for early detection. Finally, critics felt that existing facilities were inadequate for the number of alcoholics.[1] Requests for information on facilities for alcoholics and whether these provided specialist treatment came from MPs, regional psychiatrists and members of the public.[2] By the end of the 1950s, the Ministry's position on the adequacy of alcohol treatment facilities was coming under increasing criticism. In answer to the standard reply from the Ministry concerning alcohol consumption and alcohol treatment, one correspondent, Dr Smith-Moorhouse, pointed to the unreliability of existing estimates of the need for treatment. Quoting WHO recommendations on alcoholism treatment, he maintained that there was widespread and unfulfilled demand for treatment and that existing care was inadequate.[3]

The question of what kind of provision was needed was still a matter of debate and the problem of choosing between a specialist option and a generalist approach was by no means settled. Whether one perceived alcoholism as a disease entity or as a symptom of underlying problems – and the implications of each view for service provision – continued to be discussed but no longer seemed to point necessarily towards different service structures. In a letter to the *Lancet*, Max Glatt argued that:

> Therapeutically, alcoholism can be approached simultaneously as a 'disease' in its own right as suggested by Alcoholics Anonymous with therapy aimed directly at combating drinking, such as aversion treatment or disulfiram – and as a manifestation of underlying personality difficulties. (Glatt 1961a, pp. 1112–13)

His support for specialist in-patient units was unwavering but he also acknowledged that in-patient care was not always necessary; out-patient clinics – preferably part of a specialist unit – could provide adequately for some patients and 'In many cases the general practitioner may be the only medical man needed to help in the recovery programme, in particular if he is prepared to enlist the co-operation of Alcoholics Anonymous' (Glatt 1960). He also envisaged the need for a wider range of provision to cater for people such as ex-prisoners or down-and-outs who did not fit readily into clinics or therapeutic communities but might be helped in hostels, half-way houses or day hospitals (Glatt 1961b). Another commentator, Dr Basil Merriman, drawing on his experience as Medical Director of the Reginald Carter Foundation, an out-patient facility for alcoholic patients, put the case for an out-patient and day hospital approach to cater for people without gross psychopathology (Merriman 1960a; 1960b). A little later, Griffith Edwards from the Maudsley Hospital, wrote about the value of a public health perspective on alcoholism. He warned that the American trend, towards establishing treatment units as separate centres apart from general medical and psychiatric hospitals, had the major disadvantage of concentrating the treatment of alcoholism in the hands of a few doctors so that alcoholism might become seen as entirely separate from ordinary medicine (Edwards 1962a). However, the tide was turning strongly in support of specialist centres. A leader in the *British Medical Journal* quoted Parr's finding that GPs in a 1954 survey had considered that clinics for treating alcoholics were not necessary in their localities but concluded that, 'Nevertheless, these patients present special difficulties and there is a strong case for the establishment on a regional basis of special centres for treating alcoholics' (*British Medical Journal* 1960, 1, pp. 117–18). Although policy debate was still largely confined to a small group of active professionals, the exchange of ideas revealed some important differences of opinion in the developing policy community. In the early years of the 1960s, these differences were subsumed to the goal of activating a still apathetic Ministry, only to resurface before the end of the decade.

But this growing chorus of complaints, enquiries and suggestions did not constitute a coherent 'policy lobby' and ultimately exerted less pressure on government officials than other key factors. The influence of international perspectives on the medical profession, the development of both an academic window within psychiatry and a new model of treatment have already been noted. These developments were brought to a head by collaborative efforts between the British Medical Association (BMA) and the Magistrates' Committee in an alliance which united the demand for specialist treatment for alcoholism and pushed the Ministry to action.

The importance of the penal-medical interface for alcohol policy was not new. Max Glatt had noted in 1954 that, 'Drunken behaviour is the chief factor which arouses public interest and disquiet with regard to alcoholism', adding that lack of official interest in alcoholism might be because 'drunkenness has been much less evident in recent years'. But a surge in convictions for drunkenness in England and Wales, a rise of 23 per cent which took place between 1955 and 1957, and figures indicating a dramatic growth in road accidents and casualties between 1950 and 1960 (Baggott 1990; Williams and Brake 1980) were important reasons why pressure groups began to look more closely at the relationship between alcohol and these problems. Public opinion favoured more stringent control of drink driving and groups such as the Pedestrians' Association, the Magistrates' Association and the British Medical Association were united in their demands for more effective legislation.

The BMA/Magistrates' Committee 1958–61

Following a recommendation from the Council of the British Medical Association, the Joint Committee of the BMA and the Magistrates' Association had been set up in 1952, 'to consider all matters of common interest, with special reference to observation, prevention and treatment in relation to the medical aspects of legal offence'.[4] Discussion in the early years ranged over the legal aspects of illegitimacy, cruelty to children and the criminal law and sexual offenders. By November 1958, the Committee was ready to turn its attention to other matters and it was suggested that they examine the problem of the rehabilitation of vagrants and alcoholics. The proposal came from Mr Seymour Collins, a magistrate, who argued that anything the Committee could do to stress the need for treatment for vagrants and alcoholics, apart from imprisonment, would be valuable.[5] The proposal was adopted, but within the next few meetings the question of vagrancy was virtually dropped and attention focused on the response to alcoholics. Similarly, although the question of the response to drunken offenders was raised occasionally at later meetings, it was never taken on board as a focus of the Committee's work. It was not until the 1970s that the interface between health care and the penal response to drunkenness was raised again as a policy concern. Undoubtedly, the problems of vagrancy, drunkenness and alcoholism needed to be more clearly defined and their associations explored more carefully. This the Committee does not appear to have attempted.

Instead, the BMA/Magistrates' Committee chose to examine the problem of alcoholism treatment, gathering information on existing treatment facilities and approaches and focusing finally on the Warlingham Park unit as a model for future development because, unlike 'the ordinary mental hospital', it did more than simply 'sober the patient up, detoxicate him and discharge him as soon as possible'.[6] On the suggestion of T.P. Rees, the Superintendent of Warlingham Park Hospital, Glatt was co-opted on to the Committee following the submission of a Memorandum which described the Warlingham experiment and which concluded with the suggestion that 'there is a need for the establishment of special rehabilitation facilities for alcoholics, perhaps in the form of regional special units working in close contact with Alcoholics Anonymous'. The only dissenting voice seems to have been that of Dr Walter Maclay, who again advanced the 'official' view that it had been a policy of the Ministry of Health not to establish separate units because alcoholism was usually a symptom of some other disorder.[7]

By September 1959, a second draft of the Memorandum had been drawn up. It argued more directly for Ministry support for the establishment of specialist in-patient units and expressed the 'conviction of the great advantages of such a unit being part of, or directly attached to, a psychiatric hospital'. The original statement submitted to the Committee and subsequent drafts of the Memorandum have been attributed to Glatt and there was, in fact, little change in the core recommendations of the final document published as a supplement to the *British Medical Journal* in 1961. The report was relatively brief, stating that it was concerned 'only with the true alcoholic, whose whole way of life is influenced by his addiction and by his inability to break the habit unaided' (*British Medical Journal* 1961, 15, pp. 190–5).

The medical press carried very little comment on the BMA/ Magistrates' Committee Memorandum. The *Lancet* (1962, 1, p. 1169) noted that the report had not been followed by any government action and that still 'neither general nor special hospitals are providing for the needs of the alcoholic', although alcoholism seemed to be getting worse. The *British Medical Journal* and the *Journal of the College of General Practitioners* did not carry any comments or correspondence about the report. The *British Journal of Addiction* carried an editorial by Glatt (editor at the time) welcoming the Memorandum and supporting its recommendations (Glatt 1961c).

The contents of the Memorandum were known to Ministry officials before its publication and were undoubtedly the cause of some anxiety. An internal memo dated June 1960 noted that, 'If the manuscript is to be published, we can presumably expect pressure to develop for some action to be taken.' Two months later, in August, the fears were repeated in a memo which stated that, 'Alcoholism seems to be a matter about which we are gradually coming under increasing pressure and I have the feeling that it would be wise to give it some special attention'.[8] Shortly after the publication of the BMA/Magistrates' Committee report, in 1962, the Ministry of Health issued its own Memorandum entitled *The Hospital Treatment of Alcoholism* which recommended that Regional Health Authorities set up specialised hospital units for the treatment of alcoholism and alcoholic psychosis. The 1962 Memorandum (in essence, the same as the BMA/Magistrates' Committee report) is generally taken to mark the first official NHS commitment to the development of alcoholism treatment services. But the decision to develop specialist units was not favoured by everyone active in alcoholism treatment at the time and the rationale for the Ministry's choice remained unclear. It appears, however, that both external and internal events helped to produce a climate of change within the MoH so that certain aspects of the alcoholism question began to move up the policy agenda.

Inside the Ministry of Health: Preparing for Change

By the start of the 1960s, pressure on the Ministry of Health was mounting and questions of treatment provision were being raised more regularly.[9] The Department held to its opinion that special units were not necessary although now there was mention of the fact that Maclay was in favour of special attention being given to alcoholism in some existing facilities, without setting up special units.[10] A second major question concerned the division of departmental responsibility which continued to pose difficulties and which urgently required review. The perceived division between the problems of 'drunkenness' and 'alcoholism', and between 'treatment' and 'education and prevention' impeded co-operation between ministries and foiled attempts to obtain more accurate information concerning the extent and nature of alcohol problems.[11] The need to address the problem of divisive inter-departmental interests and responsibilities and the increasing recognition that, 'this is a many sided problem', led to discussions involving the Home Office. At a meeting in November 1960 between the Ministry of Health (six representatives), the Home Office (two people) and the Prison Commission (one representative), it was agreed that the Standing Mental Health Advisory Committee (SMHAC) might be asked for its advice on the best method of providing treatment for alcoholism and its opinion on the extent to which facilities met the present actual demand. Further deliberations within the MoH led to the proposal that a sub-committee should be drawn from SMHAC and from the Medical Advisory Committee (MAC). The inclusion of the latter committee was important since it implied that 'alcoholism' would be treated as of wider relevance than 'mental health' alone.[12] The Home Office, however, declined further involvement in these deliberations,[13] perhaps because the emphasis on the medical treatment aspects of alcoholism continued to dominate Ministry of Health policy initiatives.

In drawing up the terms of reference for the joint SMHAC/MAC sub-committee, it was recognised that such an enquiry was likely to strike the headlines and lead to speculation of an alarming increase in alcoholism; it was also the case that, 'whatever terms of reference we devise, that we shall get recommendations for something more to be done'. The Ministry was, therefore, concerned to limit the enquiry strictly to treatment issues since 'prevention would open very wide vistas indeed, some of them quite outside the scope of the Department'; department officials saw the use of its own advisory machinery (the SMHAC and the MAC) as advantageous since it underlined the fact that 'we are looking at the problem from a strictly medical point of view'.[14]

At the same time, in December 1960, the Ministry took action to gather statistical data on the nature and use of current facilities. Letters were sent to Regional Hospital Boards and Hospital Boards of governors requesting information concerning the prevalence of patients with alcoholism and details of available facilities. The result confirmed what was already known, that provision was scarce even in the south-east where services were most available.[15] These actions to gather information and advice were taken between September and December 1960, before the publication of the BMA/Magistrates' report. They emphasise both that the Ministry felt forced to take action regarding alcoholism and that Ministry officials were determined to act strictly within the boundaries of departmental responsibilities, by adhering to the medical aspects of alcoholism.

Within the MoH, there was still little expertise or interest in alcohol matters although the situation was beginning to change slowly. The role of medical civil servants, in this as in other areas of health policy, was soon to become a crucial mediating influence, linking in to outside psychiatric circles. Internally, however, perspectives on alcoholism and alcohol treatment were still unchanged at the start of the 1960s. The Chief Medical Officer (CMO), Sir George Godber, himself a lifelong teetotaller, had no particular interest in the alcohol field and, although in the department from 1939, was not involved in any way in alcohol issues until he became CMO in 1960. Then it 'was very much in the realms of the senior psychiatrist, Geoffrey Tooth' who had taken over from Dr Maclay on his retirement in 1961 (Godber, interview). On his appointment in 1961, Geoffrey Tooth passed over responsibility for addiction to alcohol and other drugs to Dr (Brigadier) Richard Phillipson, also newly recruited to the mental health division of the Ministry of Health (Phillipson, personal communication). This was the first occasion on which responsibility specifically for alcohol and drug issues was assigned and it is possible that the change in personnel and the new policy post in the Department of Health played some part in the swing towards the specialist approach. Phillipson came to the post without any background in alcoholism, but he was an enthusiastic and interested recruit (Madden, interview). He was attracted to the idea of alcoholism units; he came to know the leading actors in the alcohol field and became involved with developments at local level (Edwards, interview). This was the first time that policy interests outside the Ministry had had such a significant internal supporter. Certainly, by the mid-1960s, opinion within the MoH had changed. In a letter to Dr Chalke, the Medical Officer of Health for Camberwell in London, Phillipson expressed what had by then become the standard view that 'the present arrangements under which small numbers of patients are treated at large numbers of hospitals are unsatisfactory partly because they prevent the building up of staff with a special interest in alcoholism and partly because alcoholics are often more effectively treated in groups.'[16] To some extent, the notion of 'specialist treatment' was also consistent with broader trends in health policy making. Specialist, high-tech medicine, located in hospital settings was in favour (Berridge *et al.* 1993). In another respect, as subsequent discussion will show, the establishment of in-patient alcoholism treatment units went against the prevailing trend in psychiatry towards community-based care. There were, however, a number of practical reasons why the implementation of specialist units – with resource implications – became a possibility at this time.

Particularly important was the 1962 Hospital Plan for England and Wales, the developments and 'climate' of discussion which influenced the production of this plan occurring simultaneously with events leading to the 1962 *Memorandum on Hospital Treatment for Alcoholism*. In 1956, the Guillebaud Report (Committee of Enquiry 1956) had stated that there should be more money spent on hospital building and subsequent opinion from the medical profession reiterated this demand (Abel and Lewin 1959). It had been clear well before 1960 that changes in medical techniques and treatments had resulted in a decreased need for hospital beds. In one area, for instance, the need for acute beds was estimated to have fallen to 2.5 per thousand population with existing provision standing at 3.1 per thousand (Forsyth and Logan 1960). The 1962 Hospital Plan was, therefore, aimed at meeting the need for new, better hospitals, better designed and better sited, rather than with building more hospitals or providing more beds (Allen 1981).

Similarly, in mental health, the need for beds was decreasing rather than increasing (Busfield 1986). The 1950s was a decade of change in mental health care, when the move from institutionally based care towards community care – begun as early as the 1930s – was fostered by a combination of technological and therapeutic advances and changing conceptions of the nature of mental illness and its treatment. The 1957 Report of the Royal Commission on the Law Relating to Mental Illness and Mental Deficiency, of which T.P. Rees was a member, stressed a commitment to treating mental illness as covering a wide spectrum of conditions and patients, not all of whom required hospitalisation. Ideas such as the 'therapeutic community', the use of group therapy, and 'open door' policy brought new approaches to the social organisation of the mental hospital and the role of patients within it – and encouraged links with the community instead of segregation from it (Busfield 1986). As a result of these changes in medical technology and philosophy and in medical needs, around the beginning of the 1960s some Regional authorities found that they had spare bed capacity which could be re-deployed to set up specialist alcohol units. Local initiatives had already led, before 1962, to the formation of such units at Basingstoke and Chester (Madden, interview).

The prevailing view at that time also favoured a more comprehensive planned approach to hospital provision to ensure a better distribution throughout the Regions. Although Regional Boards had had responsibility for planning since 1948, without sufficient funds at their disposal they had concentrated on everyday problems rather than long-term planning (Eckstein 1958). When Enoch Powell became Minister of Health in July 1960, he and Sir Bruce Fraser, also newly appointed as Permanent Secretary at the Ministry of Health, set about determining the appropriate principles for planning hospital provision which could then be applied nationally. The principles, contained in Hospital Building Notes, were issued to Regional Boards from January 1961 and Powell personally negotiated with each Region to bring about a national plan intended to 'even up' hospital provision throughout the country (Allen 1981). A climate where planned, evenly distributed care according to need was the prevailing philosophy, was, possibly, propitious for advancing the case for a Regional approach to planning alcohol services.

The Development of Alcoholism Treatment Units 1962–80

The policy recommended to Regional Health Authorities in *The Hospital Treatment of Alcoholism* was to set up specialist in-patient units for the treatment of alcoholism and alcoholic psychosis. It was suggested that the units should have between eight and sixteen beds, a convenient size for group therapy, should run out-patient clinics and co-operate with Alcoholics Anonymous in the after-care of patients.

Within the NHS, power over the implementation of health care policy was concentrated at regional and local authority level and was often in the hands of individual consultants; health care authorities could not be relied on to impose policies designed by central government (Allen 1981). In line with this practice, it was left up to Regional Authorities to decide whether to set up specialist alcohol units and how much to spend in doing so. As a result, the response to the Memorandum varied throughout the Regions and, from the start, the units differed in their approach to treatment and in the range of services offered – a reflection, in part, of differences between Regions in perceptions of local need, of available resources, and of past history of service provision. Personalities, too, were important and the autonomy granted to local authorities and individual consultants in matters of service provision resulted in variable and sometimes idiosyncratic developments. The variability of the genesis of services is illustrated in three examples of ATUs established between 1962 and 1968 in different areas of the country.

The Welsh Hospital Board, for instance, chose to encourage the development of a specialist unit which built on a service already established in Cardiff. This had been initiated in 1961 and from the start had adopted a combined team approach with emphasis on community care and inclusion of the alcoholic's family. When the Regional unit was established in 1963, it was agreed to continue the same emphasis on family needs and on supportive work in the community, making the Cardiff unit a forerunner of later developments in the alcohol field. Unit staff also engaged in research, expressing a special interest in alcoholism in women at a time when this was generally a neglected issue, took part in teaching and the training of medical, social and voluntary workers, and became involved in educational work aimed at the general public (Evans 1967).

Other Regions responded more slowly and reflected newer concerns towards the end of the 1960s. The second example is Sandown House, established in Chichester in 1967. Sandown House reflected the personal interests and working methods of the consultant in charge, Dr Raj Rathod, as well as local conditions and national trends. Dr Rathod, a Maudsley Hospital trainee who had succeeded Glatt at Warlingham Park Hospital, found his first years at Chichester frustrating. Finding himself without a specialist unit, he tried to treat alcoholism within general psychiatry until 1967 when his repeated requests for resources to start a unit were granted. By then the problem of illicit drug use was attracting attention. On condition that he treat drug users as well as alcoholics, Rathod was given a house, a staff nurse and a part-time social worker, possibly, he recalled, because colleagues wanted rid of the alcohol and drugs patients. Sandown House thus became one of the first units to combine treatment for alcohol and drugs, an approach which later gave rise to much consideration and discussion (Rathod, interview).

The third example illustrates again the idiosyncratic emergence and development of alcohol units in some regions; but it also shows how larger forces such as the increasing policy concern with illicit drugs and the changing face of mental health care impinged on the opportunities to provide alcoholism treatment and on the resources available to do so. This service 'biography', which covers twenty years in the life of an ATU, is recounted in a letter from Dr Norman Imlah. He was a consultant at All Saints Hospital in Birmingham for nine months before succeeding Dr J.J. O'Reilly as Medical Director in 1964.

Biography of a Service

To give you some background, I was appointed Medical Director of All Saints from 1 January 1964, having been a Consultant at the hospital for the previous nine months. My predecessor was Dr J.J. O'Reilly, who for the previous quarter of a century had wielded all the total powers of the Medical Superintendents, and he was one of the most powerful, with a place on the Regional Health Authority from the start of the NHS. He was a man of considerable ability who confined his influence to the local scene, but he made a considerable reputation in the forensic field, partly because the hospital adjoins Winson Green Prison and I think there was a tendency to link alcoholism at the time with forensic work because so many came to hospital via court offences.

Very few psychiatrists had any practical experience of alcoholism at the time, but I was not among them. During my post-graduate training in Edinburgh I spent the majority of my time as a Registrar at Bangour Hospital, sixteen miles outside Edinburgh and at that time 1957–59 it was the designated hospital for alcoholism in South East Scotland. I am told that one of the reasons for basing it at Bangour was the fact that the nearest small town was one of the Scottish 'dry' towns, and therefore there was no immediate access to pubs – not that that made any difference. There was no specially designated unit within the hospital and the alcoholics were dealt with in the admission wards and two Consultants, the Medical Superintendent and his Deputy shared clinical responsibility. As their Registrar I had plenty of exposure to the problem and the existing approaches to treatment, but unless one happened to rotate to that post, the remainder of the post-graduate trainees had no practical experience, and in many other places there were even less opportunities. I also acquired some knowledge of drug addiction, as the professor of psychiatry, Alexander Kennedy was one of the few who had a special interest in the subject, and used to get cases referred to him from all over and he regularly demonstrated the problems, particularly at post-graduate meetings.

So this experience was relatively unique, but I came to Birmingham in 1959 and had little or no dealings with alcoholism or drug addiction, until about six weeks after I took over as Medical Director. Although the powers of the Medical Superintendent had been reduced, and the post redesignated to mark that change, I found in fact that for a number of years the aura of the Medical Superintendent persisted, and I enjoyed a few years of comparative autocracy. This certainly lasted until 1969 while we had a separate management authority, but changed after we were amalgamated into a large authority based on the adjoining Dudley Road Hospital, and had to compete with a large general hospital. I make this point because without that autocracy from 1964 to 1969 I don't think I could have developed the service I am about to describe.

In February 1964 I received a telephone call from the Medical Superintendent of Rubery Hospital, Birmingham. He, Dr James Mathers, said he had an alcoholic whom he wished to transfer to the new regional unit at All Saints. I told him I knew nothing about a regional unit and he, a trifle sarcastically observed that I may not have had time in my new post to have come across it, and said all hospitals had been circulated three–four months previously telling them that the new regional unit for alcoholism was in existence at All Saints, and this had been on an official circular from the Regional Board. I said I would phone him back.

I sent for the Chief Male Nurse and asked him if he knew anything about a regional unit for alcoholism. He laughed and said, 'Let me show you something'. He took me to a small side ward in a remote part of the hospital, unlocked the door, and the sole content of the room was a brand new cocktail cabinet. 'Behold the alcoholic unit' he exclaimed. He then told me that Dr O'Reilly had returned from a meeting of the Regional Hospital Board the previous September, sent for the Chief Male Nurse and said, 'Bryden we have to set up a regional unit for alcoholism. Buy a cocktail cabinet'. Popular treatment at the time consisted of creating the authentic drinking background where the alcoholics drank and received apomorphine or other drugs to induce an aversion. When the cocktail cabinet arrived, Mr Bryden asked Dr O'Reilly what he should do with it and was told to lock it up somewhere safe until he, Dr O'Reilly had had time to plan a unit. A month or two later he retired and no doubt the unit did not figure largely in his thoughts. In fairness to Dr O'Reilly, it was by no means certain that he was retiring as he already had an extension and if they were not satisfied that they could find a suitable successor, he was probably on another extension.

I returned the call to Dr Mathers and told him that the unit did not in fact exist, although there was some evidence of intent. Predictably he informed the Regional Medical Officer, Dr Christie Gordon and I received a call immediately from Dr Gordon expressing his deep concern that the unit did not exist. He asked me to call at his office at six o'clock that evening and when I arrived all the other staff had gone home. It was the first of many evening meetings with Dr Gordon, whom I regarded as a very fine administrator. He prefaced this first of these meetings as he often did with the remark, 'Now this meeting has never taken place', his way of saying that it was off the record and did not bind either of us officially. He explained the region's embarrassment, as it had not only circulated the region, they had informed the Ministry of Health that they had set up the unit. I think there must have been a directive to Regional Health Boards sometime in 1963 to set up such units, but he made it clear that the decision to site it at All Saints Hospital was based on their view that Dr O'Reilly was the only possible man around at the time who had the knowledge and the background, both clinically and administratively. The purpose of the meeting was to see whether I was prepared to set the unit up instead, and as soon as possible to avoid the necessity of telling everybody that it did not exist. Dr Gordon and I had a very good rapport and we were both natives of the small county of Banffshire and he knew my background and the fact that I had spent two years in a hospital designated for the treatment of alcoholism.

We formed a mutual informal agreement to get the unit off the ground as quickly and quietly as possible, and he promised to give me as much backing as he could from existing resources from staff and capital conversion. He asked about a suitable building that could be seen to be a distinct unit and I promised to come up with one. Next day I went around the hospital and settled for a prefabricated ward standing on its own that was a designated female sanatorium. It had been past custom to send all tuberculous patients with mental disorders to the same hospital in the city and one hospital took males and All Saints took females. As anti-tuberculous drugs were in, the condition was on the way out, and this twelve bed sanatorium had four residual patients in a relatively quiescent state. After consultation with the visiting Chest physician he agreed that I could transfer the four to an appropriate side-ward in the main hospital. I told Dr Gordon that we had a building and he came and saw it, agreed, and promised a sum of money from region to convert it to a twelve bedded male alcoholic unit. It did not lend itself to a both sex conversion, but I made four beds available in the female dormitory of an adjoining admission ward, and Dr Gordon promised that when I could free a larger ward the Regional Board would consider the conversion to a more suitable purpose built unit.

Staffing was the other problem. All Saints was overcrowded, and I had considerable administrative responsibilities, and I told Dr Gordon that I could not devote the clinical time to running the unit, although I would keep a special interest, and be prepared to work closely with a consultant in charge. At the time we only had three Consultants at the hospital, and one of those was my own vacancy when I succeeded Dr O'Reilly, and which was in the process of being advertised. I was already campaigning for an additional Consultant appointment, and this proved the clinching argument. I was given an additional Consultant who would have four sessions specifically allocated to alcoholism. In addition I was given a full time Registrar for the unit. At some point we also got money for a psychologist, but I think that came later. The rest of the staffing I agreed to find from the considerable nursing establishment, and I was able to simply request the chief Male Nurse to allocate sufficient nursing staff to run the unit, and he submitted a list for approval. I also transferred one of the hospital's social workers to the unit on a full-time basis.

The Chairman of the Hospital Management Committee was kept aware of these developments, and it was all passed through the hospital management committee without difficulty, basically because it did not have to find the capital, and region promised to honour the agreed staffing and running costs in the revenue allocations. To the best of my knowledge that original revenue allocation was never revised after we were amalgamated into the larger group in 1969.

In the course of my frequent discussions with Dr Gordon while this was happening I suggested to him that we should designate it as a Regional Addiction Unit, and be prepared from time to time to take drug addiction problems that came to light in the region. My motivations for this were based on the following: (1) I had an interest in the subject from my time with Alexander Kennedy, and was prepared to have some clinical involvement with that side of the unit. (2) Kennedy emphasised the importance of having unusual teaching material, and as we had a new Professor in Birmingham I saw it as an opportunity to strengthen teaching links with the University, and enhance the prestige of the hospital. (3) The early rumbles of a growing problem in narcotic addiction in London were appearing and I thought that if this came to Birmingham we would be in a position to deal with it, and if we were we might well be able to increase resources. This latter was prophetic, as with one exception which I will mention, all the subsequent funding was built on the drugs issue and not the alcoholism.

When the appointment committee was held to appoint two Consultants, out of about forty applicants, only one had the necessary qualifications and some real experience in alcoholism. This was Dr John Owens who was a research senior registrar in South West Scotland, studying alcoholism. He was appointed to the post with four sessions in the new unit. I don't think he had any specific experience in drug addiction, but neither did any of the other candidates. By September 1964 the new addiction unit was opened and received some publicity in the local press. About a year later, events occurred which had a very considerable bearing on the future of the unit. We began to admit young narcotic addicts in the autumn of 1965, and as the numbers steadily grew in the next few months the local press heard of the situation and we became front page news in the local papers. From then onwards for some time we were seldom out of the news, and some of it spilled over into the national papers. In fact the Regional Hospital Board became concerned about the amount of press coverage and Dr Gordon asked me to specifically monitor the information going to the media on the subject. One local feature writer in particular had contacts in the unit, and became highly specialised in the topic. All of this completely overshadowed the alcoholism side although the majority of the beds continued to be used for alcoholism. However, Dr Owens became very innovative in his approach to the management of the rapidly increasing narcotic problems, and we were eventually visited in a short period of time by the Health Secretary, Kenneth Robinson, the Home Secretary, Roy Jenkins, and the Liberal Leader, Jeremy Thorpe. All of this created a very high profile for the unit and on the basis of the numbers of drug addicts, and the government policy of setting up special units to deal with the growing problem, the Regional Board honoured its commitment to set up a purpose built unit. In fact, I had been running down the psychiatric population of the hospital by setting up rehabilitative schemes in the community such as day hospitals, workshops and hostels and I was able to empty a chronic ward block adjacent to the existing unit. Region provided capital to convert that block to a 27 bedded unit to take both sexes, with dormitories of varying size so that the sex ratio could be changed according to need. It was agreed that of the 27 beds, eight should be reserved for drug addiction and the remainder for alcoholism. In addition to the conversion of the existing building, an extension was built on to the building to serve as an out-patient clinic, administrative offices, and teaching area. In the mid-seventies I obtained another capital sum to add a further extension on to the end of the original extension. This was on the basis of the greatly increased number of addicts we were maintaining, and the need for more office space to house the increase in staffing that had taken place. That extension added another six rooms and a seminar room for teaching.

I think there is little doubt that those capital developments came through the need to be seen to be expanding the services to deal with drug addiction. With one exception, which I am coming to, I do not remember any subsequent money being made available specifically for alcoholism, apart from the capital money when we made the original move to the expanded unit, and region announced it was part of a government allocation to increase the number of beds for alcoholism.

The exception took place in 1978. Due to difficulties within the unit, I took overall clinical charge of the unit in 1976 as well as administrative control. By this time the Consultant sessions had been increased to 11, but I kept my formal commitment clinically to four, and two other consultants worked in the unit to make up the total, Dr Owens having moved out of the unit. In 1978 there was some capital money available and not taken up, and at the same time the former home of the District Nursing Service had been vacated due to reorganisation. This was a large house less than a mile from All Saints Hospital. Many of the rooms were self contained for resident district nurses. It became the property of the newly formed West Birmingham Health Authority, of which we were a part and nobody knew what to do with it. I made a bid for it and the money, and it was agreed that it should be a twelve bedded rehabilitation hostel, specifically for alcoholics, attached to our regional unit. Some time later it was formally christened Norman Imlah House!

I retired from All Saints Hospital three years ago. The unit remains 27 bedded but there have been increases in Consultant establishment, and additional staff in recent years from drug central funding initiatives, dating from Norman Fowler's time as Secretary. It is now involved in the new purchasing of services funding system, and I believe that from time to time administrators have to be reminded that it is still a service which caters more for alcoholism than it does for drugs.

To summarise, it seems probable that in 1963 there was some direction from the central government to make special provisions for alcoholics, and in this region there was a response to that direction, although due to the circumstances I have outlined, the response was somewhat delayed. I don't know whether any money was available from central funding, but the initial money when it came, was found locally. When we moved from our prefabricated building to the larger purpose converted unit, the capital was found from a sum that had been allocated by the government to improve facilities for alcoholics. The money obtained for a hostel in 1978 was not specifically earmarked, and was used on my own initiatives for that purpose. Staffing monies were provided initially, but most of the increased staffing over the years was either through my administrative power to move staff into the service from other areas, mainly nursing staff, or in the case of medical staff by gradually increasing the overall establishment of the hospital, and allocating part of that to the special unit. A considerable number of general practitioner clinical assistant posts were added over the years by those means, and we did manage to get a senior registrar allocated from the regional training scheme.

The growth of bureaucracy in the health service, and the need for endless committee meetings in my latter days in the service, make me inclined to that view that it would be very difficult to get such a unit off the ground as we did back in 1964. (Imlah, personal comunication, 1992).

The account given by Dr Imlah and the examples of the Welsh unit and the Sandown unit illustrate well the many factors which determined both the establishment and the subsequent fate of the Regional alcohol units. In effect, as we shall see below, changes were proposed soon after the initial 1962 policy statement and the centrality of in-patient care as the core of a treatment response came under question.

Alcoholism Treatment Units Prior to 1970

There are only a few contemporary accounts of ATUs established before 1970 (Glatt 1959; Evans 1967; Ritson 1969; Hore and Smith 1975) and these provide details of individual services rather than an overview of provision throughout the country. One review reported thirteen official Regional units by 1969 (James *et al.* 1972); another source, which documents the establishment of the units by year, gives a figure of fifteen. The latter estimate is based on data gathered retrospectively from units existing from 1978 to 1982 (Ettorre 1985b). Possibly, lack of consistency in the figures is due to factors such as problems in defining whether or not a service should count as an ATU, to doubts as to when exactly a unit was established and to the fact of changes in service provision which led to some units falling by the wayside. There is no contemporary overview of the kind of treatment offered by the early ATUs although examples described in this chapter suggest the variability of approaches which was possible within the broad outline recommended in the 1961 Memorandum. Later research by Ettorre documented 'types of thinking' which were reported retrospectively as having influenced ATU treatment approaches before 1979. The data from Ettorre's study, given overleaf in Table 3.1, indicate the importance of 'group work theory', 'eclectic thinking' (a mixture of theories), 'psychodynamic theory' and 'behaviour modification' as the most influential types of thinking (Ettorre 1984). This, along with descriptions of treatment approaches in specific units (such as the examples given earlier), provides a hint of the types of methods adopted by ATUs prior to 1979. More precise documentation of the evolution of therapeutic approaches within the ATUs and the factors which influenced the adoption of different treatment methods is an area for future research.

Documentary and oral sources indicate that units established before the 1970s, were attended predominantly by male patients (one in five to one in three patients being women); that patients were likely to be in their forties, to be from the higher social classes and to have a high degree of social stability except in terms of marriage breakup (Hore and Smith 1975). Comparison with people attending other types of services – AA, information centres, and with skid row populations – indicated a close resemblance between attenders at ATUs and treatment populations at AA and information centres. The characteristics of skid row drinkers were very different. Oral accounts of the period confirmed this picture, indicating a reluctance on the part of skid row drinkers to use the services and of consultants and staff to admit such patients to the wards. Interestingly, although the

Table 3.1
Question: In the past (prior to 1979) what types of thinking influenced the unit?

Influential thinking	Number of units influenced				
	A great deal	To some extent	Not at all	No answer	Total
group work theory	18	6	2	4	30
eclectic	13	11	3	3	30
psychodynamic	12	14	2	2	30
behaviour modification	7	15	4	4	30
AA philosophy	5	16	4	5	30
psychoanalytic	5	9	11	5	30
transactional analysis	3	7	12	8	30
gestalt	3	7	15	5	30
systems analysis	–	6	18	6	30

Source: Reproduced from Ettorre (1984) Table 10.

ATUs changed in many ways over the years, the characteristics and composition of the in-patient population appears to have remained remarkably stable into the 1980s[17] (Edwards *et al.* 1973; Ettorre 1985c). Clearly then, ATU provision catered for only a proportion of those who were thought to need help for alcoholism. This was recognised in the next policy statement from the Ministry of Health which began to look towards out-patient care and community services.

When, in general psychiatry, attention was turning towards a community approach to care, the emphasis on in-patient treatment for alcoholism seems already out of tune with the times. Only six years after the first Memorandum, a second document, *The Treatment of Alcoholism* recommended a broader approach which would involve a patient's family and community and which placed the specialist unit within the context of a whole range of statutory and voluntary services (MoH 1968). Official sanction for the trend away from in-patient treatment was to strengthen in the years to come.

Modifying the Role of the Alcoholism Treatment Units
It is not clear to what extent opinion on the appropriateness of a specialist approach actually changed within the Ministry of Health in the early 1960s or whether the actions taken – and the subsequent 1962 Memo-

randum – were largely a strategic response, 'being seen to take action'. Evidence from Ministry files tends to point to the latter explanation. As Robinson and Ettorre (1980) suggested in their account, the 'visibility' of the model developed by Glatt at Warlingham Park and Glatt's success in pioneering a new approach which could be replicated undoubtedly influenced the course of events. There was no competing vision of alcohol services. To follow D.L. Davies' approach at the Maudsley hospital was simply to have more of the same, to continue the trend of the 1950s and treat alcohol patients in general psychiatric wards. With strong currents of national and international opinion pushing in the direction of developing specialist units, the Glatt model offered a way of being seen to take action. Moreover, pressure on the Department of Health came also from practitioners who remained unconvinced of the need for a specialist approach but who saw proposals to set up specialist units as a means of activating alcohol policy and initiating change (Edwards, interview). Thus in a policy vacuum as existed in the 1950s for alcohol in the Ministry of Health, a relative outsider like Glatt could have influence.

Soon after the dissemination of the Ministry of Health's Memorandum to regional authorities, doubts were being cast on the recommended support for specialist in-patient treatment. The catalyst was the publication of a pamphlet from the Scottish Home and Health Department and the Scottish Health Service Council reviewing provision for the treatment of alcoholics in Scotland and suggesting policies for future service developments (Scottish Home and Health Department and Scottish Health Services Council 1965). The Scottish report suggested that treatment results at the Crichton Royal in Edinburgh, where alcoholics were treated in a general psychiatric setting, were similar to results obtained at Warlingham Park. The report recognised that differences in selection criteria might be a complicating factor, but argued, nevertheless, that there was no sound evidence for the superiority of specialized units. It went on to suggest that different types of treatment facilities be set up and emphasised the place of out-patient care and after-care. The Lancet regarded the Scottish report as 'a welcome breeze' noting that the English approach to alcoholism seemed to be in danger of becoming stereotyped. The assumption of the 1962 Memorandum that the key to treatment lay in in-patient units was, claimed the Lancet, perhaps based on insufficient evidence; little attention had been given to the WHO emphasis on out-patient care or to the results of a study undertaken at the Maudsley Hospital, which reported positive outcomes from treatment delivered in a general psychiatric ward (Lancet 1966, 1, p. 86).

Around the same time as the Lancet review was published, the results of studies undertaken at the Maudsley Hospital by Griffith

Edwards and a team of researchers were beginning to appear. Interest in conducting both clinical and epidemiological studies of alcoholism was gathering momentum in the 1960s and was being used to inform policy decisions. Edwards' research compared hospital out-patient with hospital in-patient care, reaching the conclusion that less intensive out-patient based care was as effective as in-patient treatment (Edwards and Guthrie 1966; 1967). Edwards recalled how the results of the research were 'already doing something to dismantle a narrow hospital view' (Edwards, interview) and there is no doubt that the findings from the study influenced the move towards an out-patient, community-care approach in the latter half of the 1960s. Over subsequent years, the research continued to have a decisive impact on policy thinking and on treatment practice.

Criticisms of the perceived focus on in-patient treatment in the 1962 Memorandum were taken on board by the Standing Mental Health Advisory Committee of which D.L. Davies was a member. The Committee expressed the opinion that hospital units should form part of a comprehensive service covering prevention, assessment, treatment and after-care, and this view was taken up by the Ministry of Health in the second Memorandum issued in 1968 (MoH 1968). Significantly, the word 'hospital' was dropped from the title and the Memorandum discussed 'The Treatment of Alcoholism'. It was still felt necessary to increase the number of hospital units to at least one in each Regional Health Board area to provide specialist treatment and training for staff. However, it was also stated that there was a need to increase counselling and information centres, to expand hostel accommodation and to encourage alcoholism units to act as catalysts in establishing other area facilities (Sippert 1975). These developments were given impetus by parallel events in the 1960s which pressed for rehabilitation facilities for groups – such as habitual drunken offenders – who, as mentioned above, were not reached by specialist hospital services. The allocation, in 1970, of £2 million to extend community-based facilities for the treatment and rehabilitation of alcoholics was a further move in shifting service delivery outside specialist units (Sippert 1975).

A still more decisive step away from the philosophy of specialist in-patient treatment for alcoholism was marked by the publication in 1978 of the report from the Advisory Committee on Alcoholism, *The Pattern and Range of Services for Problem Drinkers* (Advisory Committee on Alcoholism 1978b). The circumstances giving rise to the Advisory Committee and the ensuing report will be examined in more depth in a later chapter. Most importantly, the report marked a decisive move to community-based care provided at district level and was undoubtedly a challenge to the centrality of Regional in-patient treatment units as the core state response to alcoholism. Whether specialist alcoholism treatment units should be retained at all and whether they could operate as district services were separate questions which tended to be confused. Max Glatt expressed his concern at the recommendation to 'localise' specialist units by basing them on health areas or districts rather than regions. He argued that the need for specialist services might even increase if diagnostic and early intervention strategies were to succeed and suggested that the answer might lie in 'comprehensive units' – specialist treatment units with a constellation of attached services, including community services, detoxification facilities and a mobile nursing team or 'flying squad' (Glatt 1979a). As we shall see in subsequent chapters, this type of service constellation had begun to happen already with the piloting of Community Alcohol Teams – often attached to specialist units, with the attempt to introduce detoxification units, with the employment of community psychiatric nurses within specialist alcohol units and with the development of close links between statutory and voluntary services. Certainly, by 1980, ATUs had developed many and varied links with other community services and agencies (Ettorre 1985a). Moreover, specialist treatment units had never been intended as more than a partial response to the problem, nor were they meant to be solely in-patient treatment services. From the start, Glatt had envisaged the units as centres for research and training, with close links to community services and with out-patient facilities and, as the example of the Cardiff unit described earlier illustrated, some ATUs functioned in this way from the early 1960s.

Equally, the development of in-patient units and community facilities was not always a separate process involving different individuals. The development of services in Manchester provides one example of the connectedness of individuals and processes. Dr Brian Hore, a psychiatrist trained at the Maudsley in London, arrived in Manchester in 1971 to run a small ATU situated in an old mental hospital. The treatment unit already offered an intensive in-patient programme as well as out-patient groups and a relatives' group and Hore set about broadening service links in the community. While training as a registrar at the Maudsley Hospital in London, Hore had been involved with Helping Hand (later renamed Turning Point), a voluntary organisation working with homeless alcoholics. He described how he had been 'keen to develop the first Turning Point hostel of a therapeutic nature outside London' and had become involved in a lasting relationship with that organisation. He also established a close working relationship with Alcoholics Anonymous and, over the course of four years, brought a number of community agencies together to form the Council on Alcoholism. Collaboration with social services was facilitated through Clifford Hilditch, an Assistant Director of Social Services, who had also worked in the Camberwell area of London and had been influenced by Maudsley approaches to alcoholism treatment. Together Hore and Hilditch initiated the first therapeutic hostel in the Manchester area to be paid for by social services and run by a social worker specialist in alcoholism (Hore, interview). This kind of community orientation to service provision, centred around a specialist core, was by no means an unusual vision within the ATUs although perceptions of what was meant by 'community' approaches began to differ markedly between practitioners as the alcohol treatment field grew larger. Further examples will be given in the next chapter which examines the role of Maudsley Hospital psychiatrists in the development of community approaches in the Camberwell area of London and the network of alcohol specialists, such as Brian Hore, which spread to the Regions from Maudsley roots.

By 1978, there were twenty-five Alcoholism Treatment Units and this grew to thirty-four by 1980 (a further unit opened in 1986) but the 1978 Advisory Committee on Alcoholism Report marked a crucial change in policy and the expansion of ATUs came to a halt (Baggott 1990).

Twenty years after the 1962 Memorandum, the development of ATUs was examined by Ettorre in a series of articles which described the units, the staff and patients and the links with community agencies for the period December 1978 to March 1982 when the data was collected. Twenty-five of the thirty units then in existence were attached to psychiatric hospitals – as originally recommended in the 1962 document – four units were located at district general hospitals and one within the grounds of a psychogeriatric hospital (Ettorre 1984; 1985a; 1985b, 1985c).

The data suggested little change over the years in the therapeutic theories informing practice although this finding may have been a product of the way in which the information was collected. Of the thirty ATUs answering the survey, all reported some kind of in-patient programme and all treated out-patients; twenty-one had either a formal day-patient programme or accepted day-patients, and thirteen had a formal detoxification programme. For in-patients, total abstinence, full participation in groups, attending every appropriate part of the treatment programme, helping with daily chores and absence only with permission were regarded as important. The most frequently used procedures and activities varied for in-patients, out-patients and day-patients in their rank order but were otherwise similar (see Table 3.2). Use of aversion therapy was, by now, rarely reported; vitamins were prescribed by most ATUs and the use of other drugs, mainly heminevrin, hypnotics and anti-anxiety agents was reported by half or more of respondents.

As well as differences in treatment activities shown above, diversity was reported in treatment objectives (total abstinence or controlled drinking), the use of drug therapy, and treatment philosophies, and in the planned length of in-patient care which varied from three to thirteen weeks. Thus, as Ettorre noted, the ATUs were 'far from being 'stereotypical' in their treatment activities' (Ettorre 1984, p. 253).

However, despite constituting the 'official' response to alcoholism treatment, comparison with figures issued by the Department of Health and Social Security (DHSS), indicated that less than half the total of patients admitted to NHS psychiatric hospitals on account of alcoholism were routed towards ATUs. Ettorre (1985c) suggested two possible explanations for this seeming departure from the 'good practice' advised in 1962 when it was stated that alcoholics would fare better in a specialised setting. First, developments subsequent to 1962 had emphasised the community approach to service delivery and, particularly in the report issued in 1978, had increasingly assigned a supportive role to ATUs while the central role went to community and primary care services. But the swing towards a community approach in health care (within the NHS as a whole) was hardly sufficient to explain why half of those who were referred to hospital were treated within general psychiatry. Ettorre's second suggestion seems reasonable, that it might be a process of drift within a system where appropriate sharing of responsibilities

Table 3.2
Six most frequently used procedures and activities in ATUs
(used for 75–100% of patients)

In-patients	Out-patients	Day-patients
group psychotherapy	counselling by staff	group psychotherapy
counselling by staff	telephone support	counselling by staff
occupational therapy	group psychotherapy	relaxation sessions
relaxation sessions	individual psychotherapy	occupational therapy
physical exercises	social skills training	social skills training
social skills training	assertion training	telephone support

Source: Adapted from Ettorre (1984).

between ATUs, general psychiatry and primary health care had not been adequately realised. Other factors, too, were at work to curb the growth of ATUs and to question their dominance in the scheme of service provision, not least, as Ettorre noted, the cost of supporting ATUs which were possibly more staff intensive for consultants than other psychiatric settings. Changes in perceptions of the problem (which will be examined in Chapter 6) – towards looking at alcohol problems rather than alcoholism – may also have encouraged some doctors to review their practice. Dr Rathod, for example, despite his early disappointment with attempts to treat alcoholics in general psychiatry later made a second attempt. He found to his annoyance that the results were no different. With hindsight, he had come to the conclusion that, 'All these changes happened not because of great scientific reason' but because, by then, 'it suited everybody very well that we could treat them without hospitalisation' (Rathod, interview). His comment aptly conveys both the minor, 'advocacy' role of research as evidence for policy change and the importance of factors extraneous to alcoholism treatment in influencing the course of events.

By 1980 the era of specialist hospital units appeared to be over. Factors of cost, the results of research from Scotland and England which questioned that the units were necessarily better than other treatment systems, changes in perceptions of the problem and of the target population, and the personal experiences and philosophies of those active in the alcohol field, all seemed to demand different treatment approaches, and different treatment systems in responding to alcohol problems. However, the question of the role of specialist alcoholism treatment units within the service delivery system was not dead. Debate concerning the need for dedicated in-patient units for both alcohol and drugs was to continue into the 1990s and there continued to be advocates of the view that a regionally based service was valuable in ensuring the availability of specialist, intensive care for patients who need it (Hore, interview).[18] There is no doubt, however, that policy directives pushed for district rather than regional level provision and that, by the 1990s, remaining regional units had to sell their services to district purchasers.

Policy Formulation and Implementation: The Wheels of Power

In a discussion of the relationship between policy formulation and policy implementation, Walt makes the point that it is 'a complex, interactive process in which implementers themselves may affect the way policy is executed, and are active in formulating change and innovation' (Walt 1994). The alcohol policy community emerging in the early 1960s contained powerful 'implementers' – Glatt, Davies and, later, Edwards (Davies' successor), among others – who clearly drove policy first in the direction of specialist hospital units with an emphasis on in-patient care, and subsequently in the direction of out-patient and community care. Access to the seat of power was open, especially to the Maudsley-based psychiatrists. According to Edwards, 'The Secretary of State dropped in to see us, that sort of thing. And at a later stage, I could go out and call on Keith Joseph and get an audience if I wanted to. There was a sense of accessibility' (Edwards, interview). At a time when Ministry of Health officials themselves had little knowledge or experience of alcohol matters, they were reliant on a small circle of knowledgeable professionals and policy formation was largely reactive to pressures applied by these 'policy sponsors'. Those same implementers, as mentioned earlier, were also the producers of much of the research evidence which informed policy.

However, when we look beyond the core of the policy community, the fate of the ATUs lay in the hands of implementers who were not involved in policy formation at the national level and who were possibly subject to quite different personal, professional and local forces. The examples given above of regional developments indicate both a concern to respond to centrally recommended action and a tendency to implement recommendations in a highly flexible manner. Ettorre's findings – that the majority of alcoholism referrals were not to the specialist units – could be seen as an illustration of the gap between policy formulation and policy implementation and of social and professional distance between the psychiatric 'implementers' at the policy core and their colleagues in psychiatry and medicine outside or nearer the periphery of the policy community.[19] Moreover, in the time lag between the 1962 policy statement and its implementation in different regions, changes were occurring which had a bearing on the way ATUs were expected to function (these changes will be addressed in subsequent chapters). Even within the core of the policy community itself, the consensus which had helped to activate policy through support for the 1962 Memorandum was tenuous. Davies himself acknowledged that he had always entertained doubts about the need for specialist alcoholism units (Edwards 1991), although he had not voiced his disagreement in the early 1960s because, according to one account, he believed it was necessary to activate government responses to alcoholism in some way (Edwards, interview). Once alcoholism treatment was on the policy agenda, it is possible that Davies, armed with the results of the Maudsley research, would have felt freer to exercise his influence through the Standing Mental Health Advisory

Committee. By the early 1970s leading policy 'implementers' were directing alcoholism treatment away from intensive in-patient care. A further factor in the shift in policy was the more proactive approach taken by civil servants to policy formulation, including the initiation of research and the collection of policy-relevant 'evidence'. Although leading policy 'implementers' were still highly influential, the policy community was expanding and its composition changing. Contrary to analyses of state provision for alcoholics in the early twentieth century, which found that the inebriate asylums failed (Hunt *et al.* 1987), examination of the development of specialist treatment units post-1960 shows that the units changed, at least in some respects, in response to national and local contexts and changing policy demands. The 'demise' of the ATUs might better be seen as a series of metamorphoses as the core members of the psychiatric policy community adapted to a more shared and diffuse power base.

In the next chapter, we return to the 1950s and early 1960s to trace the emergence of a new alliance between the voluntary sector and psychiatry, an alliance which was to have an important impact on treatment policy directed towards the 'lost' population of habitual drunken offenders and recidivists, the group of drinkers only fleetingly considered by the Committee of the British Medical Association and the Magistrates' Association and neglected in the development of specialist units.

4   The New Voluntary Sector

Overview

Chapter 4 tells the story of the emergence and development of interest in alcoholism treatment in the voluntary sector over the 1950s and 1960s. At this time, a partnership was developing between professional and voluntary workers which was to have an important influence on policy action and a decisive effect on the expansion of the alcohol arena and the policy community. A general acceptance of the disease concept of alcoholism as the dominant treatment model provided a sense of consensus and unity in the field and facilitated the partnership between voluntary and professional agencies; much of the concern was directed towards helping skid row drinkers. In particular, the work with habitual drunken offenders linked the probation services, voluntary services and professional services, influencing policy action in the late 1960s and the Home Office policy document *Habitual Drunken Offenders* published in 1971. The chapter documents the history of two organisations, the Camberwell Council on Alcoholism and the National Council on Alcoholism. Emerging from different roots, the first closely linked to statutory service provision and the second to temperance concerns, both networks drew together individuals from different institutional bases and professional backgrounds. Although developing in different ways, these two networks were linked through cross membership and a common concern to activate policy action. Both played a significant role in the evolving partnership between statutory and voluntary sectors and, longer-term, in the formation of policy on alcohol services.

State and Voluntary Sectors: Establishing the Partnership

The major changes in access to health, welfare and educational provision which followed the establishment of the Welfare State in 1948, are generally taken as the catalyst which prompted examination of the role of philanthropy and the voluntary sector in responding to public need. This also stimulated the drive to redefine the increasingly blurred boundaries of responsibility for public services in domains shared with the Welfare State. But the partnership between the voluntary sector and the state had been evolving since the nineteenth century and the post-war emergence of the state as, initially, the dominant partner in welfare provision was to change again as considerations of cost (allied with Right-wing political perspectives) and ideology (allied with Left-wing perspectives) combined to rediscover the value of voluntarism (Owen 1965; Finlayson 1990; 1994). Initial doubts as to the survival of philanthropic effort within the new Welfare State were soon replaced by an emphasis on the importance of partnership and the establishment of complementary roles. Lord Pakenham, speaking for the Labour government, assigned to voluntary organisations 'a part as essential in the future as they have played in the past' (quoted in Owen 1965, p. 256), but their role was to be complementary rather than primary; supplementing statutory provision, acting as the initiators and pioneers of new approaches too uncertain or controversial to risk spending public money; covering emergencies and the needs of small or atypical groups; and acting as a watchdog of individual rights within the state system (Owen 1965; Finlayson 1994). A number of government reports both prior to and post the establishment of the Welfare State, supported the supplementary and complementary role of voluntary effort (see Finlayson 1994, pp. 287–304). By the early 1960s, the voluntary sector appeared confident of its new relationship with the state, claiming in one statement that, 'Effective community care depends upon enlightened statutory action in combination with skilled voluntary service. This doctrine of partnership is now widely accepted' (National Council of Social Service 1961/62).

The emerging field of alcoholism treatment offered ample opportunities for partnership between statutory and voluntary provision, in particular with regard to providing help for the skid row or habitual drunk. As previous chapters have shown, the 1962 Memorandum had signalled official acceptance of the need to improve services for alcoholism treatment but the response from Regional authorities was variable and slow and there was little increase in statutory provision throughout the decade. In any case, the needs of the vagrant drinker, raised in the considerations of the British Medical Association/ Magistrates' Committee at the end of the 1950s and again in the 1962 Memorandum, had been caught at government level in the grey interface between penal and health responsibilities and had remained neglected. It was known that at the Maudsley Hospital in London, 'Davies would not admit such people to his wards. Thought they weren't "real alcoholics"; they were drunks' (Edwards, interview). Patients at Warlingham Park tended to be middle class with relatively intact social networks and Alcoholics Anonymous was predominantly a middle-class network at that time. An out-patient clinic, opened in 1953 by Dr Beresford Davies in Cambridge, was not aimed at skid row

drinkers and elsewhere in the country there was a similar lack of
service provision for this group (Glatt 1955b; Edwards *et al.* 1965;
Cook 1989). Evidence given to a Home Office Working Party stated
that Dr Bewley at Tooting Bec Hospital in London took drunken
offenders from the courts or prisons either on a voluntary basis or
under the compulsory powers of the Mental Health Act. 'He takes up
to 60 skid row type alcoholics at a time but reports his overcrowded
hospital can give only short term attention and that this is ineffective
due to lack of the essential indefinite support in the way of after-care
these individuals need'.[1] The Supplementary Benefits Commission of
the Department of Health and Social Security was responsible for
running 'reception centres' to provide nightly shelter for vagrants.
These reception centres had evolved from the workhouses of the
nineteenth century and were maintained first of all by local authorities, then by the National Assistance Board until it amalgamated with
the Ministry of Health in 1968 into the Department of Health and
Social Security (Zacune and Hensman 1971). Despite the limitations
of the help provided, one such centre, the 'Spike' in Camberwell, was
described as 'a vital part' of the rehabilitation system since it offered a
safety net for men forced to leave rehabilitation houses when they
resumed drinking (Cook, interview).

Help from the voluntary sector was equally sparse in the 1950s and
early 1960s. Throughout the nineteenth century, philanthropic and
charity efforts, fuelled by the visibility of public drunkenness, had been
directed towards the inebriate. Evangelical zeal was an important
ingredient in much of the voluntary effort at that time, epitomised in
the work of the Salvation Army (Booth 1890). From its inception in
1878, the Salvation Army was concerned with drunkenness and in the
1960s still provided shelter for many alcoholics in the sixty hostels it
managed. A 'Harbour Light' hostel, for alcoholics only, was still in
existence in Wiltshire in the late 1950s and Edwards, then a registrar
at the Maudsley Hospital, recalled his visit there as a new recruit to
the alcoholism treatment field:

> I went down to see it – an archaeological relic. I met a lovely old
> Captain wearing a Salvation Army uniform, who was himself a
> reformed drunk. When anyone started to think of drink in his
> home, he would take them by the arm and march up and down and
> they would sing a hymn together. (Edwards, Interview)

Harbour Light Homes, liable to be seen as religious, working class
and suited to helping a particular type of alcoholic, ceased to exist
shortly after Edwards' visit. But the Army continued its provision for

alcoholics with the opening in 1968 of Booth House in London which included a specialised detoxification unit.

The involvement of the churches, which had played a major role in nineteenth-century temperance movements, also survived into the post-war era. In London, the Salvation Army grew out of the East London Mission; the Southwark Diocesan Church of England Temperance Society sponsored The Harry Lloyd Foundation, an out-patients' clinic; the Catholic Total Abstinence Society offered help which 'concentrates on strengthening sobriety through religious observance and discussion'; Methodist Missions gave rise to some of the earliest hostels for alcoholics (Chalke 1970). One of these, set up in the 1960s, was St Luke's House which became particularly influential in the emerging partnership between voluntary and professional activists. St Luke's grew out of collaboration between the West London Mission, the Methodist Church and the probation service. The house itself was provided by Donald Soper (later Lord Soper), a Methodist preacher with an interest in ex-offenders. Brought up as a member of the Band of Hope, the children's section of the temperance movement, Soper was described by a contemporary as 'a remarkable man, more like a high powered business man or politician' (Richards, unpublished). He was to remain involved throughout the decade with the circle of people working to place the habitual drunken offender on the policy agenda. The man appointed to run St. Luke's, Norman Ingram-Smith, was also to play an important role in the development of hostel provision. Coming from a background in probation work – an interest he shared with Donald Soper, Ingram-Smith was 'a gent. He had a flowery voice and always wore good suits and had lovely antique furniture in his little flat in this hostel' (Edwards, interview). St Luke's was not specifically 'skid row' and Ingram-Smith, himself, admitted that at the time he had 'no idea about any kind of therapy or what we were going to do ... in the main it was antabuse but some people had apomorphine. I can't tell you how we chose one from the other ... I think we just used to try.'[2] The medical input into what was basically an approach grounded in the philanthropic tradition, came initially from Yerbury Dent, a consultant to the house, well known for his use of apomorphine in the treatment of alcoholism; later, around 1960, Ingram-Smith met Griffith Edwards, at which point 'the word therapy kind of crept into my thinking'. Again this was an alliance which was to prove influential.

In the years following its establishment in 1960, St Luke's and Norman Ingram-Smith became an important source of experiences and ideas for the development of hostel provision for habitual drunken offenders and skid row drinkers. St Luke's provided one of the first 'training grounds' for Maudsley psychiatrists interested in hostel rehabilitation and became a source of information for others aiming to set up hostels for skid row drinkers. Ingram-Smith was in touch with Anton Wallace-Clifford, also from a background in probation, who founded the Simon Community in 1963 to provide 'wet' accommodation[3] for street drinkers unable or unwilling to sustain sobriety (Trench 1969; Leech 1990). One of the houses was Simonlight in Cable Street, London – later a source of complaints regarding public nuisance.[4] It was described by Edwards as 'chaotic' but nevertheless run by 'very good people struggling to deal with homeless people and keen to know what to do about the large proportion of people with drinking problems'. The Cable Street centre in East London became the base for research into skid row drinkers conducted by Edwards and used to inform later policy debate (Edwards, interview; Edwards et al. 1966).

The Simon Community itself did not survive the decade; it grew to six houses by 1966 but by then it was in financial trouble and its houses closed down (Trench 1969). But over the course of the 1960s, voluntary effort directed towards the vagrant drinker grew and a variety of crypts, shelters, clubs and 'soup kitchens' were opened to offer temporary relief to homeless alcoholics in various parts of the country (Trench 1969; Chalke 1970; Zacune and Hensman 1971).

Collaboration between statutory and voluntary services was not confined solely to helping the skid row drinker. Alcoholics Anonymous had been building close links with the medical profession since the start of the 1950s. In 1955, an out-patient clinic (the Carter Foundation), opened as a result of collaborative efforts between medical members of the Society for the Study of Addiction, the Church of England Temperance Society and the National Association of Mental Health (Chalke 1970; Berridge 1990) and was reported as dealing with 'large numbers of men and women from all walks of life' (Chalke 1970, p. 135). But it was the perceived plight of the homeless drinkers living on the bomb sites in London which was to unite philanthropic and professional effort, place the habitual drunken offender on the policy agenda and call into question the appropriateness of official boundaries between alcoholism (a Ministry of Health concern) and drunkenness offences (a Home Office concern).

Many of the developments that took place in the 1960s were influenced by a small network of people, some of whom have been mentioned in previous chapters, drawn from among professionals in health and welfare as well as the more traditional philanthropist groups and voluntary workers. Two areas of co-operation in particular began to develop between the statutory and voluntary sectors.

The first was the provision of adequate hostel rehabilitation care, directed specifically at homeless alcoholics and drunken offenders. Provision for the habitual drunk in the early 1960s had much in common with nineteenth-century approaches, relying largely on the offer of stable accommodation for a period of time and the opportunity, under supervision and with friendly 'advice', to adopt a new, alcohol free lifestyle (Cook, interview). In the years to come, this approach was to change dramatically as many workers in the voluntary services concerned with rehabilitation collaborated with professionals in the alcohol field, accepted the disease theory of alcoholism and espoused more 'scientific' approaches to treatment. Collaboration with the statutory sector, especially with psychiatrists and influential doctors working in the alcohol field, moved the voluntary sector away from its philanthropic roots and from its perceived links to the temperance movement and to religious organisations. These were factors which impeded its access to policy-making circles in the early days of the new alcohol arena. Just as international influence through the WHO had been a significant factor in legitimising medical concern with alcoholism, so too the 'professionalisation' of the voluntary sector, at least in part through joint action with the medical profession, helped to legitimise the voluntary role in alcoholism treatment and to reinstate the policy relevance of the voluntary sector. But the alliance between statutory and voluntary activists was to prove mutually beneficial. Through involvement with philanthropic leaders and with issues and clients traditionally the concern of voluntary work, individuals active in the statutory services became part of a process whereby new population groups were defined as relevant to health policy and in need of 'specialist' services (although of a different sort from ATU provision). This represents one of several examples of expansion of the alcohol arena through, in Wiener's words, 'legitimising' and 'demonstrating' the problem of alcoholism (Wiener 1981). Collaborative efforts to place the issue of treatment of habitual drunken offenders on the policy agenda, and the development of services for this group are examined in the next chapter.

The second area of co-operation between the two sectors was the development of a community-based response to alcohol problems which incorporated a preventive, public health perspective and supported the delivery of care in community-based settings. In the move towards a 'community' response, one might expect the role of public health and of the Medical Officer of Health to be crucial. But for most of the post-war period, the potential of public health to play an active part in the alcohol arena was curtailed by the conflicts and confusion which beset this area of health care and by the failure of public health doctors to carve out a distinct identity and function for themselves (Lewis 1987). By the 1950s, Medical Officers of Health were little more than 'administrators with medical knowledge' (Lewis 1991, p. 103) and the profession was in a state of flux and administrative change with Medical Officers of Health becoming Community Physicians by the end of the 1960s. But the concepts of 'community medicine' and 'community care' were unclear and tensions arose from variable use of the terms in relation to changes in the role of public health doctors. Lewis suggests that increasingly the term 'community' came to describe the non-hospital services, linked to the administrative structure of the NHS, without any clear definition of the role of the public health physician (Lewis 1991). Certainly during the 1960s, there is no evidence of interest in alcohol issues from public health physicians as a profession, although some individual doctors became involved in alcohol related activities initiated by other groups.[5]

Within health care more generally, the 'prevention' approach was beginning to target individual lifestyles rather than tackling the environmental and community aspects of health and illness (Baggott 1994; Lewis 1994), a trend which was to strengthen in the coming years and which influenced prevention approaches in the alcohol field. Moves towards preventive, community approaches within psychiatry and within health care generally, in particular the pressures to provide care outside large institutions and to mobilise community resources (Ministry of Health 1959; Shepherd 1980), set the context for similar developments in responses to alcoholism. More specifically, ideas about how community-based approaches to alcohol problems could operate were derived from the American experience. For example, the idea of setting up community 'councils' on alcoholism, first proposed in the early 1950s, was borrowed from the American Council on Alcoholism, a network of alcohol advisory services established by Mrs Marty Mann, a recovering alcoholic. It led, eventually, to the establishment of the National Council on Alcoholism in the UK which is discussed below. Similarly, ideas which resulted in the formation of the Camberwell Council on Alcoholism were generated, partly, by a London consultant following a visit to the US. As we shall see, although these two organisations had much in common, they differed both in their genesis and subsequent development. Both organisations drew together members from voluntary and professional groups, but the early relationship between them is less clear than in the case of statutory–voluntary collaboration around the drunken offender issue and they developed different, although inter-linked, networks of influence. Again, as in the case of hostel development for drunken offenders, activists in the statutory sector – often psychiatrists – played a leading role in initiating a range of community-based treatment and prevention approaches. But the major service development to emerge in the 1960s was the creation of Councils on Alcoholism, a service delivered mainly by non-medical professionals or volunteers, emphasising counselling[6] and education approaches, and providing help to drinkers and their families living in the community.

Through activities aimed at strengthening those two areas of treatment provision, the 1960s witnessed the emergence of a new form of voluntarism in the alcohol field which was to become increasingly 'professional' in its approach, increasingly integrated into statutory frameworks and increasingly concerned with a widening range of target groups. The new partnership did not mature until a decade later when the availability of funding, greater official recognition of the importance of voluntary work and greater dependence on the voluntary sector for the delivery of community-based services resulted in the voluntary sector, 'in effect acting as agents of the DHSS, supplying a service on its behalf' (Baggott 1990, p. 20). However, the seeds of its development were sown in the early 1960s. This can be illustrated clearly in the emergence and activities of two organisations, the Camberwell Council on Alcoholism (CCA), established in South London in 1962, and the National Council on Alcoholism (NCA) set up in the same year. Although these were not the only organisations to address the problem of alcoholism throughout the country, through their espousal of a common perspective on the problem of alcoholism, through their inter-linked membership, and through their advocacy of specific issues such as the need to provide a community-based response to alcoholism, both organisations played a decisive part in local and national policy making and were to influence the course of events for the coming decade.

The next two sections examine the emergence and development of these two organisations before turning to a discussion of their importance for the alcohol policy community and the expansion of the alcohol treatment arena.

The Camberwell Council on Alcoholism

A new development in civic concern was seen in Camberwell, in south east London, on February 19 when some 65 citizens gathered in the Town Hall under the chairmanship of Alderman George S. Burden, to consider the problem of alcoholism as it presented to the borough. The Rev. J. McGregor Lewis, chairman of a steering committee, said that Dr Griffith Edwards, of the Maudsley Hospital, had the original idea during his survey of alcoholism programmes in the USA, and a small committee which had been set up had outlined some initial projects. (*Lancet* 1962, 1, p. 491)

The announcement in the *Lancet* carried the heading, 'A Council on Alcoholism' and the new venture, the first of its kind in the country, marked the culmination of discussions which had begun in December 1961. Impressed by work in the US in aid of homeless alcoholics and by the extent of community action in responding to alcoholism, Edwards had initiated discussions with able individuals in the Camberwell area. He recalled that,

> Actually, one morning over in outpatients, a patient of mine who happened to be the vicar of Camberwell – he's dead now – a man called McGregor Lewis – a big, shambling man of great humour and warmth who'd run into terrible drinking problems, now recovered – said, 'We'll do something. Have a meeting in the Town Hall!' And he got hold of Herbert Chalke who was the Medical Officer of Health and Lord Soper and we had a meeting. (Edwards, interview).

A year later, in 1963, at the first AGM, the constitution of the new organisation was approved and the executive committee was appointed. It included representatives from psychiatry, general practice, preventive medicine, the churches, the probation service, professional and voluntary social work and prisoners' aid (Chalke 1970).[7] The membership represented the emergent policy community and included many individuals who were to remain at the heart of policy making in the coming years. The Council's aims were to increase awareness about alcoholism and the problems of alcoholics among professionals and the general public, to stimulate the growth of treatment services in the area and to develop a model of a community's response to alcoholism.[8] Although set up as a local council, the group quickly established a national reputation and became an important information link between the wider alcohol arena and the policy field. One of the reasons for its national prominence may simply have been the lack of other strong policy relevant interest groups in the alcohol arena. Another was the influential group of people it attracted. Early in its existence, deputations from the Council met with interested MPs and medical civil servants, the latter regularly attending council meetings and events.[9] According to Edwards, Dr Richard Phillipson, a recent recruit to the MoH – although coming from psychiatry – was attracted to the group by the 'slightly prevention, socially embedded, public health view' pressed by Edwards in a number of publications and reflected in the aims and approaches of the Camberwell Council (Edwards 1960; 1961; 1962a; 1962b). The Rt Hon. Samuel Silkin QC, MP for Dulwich, became president; and D.L. Davies, of the Institute of Psychiatry, was one of the vice-presidents.[10] Through these powerful connections, the Camberwell Council on Alcoholism (CCA) quickly gained access to the seat of policy. The Council's programme included a wide range of activities which covered prevention efforts, research, and the stimulation of services for alcoholics (Chalke 1970). The Council did not see its role as the provision of treatment or intervention services, a feature which was to mark it out from the National Council on Alcoholism and was to create some tension between the two organisations (Kyle, interview).

In 1963, Edwards had set up a research team – the Alcoholism Impact Project, which became the Addiction Research Unit in 1967. The initial funding for the group came from the DHSS and was brokered between Edwards, D.L. Davies and Richard Phillipson over lunch in the Maudsley canteen (Edwards 1989). Studies from the Alcoholism Impact group furnished some of the first UK research evidence on patterns of drinking in a community and on the needs of the homeless alcoholic and provided the CCA (and other groups) with 'scientific' support for claims for policy action. It was from this alliance between academic research, psychiatry, and a wide range of professional and voluntary workers revolving around the Camberwell Council that research and experimental treatment projects emerged which were to influence the future direction of policy on alcoholism treatment for the next decade.

Of two main strands of research and activity sown in the Camberwell initiative, the provision of hostels for homeless and offending alcoholics, received speedier attention at policy level. The Camberwell Council provided the debating ground and a supportive institutional framework for much of the activity driving policy considerations on the habitual drunken offender and members of the CCA played a leading role in the Home Office working party which issued the report, *The Habitual Drunken Offender* (Home Office 1971). This was the main policy statement to derive from the concerns of the 1960s. A fuller examination of policy developments regarding the habitual drunken offender is undertaken in the next chapter.

The move towards a public health, community-based response to alcohol problems took longer to establish and branched into many different strands of activity in the mainstream of developments in the 1970s. One branch of activity, for instance, was the stimulation of public and professional awareness of alcoholism and the development of education and professional training. Again, the CCA was involved in these trends. From its inception, the Camberwell Council had arranged public meetings and run seminars attended by a wide range of local professionals. The importance of the Council's educational role was emphasised by Edwards in 1967 when he stressed that 'our aim as the CCA should be to educate a local community'.[11] But the Council also acted as an organisational base for national activities. In February 1967, drawing again on American experience, Edwards suggested running a summer school on alcohol studies in England.[12] The suggestion was taken up and under the leadership of D.L. Davies, with part sponsorship from the National Council on Alcoholism (NCA 1978/79), the first summer school took place at Birmingham University in September 1969. It was deemed to be a resounding success; the 120 participants included 27 doctors, 23 social workers, health and welfare workers, 16 nurses, 12 prison officers, 11 probation officers, 8 members of the clergy, 8 executive officers of information centres, and 5 other people; also attending were visitors from Iceland and the US.[13] The summer schools became an important feature of the alcohol field and an important forum for discussing new ideas and approaches. Stemming from them, again under the leadership of D.L. Davies, was the creation of the Alcohol Education Centre (AEC) in 1972, regarded by one commentator as 'absolutely key' in creating a sense of identity in the field (Kyle, interview). Eventually, the AEC, took over from the CCA the national role in information dissemination and education.

Over a fifteen-year period, the CCA continued in its role as pioneer and stimulator of services and supporter of co-operative partnership between the statutory and voluntary sectors. In Chapter 8, its role in the initiation of services for women will be examined. Despite its stated brief to stimulate local responses to alcohol problems, the Council's role had quickly widened to embrace issues on a national and international scale and by the end of the 1960s, there was concern that the emphasis of the CCA should be to remain 'a truly local community-based organisation'. As part of this aim, a Community Council was created, made up of lay members of the public as distinct from the executive committee, which was composed mainly of medical and social workers. However, it was not until the mid-1970s when the Camberwell Council was drawing the criticism that, 'The CCA is better known in Cincinatti than in Camberwell', that the CCA funding sub-group suggested that efforts should be channelled towards more local activities.[14] The pioneering days of the Council had ended.

The National Council on Alcoholism

While the Camberwell Council espoused the notion of the provision of community-based care for alcoholism, it did not develop or run a service until much later. The evolution of other Councils on Alcoholism developed separately, forwarded initially by the National Council on Alcoholism (NCA), an organisation which had grown out of the activities of the Rowntree Trust in the 1950s. The Joseph Rowntree Social Service Trust had been actively interested in the problem of alcoholism since the beginning of the century when the Trust had opened the Norwood Sanatorium Company which ran a home for alcoholics at Beckenham.[15] Shortly after the end of the Second World War, an attempt was made to establish a Council on Alcoholism similar to the American National Council on Alcoholism started by Mrs Marty Mann (NCA 1978/79). Correspondence from Mrs Mann to individuals involved in the UK effort, encouraged attempts to set up a similar organisation but stressed the danger of creating confusion between Alcoholics Anonymous and the planned Council. Mrs Mann recommended that:

> this work must be kept very separate and labelled clearly as health work, just as it would for cancer, diabetes or whatever. AA must be played way, way down – IF we want to get non-alcoholics interested.[16]

Despite this concern, the individuals involved initially in the UK were largely recovering alcoholics and members of the temperance movement usually linked to the churches. They formed an Interim Committee on Alcoholism which led, in February 1952, to the formation of the Advisory Council on Alcoholism. The chairman was Dr T.A. Munro and the Committee contained such well known names as Dent and Hobson, private medical practitioners with established reputations in alcoholism treatment. Others such as Lincoln Williams appear at first to have declined the invitation to join[17] but became involved later. The aims of the Advisory Council were to promote understanding of alcoholism as a disease and as 'a public health problem and therefore a public responsibility'.[18] The campaigning role of the new organisation was clearly stated in a letter to the chairman in January 1953:

> A further suggestion was that we ought to have at least one MP on our books, and that MPs should be contacted with a view to bringing pressure to bear on the House to give assurance that the provisions of the NHS are sufficiently wide to cover advice and treatment for alcoholics and that alcoholism should be recognised by the NHS as a disease.[19]

However, lack of funds and the difficulty of involving Council members in more than name appear to have stifled activity so much so that, a few years later, Pullar-Strecker was to write that the Council had been 'stillborn from the start'.[20]

It was the interest and involvement of W.B. Morrell, a member of the Rowntree Trust, which reactivated voluntary effort. Forbes Cheston, the secretary of the Advisory Council, had been in touch with Morrell throughout the early 1950s and had hoped to enlist his support in applying to the Rowntree Trust for funds for the Advisory Council on Alcoholism.[21] Morrell, however, appears to have been cautious about soliciting the Trust's directors for support. In a letter to Philip Rowntree, he stated his interest 'that there should be an organisation in existence which would make both the authorities and the public better aware of the problem of alcoholism as a disease and the facilities that exist for its use'. He added, however, that, ' So far the groups which have been set up with this object in view have been weakly constituted and not worthy of support'.[22] Finally, in 1956, Morrell persuaded the Rowntree Trust to set up a Steering Group on Alcoholism, 'to secure public recognition of alcoholism as a disease and the responsibility of the health services' (British Journal of Addiction 1966, 61, pp. 295–9). Members of the Steering Group included social workers, doctors and representatives of churches and societies working in the field. Again, well known personalities from the alcoholism treatment field, such as Pullar-Strecker, Glatt and Hobson, became involved. The group adopted a wide brief for its activities gathering ideas from contacts and visits abroad – especially to the Brookside Clinic in Toronto, run by the Alcoholism Research Foundation (NCA 1978/79).

The Steering Group appears to have established itself with some success as a 'support group' for individuals interested in alcohol policy or the delivery of alcoholism services. For instance, on the agenda for the March meeting in 1961, we find a letter from Dr Smith-Moorhouse, whose correspondence with the Ministry of Health regarding the lack of facilities for alcoholics was noted in Chapter 2. He wrote that he was not making enough progress in establishing a service on his own, and continued:

As a single individual, I felt that more progress could be achieved if I was supported by a pressure group, especially if that group could have influence in the right quarters. (Smith-Moorhouse, letter)

He had approached Leeds Regional Hospital Board hoping to set up a specialist clinic and received an encouraging reply which acknowledged the need to develop facilities for alcoholics and stated that 'in time it may be possible to develop these facilities within the region'. But there was no promise of action. The results of his next approach to the Medical Officers of Health of various towns in the region were more successful:

> I suggested that existing premises could be used, say in an evening; I volunteered my services free, and undertook to provide my own staff, secretary cum organiser, group discussion leaders, canteen helpers from friends and sober alcoholics who were willing to help me .... The only interest I received was from Dr Davies, MoH Huddersfield. (Smith-Moorhouse, letter)

A six-month trial of a specialist out-patient alcoholism treatment clinic was agreed and Dr Smith-Moorhouse hoped to use the results from the trial to press for an in-patient unit. The Steering Group agreed to send a supporting letter to NHS officials,[23] but it is unclear, at this point in time, to what extent the Steering Group had any real influence or contact with policy makers.

Besides providing a focal point of contact for individuals such as Smith-Moorhouse, the group was proactive in its stated aim of promoting the concept of alcoholism as a disease, for instance, by disseminating information about alcohol to GPs and other professionals.[24] There was also support, at least from some members, for a community-based delivery of services. This was expressed as early as 1956 in a letter from the Rev. J.B. Harrison, General Secretary of the Church of England Temperance Society and a member of the Steering Group. Commending the work undertaken by Dr Basil Merriman at the Reginald Carter out-patient clinic in London and requesting Dr Merriman's participation in the group – which was granted – the Rev. Harrison went on to express the opinion that, 'Undoubtedly the outpatient clinic rather than the residential institution is now the accepted modern approach to treatment.'[25] Again, as we saw in the last chapter, even within networks, different interest groups shared a concern to stimulate policy and practice on alcoholism treatment, but held diverse views on the kind of alcoholism treatment facilities required.

The focus of the Steering Group's work, for which it was subsequently best remembered in the literature, centred around the collection of information on the incidence of alcohol problems in the community and on the social implications of alcoholism. The idea for the study appears to have come from Morrell.[26] It was intended to assess the incidence of alcoholism from data provided by health visitors and probation officers in five localities (Harrow, Peterborough, York, Salford and Gateshead). In this way, it was hoped to build on Parr's earlier study of the incidence of alcoholism seen in general practice (Parr 1957), and include population groups, such as women and the unemployed, who were likely to have been missed in Parr's research. The survey, carried out between 1960 and 1963, and published under the title *Chronic Alcoholics*, was attributed largely to G. Prys Williams, an economist and statistician working for the Christian Economic and Social Research Foundation. The results of the study confirmed that the incidence of 'hidden' alcoholism was greater than the much quoted evidence from Dr Parr's survey of general practitioners had suggested (Joseph Rowntree Trust, 1960–63). By this time, a National Council on Alcoholism was poised to replace the Steering Group on Alcoholism. It was established in 1962 with Richard Percival as Director of Field Work. With the establishment of the NCA and the completion of their survey, the work of the Steering Group on Alcoholism came to an end although the Rowntree Social Service Trust continued to provide financial support for the NCA until 1974, by which time government funding had been secured (NCA 1978/79).

From the outset, the Steering Group had been concerned with the social implications of alcoholism and had aimed to encourage 'a picture of the alcoholic in relation to the community' (*British Journal of Addiction* 1966, 61, pp. 295–9) rather than concentrate solely on the medical aspects of alcoholism. The establishment of regional information and advice centres lay, therefore, at the heart of the new NCA's plans. But, as with the ATUs, the spread of Councils on Alcoholism depended very much on the local context and on the involvement of interested individuals, especially in the early period when funds were low (Rutherford, interview).

Liverpool was chosen as the first site for a Regional Council on Alcoholism because it already boasted a structure of alcoholism services and a number of interested medical and social professionals (Kenyon 1970; Madden1988). The Mersyside Council on Alcoholism was formally opened on 23 July 1963 by Mrs Bessie Braddock, MP, 'formidable in personality and appearance' (Madden 1988). Soon after, the first director retired due to ill health and his place was taken in 1964 by Bill Kenyon, 'a dynamic person', who was to play an important role over the next decade in establishing services, training and awareness locally and nationally (Madden, interview). The council became host to a series of international conferences which it still organises in the 1990s and contributed to the foundation of a Medical Committee. The latter became the Medical Council on Alcoholism

(MCA) in 1967, with the aims of stimulating greater awareness among doctors of the problems of alcoholism and of providing information to the general public (Chalke 1970; Caldwell 1975).

Other Councils on Alcoholism followed, in Cardiff, Gloucester and Brighton in 1964, and in Glasgow in 1965,[27] but lack of secure funding meant that councils came and went. The Sussex Council (Brighton), for example, under the directorship of Lincoln Williams, was forced to close in 1965 'owing to a combination of factors, mainly financial' (NCA 1978/79). A national appeal for funds in 1964, launched at a lunch reception by Mrs Marty Mann, was a disaster, netting less than the campaign expenses, and later appeals by celebrities such as Bessie Braddock raised only modest amounts (NCA 1978/79). Early appeals to government received encouragement without financial help and by 1973 there were still only six councils (Rutherford, interview). In 1973, on the wave of a new interest in alcohol service development, the NCA received a government grant of £113,000 spread over three years. The money was to be used for administrative work, to support existing councils until local authorities and area health authorities assumed financial responsibility, and to provide 'pump-priming' to develop a network of information services and stimulate local and voluntary effort throughout the country (DHSS 1973; NCA 1978/79). The subsequent fate of the NCA and of Councils on Alcoholism is continued in later chapters which examine the changing face of alcoholism treatment and service delivery in the 1970s. By then, councils on alcoholism were no longer seen as closely associated with their early roots which had linked them to temperance approaches and temperance networks, and the NCA and local councils were becoming a major institution in the delivery of community-based interventions for problem drinkers.

Networks of Influence

During the early years, the voluntary–statutory partnership initiated by the Camberwell Council united a group of individuals drawn from professional health, social welfare and policy backgrounds working with individuals still active in the voluntary, philanthropic tradition. The individuals involved held, although to varying degrees, a common conceptualisation of the nature of the problem based on the disease concept of alcoholism which had gained increasing acceptance over the previous decade. Although services existed in different parts of the country, the drive to initiate and develop new approaches was largely London-based especially in the case of hostel and community-care approaches. Centred around the activities of the CCA, there was a feeling of consistency and coherence of aims and approaches to the problem of alcoholism which undoubtedly strengthened the emerging alcohol field and aided attempts to influence policy at that time. In the longer term, from the alliance between professional and voluntary workers in the Camberwell project and from the research and training activities developed at the Institute of Psychiatry, there emerged networks of individuals who spread to other parts of the country where they were often instrumental in policy formation and in the implementation of services.

Out of the Joseph Rowntree Steering Group on Alcoholism and the National Council on Alcoholism came another network of individuals, less clearly defined than the CCA group and, although active as policy advocates from the 1950s, less immediately connected to the core of policy formation in the 1960s. Although there was some overlap in the individuals involved with both organisations, the NCA and the CCA evolved separately and, initially, this resulted in some tension so that affiliation of the CCA to the NCA did not happen until 1970.[28] One source of tension was the CCA's refusal to set up a counselling service. Twelve years after the CCA had been established, the chairman of the executive committee, Mr Jimmy Gordon, supported the Council's continuing refusal to provide a service, arguing in the Annual Report for 1974–75 that, 'I have this dread that one day in our city high streets every alternative shop will be a specialist treatment agency'.[29] The following year the report carried the comment that, 'the reasons for the development of this unique style must include our close early links with the Maudsley Hospital and the Institute of Psychiatry ... both responsible for much of the pioneer treatment and research into alcoholism in England'. By the time a counselling service was set up in the Camberwell area in 1976, the CCA itself was already of less significance, having spawned newer organisations to further its various functions. The NCA, on the other hand, had been concerned from the start with the provision of an intervention (as well as information) service to alcoholics. The approach was one-to-one counselling although, as noted already, over the years the term 'counselling' has been used to describe a therapeutic approach which has itself undergone considerable change and, in the early days, was generally described as 'advice'. Councils on Alcoholism were to become the largest network of services for problem drinkers within the voluntary sector with over ninety regional and local councils in the UK by 1990.[30]

However loosely, the CCA and the NCA networks were interlinked from the start and links between the networks appear to have strengthened over the years. For instance, the Rev. MacGregor Lewis, one of the leaders in setting up the CCA was in touch with the NCA and when he moved to Herefordshire, he started the Herefordshire Council on Alcoholism.[31] By 1970, the NCA had Donald Soper as one of its patrons; Barry Richards, a business man, involved with Griffith Edwards in setting up a hostel for homeless alcoholic men in south London, was on the Executive Committee of the NCA as was Celia Hensman, a researcher who had joined Edwards' research group at the Institute of Psychiatry in the 1960s. Alan Sippert, a medical civil servant, attended both NCA and CCA meetings as an observer; Edwards, Glatt, Rathod and Chalke were all members of the NCA Medical Committee; and, as mentioned earlier, the NCA and the MCA were involved with D.L. Davies in organising the first summer school in Birmingham. Although the alcohol arena was expanding, these inter-connections illustrate that it was still quite small and quite cohesive in its aims of furthering alcoholism treatment policy. Policy was not entirely dominated by medical or psychiatric perspectives although individual psychiatrists were in the forefront of many of the developments which had an immediate impact on policy agendas and policy statements. This is illustrated in the next chapter which returns to the early 1960s and examines the impact of the alliance between philanthropy and professionals on policy developments in the treatment and rehabilitation of habitual drunken offenders and skid row alcoholics.

5   Habitual Drunken Offenders

Overview

The interface between health and criminal policy and the division of responsibility between the Department of Health and the Home Office became major issues in debates concerning the response to habitual drunken offenders. This chapter traces the events leading up to the establishment of a Home Office Working Party in 1965 and the report on the Habitual Drunken Offender issued in 1971. In many ways, the chapter continues the story of the emerging voluntary–statutory partnership and provides a case study of its influence on policy since this was one of the main issues which drew the partnership together in the first instance. However, the recommendations of the Working Party, especially the aim of establishing detoxification units as a response to habitual drunkenness, never passed the experimental stage. The chapter considers changes in the alcohol field and in the social context of care in the 1970s which may have influenced policy implementation with regard to the habitual drunken offender.

Skid Row: The Meeting Place of Philanthropy and Professionalism

> What was unique, you had a philanthropist meeting a professional with a vision who had identified a need for something to happen. And chemistry worked at one level. (Kitchen, interview)

At a time when interest in the problems of alcoholism and its treatment was still confined to a small group of individuals and when the vagrant, homeless drinker was subject to repeated prison sentences rather than the recipient of medical or rehabilitative care, it is interesting to examine the process which raised the profile of this group of drinkers and led to the establishment of a treatment and rehabilitation response. As the comment above from a social worker active in the services in the 1960s suggests, it marked a partnership between professionals and philanthropists; it marked, too, an inter-meshing of different conceptual frameworks regarding alcoholism and treatment approaches; and it brought together a powerful network of personalities from different walks of life with access to government and policy-making circles.

The Nature and Extent of the Problem

At the start of the 1960s attention was turning once more to the problem of public drunkenness which had been less visible during the inter- and immediately post-war periods. A number of economic, legal and social factors, which combined to reduce the real price of alcohol and increase its availability, resulted in rising consumption and a rise in public drunkenness (Out of Court 1988; Baggott 1990). Derek Rutherford, whose roots were in the temperance movement, remembered taking part in rallies in the north of England to oppose moves to liberalise further the availability of alcohol; but temperance opposition was against the climate of the times with its emphasis on personal freedom, including the freedom to drink (Rutherford, interview). By the mid-1960s, the annual figure for drunkenness convictions had peaked at over 80,000 (a rise of 32 per cent between 1950 and 1966) of which some 3000 annually resulted in imprisonment (Cook *et al.* 1969; Home Office 1971; Out of Court 1988).

There has always been considerable confusion surrounding the 'habitual drunken offender'. Statistics gathered by the Home Office report on the number of offences but do not indicate the number of individuals responsible for the offences nor how many of these might need help for alcoholism. In its 1971 report, the Home Office acknowledged the deficiencies in the available information but estimated that there were at least 5000 habitual drunken offenders in need of detoxification facilities (Home Office 1971, p. 30). More recent estimates based on studies carried out in the 1960s and 1970s suggest that the figure was much higher, probably around 17,000 (Out of Court 1988, p. 18). The extent of the problem varied in different parts of the country. Reports made to the Home Office Working Party from Chief Constables of Police indicated around 48 men known as habitual drunken offenders in the Birmingham courts; Manchester recorded approximately 30 persons in this category while Glasgow noted 112 offenders who regularly came to police notice as persistently drunk. Figures were not provided by Liverpool where the problem was acknowledged to exist but caused 'little or no trouble to other members of the public'. Brighton's problem was somewhat different; seasonal migration of habitual drunken offenders was problematic especially in summer. Evidence from the Chief Magistrates Court in Bow Street, London, suggested that 25–50 per cent of persons charged with drunkenness had a drink problem and half of those were habitual drunken offenders. Pentonville Prison in London claimed that one-third of discharges were vagrant drunks and that many others had severe drinking problems.[1]

Homelessness and vagrancy are not synonymous with excessive drunkenness, and 'skid row' includes people who do not fit the stereotype of the 'down-and-out-drunk'; but the majority of habitual drunken offenders were homeless and the increased visibility of public drunkenness in the 1960s was particularly evident in the case of homeless drinkers. A 1965 study of 17 out of the 19 reception centres, run by the National Assistance Board since 1948, found that the centres sheltered approximately 1100 homeless men in any one night; of these almost one-third were estimated to be alcoholics or heavy drinkers.[2] Leach and Barber (1975 cited in Out of Court 1982, p. 18) reported that from a sample of 277 men sleeping rough in London, 21 per cent were members of drinking schools, 26 per cent were heavy drinkers not in schools, 39 per cent were 'dossers' with a drink problem, 10 per cent were casual workers and 4 per cent were tramps.[3] In his study of skid row alcoholics Peter Archard (1975) estimated that between 25 per cent and 45 per cent of the skid row population were alcoholics.

Lay and professional perspectives displayed the simultaneous existence of different explanatory models of the problem and different stereotypes of the drinkers. Archard summarised the conceptual confusion as follows: 'The public label them meths drinkers; law enforcement officials view them as offenders; the medical profession define them as suffering from a disease; mission personnel understand them as being spiritually and morally weak; and social workers speak of them as being social inadequates' (Archard 1975, p. 16). Whatever the real size or extent of the problem, the vagrant alcoholic was generally regarded as a public nuisance, attracting public and media attention and often outrage from citizens in areas where they tended to congregate. In London, the problem appeared to be particularly acute, especially in the south and east boroughs of the city, where open spaces, high-rise housing estates and still uncleared bomb sites were used by the men. By 1967, the London Boroughs of Tower Hamlets and Southwark were campaigning for action to clear the vagrant alcoholic from the streets by compulsory detainment, if necessary. A deputation to Lord Stonham, Joint Parliamentary Under-Secretary of State to the Home Office, detailed the complaints of the citizens in the boroughs and provided examples of letters received by the councils. Descriptions were given of incidents involving fighting and indecent exposure in public parks and spaces, incidents involving children, harassment of citizens entering and leaving their homes and places of work in the area, fear of using Social Security Offices because of the 'meths drinkers', excreta and fouling left by the drinkers, in one instance resulting in the refusal of Council workers to clear litter.[4]

With the interests and wellbeing of 'normal law-abiding citizens and their families' at heart, the Councils' primary concern was to control the public nuisance aspect of homeless drinking. They were sceptical of the ability of voluntary efforts to tackle the problem, complaining that the missions and shelters opening in the early years of the 1960s had increased the nuisance by attracting greater numbers of homeless alcoholics into the area. The same document argued that, 'because of the resistance of methylated spirit drinkers the methods of voluntary rehabilitation at present available are totally inadequate', and the Councils requested 'an approach to the Secretary of State for Home Affairs and the Minister of Health with a view to centres being established under the Inebriates Acts 1879–1900 so as to compel the detention of methylated spirit drinkers in appropriate cases as a positive action towards the cure of these unfortunate people'.[5]

Efforts to address the needs of homeless alcoholics must be seen, therefore, as lying in the grey area between treatment and punishment approaches characterising responses to the group from the nineteenth century. The use of compulsory treatment to deal with the problem of the homeless, habitual drunk had been demanded by some sectors of the populace since the nineteenth century and was to be brought up again in committees and policy discussions into the 1970s.[6] But it never gained serious credence at policy level, possibly because the increasingly powerful medical lobby argued against compulsory incarceration as an effective response to the problem. Over the course of the 1960s, at least within professional and policy circles, the emphasis became more firmly fixed on a treatment model, rather than a penal model as the appropriate response. Nevertheless, the multiplicity of perspectives on the problem remained, and Archard's analysis of the situation explained changing responses to skid row drinkers in terms of changing strategies of control which, by the 1970s had resulted in an institutional structure offering simultaneously moral, legal, medical and social approaches to pulling men out of the skid row treadmill (Archard 1975, p. 18).

Helping the Homeless Drinker and Habitual Drunken Offender

At the start of the 1960s, help for skid row alcoholics was sparse and came almost entirely from voluntary effort which, as noted in the previous chapter, mainly provided traditional 'soup kitchen' help, overnight shelters and 'wet' houses (which accept individuals who have been drinking prior to entry). However, public attention and concern over the apparently increasing number of down-and-out drinkers and habitual drunken offenders was beginning to stimulate the voluntary sector to consider new approaches to managing the problem. In particular, there was a move towards providing after-care to break the cycle of recidivism and rehabilitate the habitual drinker into the community. At the time, the view was that this might be achieved by providing residential homes where the environment, the milieu, was the active agent and the drinker was treated as a dignified human being.[7] St Luke's, described in the last chapter, was one such establishment. St Luke's also presented a model for collaborative work between the voluntary sector and professionals, in this case the probation service, as well as doctors.

A report in 1963 from the Advisory Council on the Treatment of Offenders had stated that after-care in the community was part of the responsibility of the Probation and After-Care Service; that it was essential to have co-operation with the voluntary services; and that there was a need for more hostels.[8] As a result, in May 1965, the Secretary of State for the Home Office set up a Working Party on *The Place of Voluntary Service in After-Care* which was to make an important contribution to discussions on facilities for habitual drunken offenders. The Committee was chaired by the Dowager Marchioness of Reading, 'the demon chairwoman' (Lee, interview), 'a cross-bench peeress and a powerful and influential woman, who could ask the Home Secretary to dinner at any time and expect him to come' (Edwards, interview). She provided an important link between ministers and government officials, the voluntary sector and activists within the Camberwell Council on Alcoholism who became involved in moves to stimulate policy interest in this group of drinkers. Between May 1965 and June 1966, the Working Party met forty-one times to review the field of residential provision for homeless discharged prisoners. Among the considerations of the Working Party were the needs of drunken offenders who, it was stated, formed 'perhaps the largest single category of men requiring specialised hostel facilities'. Among the recommendations made by the Working Party was the provision of 'hostels, specialising in alcoholics and run on moderately authoritarian lines, such as St Luke's House in London' and 'small group centres, or family-like hostels, linked with a psychiatric hospital and providing a high degree of support and treatment, and thus able to accept a proportion of the very disturbed or deteriorated alcoholics' (Home Office 1966, pp. 9–10). It seems likely that the latter recommendation emerged from the written and oral evidence to the working party provided by Griffith Edwards who, by this time was actively involved in trying to set up services for skid row drinkers.[9]

Edwards, with the assistance of colleagues in the Camberwell Council on Alcoholism, had already laid some of the groundwork for opening a hostel which would attempt to rehabilitate the most severely affected group of homeless alcoholics. Again, the inspiration had come from the US. Encouraged by what he had seen there, Edwards had become interested in the problems of London's skid row drinkers and had admitted one of them, Fitz (Fitzpatrick), to his ward at the Maudsley Hospital. Fitz provided Edwards with a list of skid row alcoholics and told him in great detail 'about gang life, about methylated spirits, about the shop which sold religious curios and methylated spirits, the relationship with the police, the rough life, keeping yourself warm by the fire that blackened your face'; thus providing 'an astonishing view of an underworld unknown to the civilised people walking the streets'. Edwards recalled that his encounter with Fitz must have been in 1961 and it was that, too, which really persuaded him 'to get out there on the bomb sites and find out who these people were' (Edwards, interview). Another reason for the ensuing surveys which took Edwards and a research team to the Reception Centre and to the Cable Street house, as well as to the bomb sites, was noted in the minutes of a meeting of the executive committee of the CCA. Speaking of the plight of the homeless alcoholic, Edwards stated that there was a need 'to be sure that we are not inventing the difficulties and that we are right in recognising this as a social problem' (Edwards *et al.* 1966; Edwards *et al.* 1968).[10] It was an article from the early contact with Fitz and the men on the bomb sites which Edwards believes attracted the attention of Lady Stella Reading and led her to contact him. In a letter dated 28 May 1965, Lady Reading invited Edwards to present his views on provision for drunken offenders to the Working Party on *The Place of Voluntary Service in After-Care*.[11] Soon after, a draft Memorandum on hostels for alcoholics was sent to Lady Reading and circulated to the Working Party. The Memorandum acknowledged the dedication shown by the church and the voluntary organisations in their attempts to rehabilitate the derelict alcoholic, but went on to add,

> there is little evidence that voluntary action in this particular field has had more than a trifling impact on what is, in London at least, a very pressing social problem. I am totally convinced that the need here is for Government action – the Welfare State must accept its responsibility. The task is too complex and requires too many professional skills for voluntary organisations although voluntary workers should certainly play a part in state provided treatment facilities.

The Memorandum went on to sketch out the possible types of hostel provision and approaches for this group noting that, 'the needs of the alcoholic can be more effectively met if the population of each hostel is more homogeneous' than was generally the case in existing facilities.[12] Further meetings and correspondence between Lady Reading, Griffith Edwards and Celia Hensman, a researcher appointed in 1964 to Edwards' research group, established that any immediate effort should be directed towards hostels for skid row drinkers partly because of the total lack of facilities for this population and because of 'the present belief that nothing can or, even, should be done'.[13] These moves were important in prompting a re-conceptualisation of the problem of the habitual drunken offender as one where solutions could be found, and a first step towards securing the support and resources necessary to set up an experimental model service.

A few weeks later, in August 1965, Lady Reading wrote to Edwards to ask whether, given money, he could run a hostel and what the costs were likely to be. She added that any such scheme should have an attached research worker. The contact with Lady Reading, and the connections with influential individuals it opened up, was to prove crucial in furthering the vision of setting up a rehabilitation project for down-and-out alcoholics and in leading to the eventual opening of Rathcoole House.[14] There was, too, increasing public concern and publicity about the problem which came to a head when 'in the winter of '64 or '65 certainly one if not two homeless alcoholics died on the steps of St Giles' Church in Camberwell. There was a huge furore about that – a public meeting' (Cook, interview). This visible demonstration of the problem lent impetus and legitimation to the pressure for policy action.

The Memorandum submitted by Edwards, and his suggestions for providing a positive response to the needs of chronic drunken offenders were drawn, at least in part, from his experience and involvement in setting up hostel rehabilitation facilities in the early 1960s. Prior to the events described above, Edwards had already collaborated with individuals in the voluntary sector in establishing a hostel for alcoholics which had opened in 1964 with Edwards as house doctor. The opportunity had arisen when Edwards met Barry Richards, a philanthropist businessman with an interest in helping alcoholics. Richards, who was friendly with a cousin of Edwards, was involved with the Leonard Cheshire Foundation, a voluntary organisation concerned to help people with physical and mental disabilities. When the Cheshire Foundation refused to extend their work to ex-offenders and people with drink problems, Richards decided to proceed on his own. With the help of Dr H.D. Chalke, Chief Medical Officer for the Camberwell area and a grant from the City Parochial Foundation, Richards registered the name Helping Hand Organization as a charity. The first meeting of the charity was held in early 1964 and attended, among others, by Griffith Edwards. Giles House, a residential hostel for alcoholics was opened in the same year (Metcalf, interview).[15] Edwards remembered that, when they met, Richards 'had an idea that they would set up residences for middle-class alcoholics and I somewhat subverted that to Giles House'. All the same, the residents of Giles House were still 'people who were fairly together' (Kitchen, interview) rather than the down-and-out alcoholic. Links between Giles House and notable figures in the field were strong. Norman Ingram-Smith was involved in an advisory capacity and an assistant warden from St Luke's, Gerry Armstrong, was appointed to run the Giles House project after a problematic early start. D.L. Davies and Max Glatt were also in touch with the house. Throughout the 1960s registrars and researchers from the Maudsley remained involved with Giles House and with the setting up of additional houses. 'Helping Hand' became a major charity in the field and was renamed Turning Point around 1977.

Rathcoole, the hostel eventually opened in May 1966 from the collaboration between Edwards and Lady Reading, was intended as 'a constructive and positive alternative to the repeated imprisonment and arrest of the habitual drunken offender'. It was regarded as an experiment, 'to see how far and in what way the 'hopeless drunk' could effectively be helped'. Timothy Cook, a graduate in law from Cambridge, became the warden of Rathcoole and he was to play a part in the campaign to gain acceptance of a medical-social response rather than a penal response to habitual drunken offenders. The role of the psychiatrist and of the GP in the rehabilitation process was possibly more prominent, for a start, than in other hostels, but over the course of the first years of the house, the role of the psychiatrist decreased and became more focused on providing help in specific cases. The rehabilitation offered at Rathcoole was monitored and changes were made as different methods and approaches were tried out. These were discussed in journal articles and reports,[16] thus gaining considerable publicity for the venture.

As with St Luke's and Giles House, the help offered at Rathcoole had its roots partly in traditional nineteenth-century approaches to rehabilitation, partly in the group therapy and self-help approaches which had been introduced into alcoholism treatment in the 1950s and partly in emerging social work techniques. The work of Maxwell Jones, in particular, was remembered as significant in the development of a 'new' model of rehabilitation and visits to the Henderson Hospital, where his therapeutic approach was pioneered, provided fresh ideas for workers trained in the more traditional worker–client approaches used in St Luke's. Residents of hostels employing the 'new' model of rehabilitation were expected to seek employment, to contribute to the running of the house and attend group meetings; individual help was offered in the form of 'case work' by social workers employed at the hostel, leading to 'some interesting and relevant debates about the place of case work and group work in social work' (Kitchen, interview). This was just a few years before the 1968 report from the Seebohm Committee was followed by a massive expansion in social work and a drive towards professionalisation. The Seebohm Committee had been appointed in 1965 'to review the organisation and responsibilities of local authority personal social services in England and Wales, and to consider what changes were desirable to secure an effective family service'. As a result of the 1968 report, new social service departments were created in 1971 and the reorganisation was accompanied by moves to improve the status of social workers as a profession. Eventually, this was to bring an increase in social workers' involvement in the alcohol field.[17] But in the mid-1960s, professionals, as much as voluntary workers, were feeling their way and testing the effectiveness of different kinds of intervention for the rehabilitation of hostel residents (Edwards, interview; Kitchen, interview). Timothy Cook recalled that most of the workers at the time had no qualifications specific to the work and there were few standardised guidelines for running a hostel. At Rathcoole, there was no time limit for residence at the hostel.

A year or more for those who stayed sober was not uncommon ... almost all of them got jobs ... I suppose at the heart of it was that they were more capable and more responsible than they realised and other people said they were. No live-in staff after a year. That was a big shift from staff looking after them to them looking after the place. You spent a lot of time talking with individuals. Counselling was really not needed ... it was not appropriate for this group ... We didn't have the skills and we wouldn't have had the time to do what is now known as counselling ... the more structured counselling came in later and had more to do with the needs of the social workers than with the needs of the clients. (Cook, interview)

This approach to helping the homeless chronic drinker, which seems to have been fairly typical of its type, lasted throughout the period when Cook was warden from 1966 to 1975 by which time Rathcoole House had become Alcoholics Recovery Project (ARP) (in 1969), the second major charity along with Turning Point to cater for the rehabilitation of alcoholics in London. Again American influence played some part in 'professionalisation' in the alcohol field, notably in increasing awareness of counselling as a therapeutic approach. For instance, the director of Alcoholics Recovery Project in the late 1970s was an American social worker who introduced new ideas into the service (Graham, interview). By the 1980s, then, professionalism had overtaken philanthropy.

Policy and Personalities

It is not possible to understand fully the events and processes leading to the initiation of services for skid row alcoholics in the early 1960s without examining the personalities of the individuals involved and the networks which emerged in the Camberwell area and which were to spread subsequently to other parts of the country. Clearly, the way in which the issue of the habitual drunken offender acquired policy attention bears out Smith's observation that political life works 'through who knows whom' (Smith 1991). As earlier discussion has indicated, although not the only source of concern with helping vagrant alcoholics, and not the only source of pressure for a review of policy in this sphere, the voluntary–statutory partnership in the Camberwell area was important because of its access to policy makers and because it helped to 'politicise' the problem through action which went beyond the more Christian charity work approaches adopted by other concerned organisations. It was also this network which drew health and 'charity' arguments together. According to accounts given by individuals working in the alcohol field at that time, policy leadership played a significant role in mobilising awareness of and action on the habitual drunken offender as relevant to health policy and health care; one of the leaders was Griffith Edwards. Shirley Otto, a researcher who joined the group in 1970, saw herself as coming in 'at the end of Griffith Edwards' great campaign to do things for vagrants ... He was the person who got it going ... galvanised the statutory and voluntary services' (Otto, interview). Edwards, according to accounts from his colleagues at the time, seemed able to form special relationships with old tramps and 'was tickled pink about talking to them'; he could get 'fellows from Bogside to articulate their feelings', and 'had an almost holy attitude to the perfectibility of men, taking one man back 14 times into his ward'. 'Every skid row who met Griff thought he was fantastic.' His readiness to 'get his hands dirty' in forming partnerships outside the hospital and academic spheres and his ability to gain the respect and liking of professionals and government officials, enabled Edwards to gather around him a group of people with a similarity of outlook and background.[18] They were individuals who, according to the views of one contemporary, shared an interest in Left-wing politics and a belief in the Fabian and Labour

Party approaches, that it is the material context of people's lives which creates individual problems (Otto, interview).

On the whole, they were also people from privileged backgrounds (Edwards, interview; Otto, interview) and their willingness to work with derelict alcoholics who were largely ostracised by the public and ignored by statutory health and social welfare workers has to be seen in the light of the 'upper class romance with the fallen' inherited from Victorian philanthropy (Otto, interview). To the glamour must be added the 'immense sense of excitement' generated by the commitment of those 'heady times' working in a pioneer field (Cook, interview). To some extent, it was also 'an eccentric subject' which attracted distinguished visitors such as John Profumo to the invited dinners with the residents of Rathcoole. These occasions, again reminiscent of philanthropic approaches, helped to gain a more acceptable public image for work with skid row alcoholics although, according to the house doctor at the time, 'they [the alcoholics] were dumbfounded and they didn't say very much. Most conversation was going on between the invited guests' (Pollak, interview). On the periphery of the Camberwell group, there was, therefore, a wide range of interested, influential people from very different walks of life. Edwards remembered how the issue of 'the drunk' brought in people like David Napley, 'a senior partner in Kingsley Napley, a most distinguished firm of solicitors'. There was also John Havard who was the secretary of the BMA and, of course, Lady Reading who opened many doors. Access to policy-making circles was easy – 'It was possible to dine with Jim Callaghan, the then Home Secretary to discuss contacts with the DoH. We had the attention of the press and we had all manner of people compassionately concerned' (Edwards, interview).

A more cynical interpretation might argue, as Marland (1991) does in the case of nineteenth-century medical–charitable collaboration, that charities (or voluntary organisations) offer opportunities to the medical profession to establish new types of medical care and to forge individual and collective reputations. As in other spheres of collaboration between charity, medicine or the state, compassion, excitement, professional ambition and intellectual challenge undoubtedly interacted in the move to activate policy on the chronic drunken offender. By the time Rathcoole was opened in May 1966, there was a well established network of individuals with access to government ministers and civil servants working with homeless alcoholics; research to assess the practicability and effectiveness of the rehabilitative hostel approach was underway and the involvement of psychiatry along with 'gents' from the voluntary sector had helped to legitimise and raise the status of work with skid row alcoholics. It had also served to promote the medical–social response to habitual drunken offenders and had defined a new group as a legitimate concern for health policy and health professionals. Camberwell had become the centre of the alcohol world and by 1970 was receiving the accolade that 'If you have to be an alcoholic there's no better place to be than Camberwell' (*New Society*, June 1970).

In the long term, the network of psychiatrists and psychologists trained at the Maudsley was important in establishing the addictions as a specialism within psychiatry and in developing services, and training, in other parts of the country. In the short term, members of the Camberwell group played a prominent part in the Home Office Working Party on the drunken offender, organising a conference on that theme timed to pressurise the Home Office[19] and to demonstrate their understanding of the nature of the problem and of the appropriate response. Once accepted on to the political agenda, it was necessary to 'institutionalise' the still experimental response to habitual drunken offenders by formalising acceptance of the medical-social understanding of the problem at policy and practice level and by securing the development and stability of hostel provision. The Home Office Working Party provided a vehicle for institutionalisation but the extent to which the venture successfully secured a long-term stable treatment response to the habitual drunken offender is open to considerable doubt.

The Home Office Working Party on Habitual Drunken Offenders

Modern legislation dealing with drunkenness offending dates from 1872 when the Licensing Act made it illegal to be drunk on a highway or other public place or on any licensed premises. The Act covered 'simple drunkenness' (not involving other unlawful behaviour) embracing the offence of 'drunk and incapable', and a wide range of 'aggravated drunkenness' offences such as 'drunk and disorderly' and 'drunk in charge of cattle' (Out of Court 1988, p. 8). The first time the concept of the 'habitual drunkard' became incorporated in a legal statute was in the Habitual Drunkards Act of 1879. This provided for the voluntary treatment of habitual drunken offenders in 'retreats' for up to a period of two years. However, no such establishments were set up until after the passing of the Inebriates Act in 1898 which permitted the compulsory detention of any habitual drunkard convicted on indictment of an offence punishable by imprisonment, if the offence was committed when the defendant was under the influence of drink, or if drunkenness was a contributory cause. This meant that chronic drunkenness offenders could be held, against their will, for up to three years in State or Certified Inebriate Reformatories. Two State

Reformatories and thirteen Inebriate Reformatories were set up but, as mentioned in Chapter 1, the venture proved a failure and all had closed by 1921 (Hunt *et al.* 1987; McLaughlin 1991).

By the 1960s, when the habitual drunken offender again became a visible problem, moves were afoot to influence official thinking by replacing the 'moral model' – which had dismissed this group as lazy and morally deficient, to be managed by 'compulsive' means – with the 'disease model' which prompted a 'treatment ' response, and by demonstrating rehabilitative alternatives to the penal approach. The work, described above, of the Advisory Council on the Treatment of Offenders and the establishment of experimental hostels in south London was part of a more general climate of change within which legislation affecting the response to chronic drunkenness offenders was revised. In section 91 of the Criminal Justice Act of 1967, the penalty of imprisonment for the offence of being 'drunk and disorderly' was removed on condition that the Home Secretary was satisfied of the availability of sufficient suitable accommodation for the care and treatment of persons convicted of the offence. However, since appropriate facilities were lacking, consideration of the range of available facilities needed for habitual drunkenness offenders now assumed greater policy salience (it was not until 1978 that section 91 was implemented). It was in this context of shifting conceptualisation of the problem and of moves to activate policy and service changes that the activities of the Camberwell statutory–voluntary partnership entered the policy arena, and influenced the Home Office Working Party on the Habitual Drunken Offender.

In June 1967, the Secretary of State for the Home Office appointed a Working Party:

> to consider the treatment, within the penal system, of offenders who habitually commit offences involving drunkenness, to assess the extent and nature of the need for such treatment, including the use and provision of hostels, and to make recommendations. (Home Office 1971, p. iv).

The Working Party, under the chairmanship of Terry Weiler, the Assistant Under-Secretary of State for the Probation and After-Care Department, included Tim Cook, Griffith Edwards, Max Glatt and Norman Ingram-Smith among its members. It met on sixty-two occasions and took evidence from a wide range of individuals and organisations. From the start, the question of departmental responsibility for the habitual drunken offender was a bone of contention. On the one hand, the rationale for setting up the Working Party had been to examine options for taking the drunkenness offender out of the criminal justice system which had proved ineffective as a solution to the problem. The increasing acceptance of the 'disease' model of alcoholism and of the view that, in many individuals, habitual drunkenness was a manifestation of the disease, undermined the appropriateness of the Home Office as the department best suited to provide a response and suggested that it was a responsibility of the DHSS. The involvement of prominent experts such as Edwards and Norman Ingram-Smith in the debates and interest groups which generated concern prior to the Home Office Working Party had strengthened support for a treatment and rehabilitation response rather than imprisonment for the habitual drunk. At the same time, by 1970 some doubts were being cast on the 'disease' label and the psychological model of alcohol misuse as 'learned behaviour' was beginning to creep into professional and policy discourse (Lee, interview). Thus the uncertain status of the habitual drunken offender as a criminal, a sick person, or as someone who had learned dysfunctional behaviour patterns made it easy for departments to vie with one another to retain or reject this area of responsibility.

Perspectives differ on the positions taken by the Home Office and the DHSS during the considerations of the Working Party and immediately after the issue of the report. The impression gained by Timothy Cook, a member of the Working Party, was that the Department of Health and Social Security strongly resisted taking on any responsibility especially at first although, later, they 'began to see it as a health issue' (Cook, interview). Edwards shared Cook's view of events. At the first meeting of the Working Party, Edwards had been disturbed to find that they were expected to consider the treatment of the chronic drunkenness offender within the penal system and he recalled objecting – 'I said that I found this profoundly unsatisfactory because the penal system was one place where they shouldn't be treating the chronic drunkenness offender' (Edwards, interview). Richard Phillipson was present as an observer from the Department of Health and was described by Edwards as 'keeping the fences for his Ministry, saying "Of course, these are drunks and we don't want anything to do with it. The National Health Service would be overrun. It's a Home Office problem".' A somewhat different viewpoint was offered by Penny Lee, an assistant secretary in the DHSS, who had become involved with preventive health issues (including alcohol) around 1968. Although not a member of the Working Party, she was aware of the 'big to-ing and fro-ing' which accompanied discussions of the habitual drunken offender and that responsibility 'came over with great turmoil to health and eventually went back again'. As she saw it, the Home Office was generally reluctant to lose anything that was therapeutic or good;

anything that wasn't locking people up was a nice thing to do. Therefore they should hang on to it ... But their real doubts were whether the DHSS would be capable of setting up services which were likely to be seen as an unwelcome nuisance by local authorities and health services. It was the DoH's philosophy of consensus and 'let's persuade them' which was seen by the Home Office as a bit peculiar. (Lee, interview)

Lee remembered the DHSS as keen to take over the treatment of offenders from the Home Office and that there was 'a big fight with the Treasury to get the money'. At the end of the day, it became clear to those involved in the discussions that there was a therapeutic role and that the policy recommendations contained in the report could only be implemented by the Department of Health.

The Working Party published its report, entitled *Habitual Drunken Offenders*, in 1971. It made two main recommendations; to increase and improve hostel facilities for this group of people; and to set up special detoxification centres as an alternative to arrest for public drunkenness. Neither of these recommendations was to receive speedy implementation and detoxification centres never progressed beyond pilot projects. Frustrated by the inactivity which followed publication of the report, an attempt was made by some members of the Working Party to pressurise the DHSS to take action. This resulted in the establishment of a task force to oversee the piloting of a number of detoxification centres and provided modest funding for the venture; but it did not secure the group's main aim of forcing through the implications of the report on a national basis. However, in 1972, a section was included in the Criminal Justice Act which empowered police officers to take persons who were drunk and incapable or disorderly to 'a medical treatment centre for alcoholics' and in 1973, the DHSS issued a circular (circular 21/73 Community Services for Alcoholics) which is generally taken to mark an important change in perceptions of the drunken offender. It acknowledged 'sickness' rather than 'criminal' explanations of habitual drunkenness offences, and provided financial support to organisations willing to set up facilities for people with severe drinking problems (DHSS 1973). But funding was limited to a five-year period and local authorities were free to implement the recommendations as they saw fit. The result, according to one review, was that by the early 1980s the position in relation to the homeless offender was 'particularly bleak'; incentives to set up new services were virtually non-existent, and the funding framework had become more complicated than ever before. Ten years after the Home Office report was published only two detoxification centres had been set up and only one-third of the number of hostel places recommended in the report was available (Out of Court 1988, p. 25). In 1981, over twenty organisations came together to form a new pressure group, Out of Court, with the aim of working for realistic alternatives to the processing of drunken offenders through the penal system. The question of responsibility for the drunken offender was still unresolved.

A brief review of the detoxification experiments illustrates Sabatier's (1991) concern to examine the factors which influence progression, or lack of it, from one stage of the policy process to another and provides some clues as to why it proved difficult to move from a statement of policy intent regarding the habitual drunken offender towards implementing the policy recommendations.

Detoxification Units

The attempt to set up detoxification units came as a result of recommendations made in the Home Office report *Habitual Drunken Offenders* in 1971, and reiterated as a commitment in circular 21/73. The Home Office report had stated that detoxification facilities were indispensable to any system aiming to address the problem of public drunkenness and had called for detoxification centres which were 'demonstrably medical and social work facilities with a clearly therapeutic purpose' (Home Office 1971, p. 191). The centres were intended for persons drunk in public who would normally be arrested by the police. Two experimental facilities were funded by the DHSS, in Leeds (1976) and in Manchester (1977). A third was planned but never got off the ground. Both centres offered detoxification, assessment and rehabilitation facilities. The Manchester centre was attached to the Department of Psychiatry and had a large medical emphasis; the Leeds centre was managed by a voluntary agency and had a social work bias although medical care was also available (Kessel *et al.* 1984; NCVO 1985).

From the start, the provision of detoxification facilities appears to have been both an emotive and a political topic.[20] As envisaged by the Department of Health, the original concept was of a very simple, basic detoxification service, 'somewhere to sleep it off', run by trained nurses and social workers, with medical services in reserve (Lee, interview). The intention appears to have been to encourage community-based provision with an approach similar to

> something that Helping Hand did in one of their hostels. They had an American girl who worked in Harlem with alcoholics – and a group of rather nice, fuzzy young men and women. They got people in off the streets and she never had the slightest trouble with them. Just by being

disarming and ordinary and nice and relaxed and not clinical, they got good results'. (Lee, interview)

Cost was an important factor. One researcher with funding to carry out a detoxification evaluation, recalled a senior civil servant, Chris Ralph, warning him before the project started that, 'if you find that the most effective way for detoxification is a local general hospital costing £2.5 million, forget it'. Basically Ralph was seen to be saying that the findings from the research had to be community-based because that was all that could be afforded (Cartwright, interview).

It soon became apparent that the detoxification centres were not working as the department had hoped. According to one account, the department was unhappy with the hospital-based service:

All these hospital based ones had to have men to help, porters etc. ... in one, the doctors insisted on having three types of gasses piped to each bed and they saw it very much in terms of beds. It became very medical, but it wasn't the psychiatrists who were the trouble, it was the casualty people. (Lee, interview)

From the point of view of the Department of Health, there was also misuse of health facilities by the police who used hospital detoxification units for young men 'who had got themselves howling drunk' (Lee, interview) while a main objective of the units – to break the cycle of recidivism and get the habitual drunken offender into the treatment network – was unsuccessful. An evaluation of detoxification units was funded by the DHSS in 1977 but the system was deemed a failure long before the publication of the evaluation report in 1985. The report confirmed that detoxification could be carried out in community-based services without sophisticated medical facilities. But it also reiterated the conclusions of the 1971 Home Office report that habitual drunken offenders were likely to be suffering from alcohol problems and were, therefore, the responsibility of the Department of Health; and it pointed out that there was a need for detoxification facilities although it was not clear what form provision should take (Orford and Wawman 1986).

A number of reasons seem to have contributed to the difficulties in implementing the recommendations of the *Habitual Drunken Offenders* report. Limited financial support and the non-mandatory nature of circular 21/73 undoubtedly played a part; but other, less obvious, factors were also at work. For one thing, the question of departmental responsibility was never quite resolved and both the

Home Office and the Department of Health ended up funding 'wet shelters' – overnight shelter for people who would otherwise be charged with offences of drunkenness (Kingsley and Mair 1983). Second, there was a lack of clarity over the goals and functions of the detoxification centres which made DHSS officials cautious about their commitment to the experiment. In particular, the hope that the projects would act as a gateway to rehabilitation for a group which was highly resistant to treatment entry proved unrealistic (Finn 1985).[21] Finally, the Home Office report came at a time of change in the alcohol field. Already, however slowly, perceptions of the problem were shifting from an emphasis on the disease of alcoholism and its treatment, towards a concern with the level of alcohol consumption in the population and the need to activate preventive policies (Baggott 1990). Possibly by 1970 some of the passion had gone out of the alcohol issue. Concern over illicit drug use gained increasing policy importance and competed for resources and the attention of the small number of experts working with problems of substance use. Certainly, the growth of the alcohol arena meant that new areas of national and international activity were added to the existing commitments of those involved in the field.[22] Edwards, for one, committed to international work with the WHO, directing an expanding addiction research unit, and in charge of an NHS alcohol treatment service, found himself forced to pull back from some of the voluntary sector work with which he had been involved since the 1960s. As he pointed out, because of the relatively few people involved in alcohol policy and practice, 'finding enough time in any one day was often the determinant of what happened' (Edwards, interview). For many reasons, therefore, the habitual drunken offender was again slipping out of the public eye and out of the political consciousness.

The 1960s: Passion and Consolidation

The 1960s was an exciting time in the alcohol field. The small policy community which had emerged in the 1950s around the activities of the Joseph Rowntree Trust Alcohol Steering Group, the Institute of Psychiatry, and the London based voluntary sector, especially the probation service and interest groups concerned with prison after-care, grew in strength as it developed networks of action and communication between the individuals and organisations involved in the field and Ministry of Health and Home Office officials. Particularly important at this time was the collaboration between psychiatry and the voluntary sector and the intermeshing of different policy arenas around the issue of the chronic drunkenness offender. This served to challenge prevailing notions of the divide between the medical aspects of 'alcoholism' – the responsibility of the DHSS, and the social problem of drunkenness and alcohol-related problems – a Home Office responsibility. The disease concept of alcoholism, although not fully endorsed by everyone, continued to be a powerful, practical tool in recruiting support and pressurising for action, and the humanitarian vision it embodied lent passion as well as 'scientific' rigour to the debates on rehabilitating the alcoholic drinker. At the same time, beside the passion was a concern over the 'public nuisance' aspects of alcohol consumption and in particular over the visible excesses of homeless drinkers – the group around whom much of the compassionate activity of this period was concentrated. This, too, helped to raise public interest and activate the policy response. The appointment, within the professional stream of the civil service, of a senior medical officer with responsibility for alcohol and drug issues was an important step which provided an inside link to government ministers and senior civil servants. This link was to increase in importance in the coming decades especially as access to relevant ministers and senior civil servants became less easy for practitioners and researchers working in the field. The 1960s was, therefore, a period of consolidation and expansion marked by a relative consensus in the field and by inter-linked interest groups, working towards more or less compatible demands and goals in treatment policy. As Baggott (1990, pp. 59–63) has noted, it was a consensus which included the alcohol industry. An ideology which focused on alcoholism as a problem of the individual rather than as a product of social and political contexts did not threaten the market. This consensus was soon to end.

The early 1970s brought the formative stage in the development of alcohol treatment policy to a close. As subsequent chapters will show, changes in problem perception and treatment philosophies were allied to an expansion of treatment populations and the growth of the alcohol policy arena. As the alcohol arena matured, the cohesiveness of the 1960s gave way to a more diverse, complex relationship between different interest groups in the field, and between policy makers, their medical advisers and informants, and the widening groups of professional, voluntary, and lay practitioners involved in the treatment and rehabilitation services. Speculatively, the shift in psychiatric attention towards drugs left a gap which was filled by other professions and leaders from other backgrounds – although this was only one facet of the decreasing dominance of psychiatry in the alcohol arena, an issue which will be discussed in subsequent chapters. Change did not come out of the blue; changes in perceptions of the problem, in treatment approaches and in the structure of treatment services can be traced back to the debates and concerns of the 1950s and 1960s which did not mature in the context of the developing alcohol arena but which re-emerged with the greater opportunities for professional development afforded in a more established arena of activity. The next chapter begins an examination of the changes which took place in the 1970s and which were to alter fundamentally treatment approaches, service structures and the delivery of alcohol interventions.

6 The 1970s: New Perspectives On Alcoholism and Alcohol Consumption

Overview

In the two decades since the establishment of the National Health Service, the alcohol field had striven towards the adoption of a consensus view of alcoholism as a disease requiring a specialist treatment response with the leading role taken by psychiatry. With the exception of the temperance movement, which held to its traditional emphasis on controlling alcohol consumption, the new voluntary sector which emerged in the 1960s tended to subscribe to the disease model of alcoholism which fitted quite well with its tradition of providing help for 'drunks', 'down-and-outs' and 'alcoholics'. General consensus on the nature of the problem helped to cement the relationship between psychiatry and the voluntary sector throughout the 1960s and to bring combined pressure for action on policy makers. But although the dominance of the disease model and the specialist treatment response provided the basis of a consensus for action between groups with disparate interests keen to influence public opinion and policy makers, the consensus was never complete or without challenge. By the 1970s the apparent unity of the emerging alcohol arena had given way to a more diversified and fragmented field where different interest groups could challenge established concepts and treatment approaches. Of prime importance for alcohol policy development in the 1970s, was the re-conceptualisation of the nature of the alcohol problem. Change came from a number of directions. First, there had been continuing debate since the 1950s about the disease concept of alcoholism; by the 1970s, new and refined definitions of 'alcoholism' were stimulating discussion and a unitary disease theory of alcoholism seemed much less tenable than it had appeared in the 1950s. Second, moves towards a new 'public health' view of alcohol problems with an emphasis on the consumption of alcohol in the population as a whole and on the perceived link between alcohol consumption and harm gathered momentum over the course of the 1970s, with a resultant swing in policy statements towards prevention and the early identification of problems. A third trend was the emergence of an epidemiological approach to the problem. The importance of measuring the size of the problem in the country as a whole – a point made by Jellinek in the 1950s and disregarded by the Ministry of Health at the time – was now accepted and resulted in a series of national surveys. A related drive to refine ways of measuring harmful consumption at the individual level, resulted in a strong consensus on measures of harmful drinking which categorised individuals who could not be seen as 'alcoholics' as nevertheless potential targets for intervention. The new, broader vision of the alcohol problem which emerged in the 1970s found expression in three reports from the Advisory Committee on Alcoholism, often known as the Kessel Committee after its chairman Professor Neil Kessel. Set up in 1975 to examine the provision of services for alcoholism, the Committee's reports were significant in consolidating and legitimising the direction of existing policy trends and in setting the agenda for service implementation throughout the 1980s (Advisory Committee on Alcoholism 1978a; 1978b; 1979).

This chapter traces the conceptual and ideological shifts which drew the policy focus in the 1970s away from the provision of alcoholism treatment towards a concern with alcohol consumption and 'problem drinking' in the population, and which resulted in a much broader, more diverse alcohol treatment field encompassing a wider range of clients, professionals and intervention approaches. The chapter begins with a brief outline of changes in the disease concept of alcoholism and goes on to examine in more detail the factors associated with the swing towards a prevention perspective. Second, the significance for treatment responses of the Advisory Committee on Alcoholism is discussed. Finally, ways in which perceptions of the size and seriousness of the problem were confirmed are traced and noted as part of the increasing importance of epidemiology as a key element of the 'new public health' approach in alcohol policy.

Modifying the Disease Concept of Alcoholism

Since the 1950s, there had been continuing debate about the nature of the 'disease' of alcoholism and in the US social scientists had been especially active in developing a critique of the popularised version of the disease model as it appeared in the 'lay wisdom of Alcoholics Anonymous' (Room 1983, p. 50). Sociologists, in particular, questioned both the validity and the usefulness of the disease concept and, by the end of the 1960s, began to subsume 'alcoholism' under the broader term 'problem drinking' (Seeley 1962). In the American context, opposition to the disease concept was construed by some as a bid for 'ownership' – if alcoholism was not a disease it could not be claimed by doctors; it becomes 'a social problem, and the social scientists are the ones to take charge' (Keller 1981, cited in Room 1983). In the UK, the social science perspective proved less contentious; it arrived later on the scene than in the US and was, possibly, 'hijacked' by psychiatry and absorbed into already changing perceptions of the nature of alcoholism. The fact that there were few social scientists working in the alcohol field, and that those who entered alcohol research or clinical work generally worked alongside psychiatrists, may have prevented the development of widely divergent perspectives. But psychiatrists themselves did not hold a consistent or unified vision of the disease theory of alcoholism. Doubts about the disease theory had been sown early in the 1960s from observations and research within psychiatric treatment settings where central concepts of the theory – such as the need for lifelong abstinence, or the centrality of 'loss of control' over drinking – were already being challenged (Davies 1962; Kendell and Staton 1966; Merry 1966; Edwards 1970). By the 1970s, a disease theory of alcoholism seemed much less tenable than it had appeared in the 1950s, and what one commentary called 'a watered down version of the disease theory' (Shaw *et al.* 1978, p. 67) had evolved from within psychiatric circles. This was the concept of 'dependence' on alcohol which incorporated a physiological, psychological and, to some extent, a social dimension within its definition (Edwards and Gross 1976). As with the disease theory, dependence theory was not an entirely new idea and the origins of later thinking could be traced back to nineteenth-century discussions of the 'habit' of drinking. But, once again, the new version was presented as more scientifically grounded, especially in lines of epidemiological and psychological research which had developed since the 1950s. European unease with Anglo-Saxon conceptualisations of alcoholism, along with social science critiques of the disease concept, emerging in Scandinavia, as well as in the US, contributed to international debates and were influential in emphasising alcohol 'problems' rather than disease or addiction (Edwards 1992). The WHO adopted the new terminology, replacing the term 'alcoholism' with the phrase 'alcohol dependence syndrome' and highlighting the concept of 'alcohol-related disabilities' (Edwards *et al.* 1977).

Much debate accompanied the emergence and subsequent use of the concept of the dependence syndrome. To some, the new terminology implied a fluid and subtle set of phenomena so that, in any one individual, the syndrome could manifest all or only some of the phenomena; it was a 'learned behaviour' which could exist in various degrees of strength and was, therefore, a dimensional definition rather than a categorical definition of a condition; it represented a significant step away from the disease model of alcoholism since it appeared to widen the scope and importance of social and health problems associated with alcohol and to require a response to alcohol related disabilities whether an individual was regarded as 'dependent' or not. To others, adoption of the 'alcohol dependence syndrome' appears to have rested on the reputation and influence of prominent individuals in the alcohol field and in the WHO rather than on 'scientific' evidence.[1] The 'new' concept merely represented a revised version of the disease model and maintained 'an essentially medically-oriented explanation of drinking problems' which 'discriminated against the ability of non-medical agents to recognise and understand the effects of alcohol' (Shaw et al. 1978, pp. 67–8). It was, in effect, 'a political rather than a scientific achievement' (Heather and Robertson 1985, p. 78). The incorporation of the 'alcohol dependence syndrome' into the International Classification of Diseases in January 1979 (WHO 1979) appeared to confirm the continuing strength of a disease perspective 'owned' by the medical profession.

Although the dependence syndrome and the alcohol disabilities concept became the subject of professional and research debate, again, as with the adoption of a popularised, easily promoted version of disease theory, reframing the concept of 'alcoholism' had important implications for policy and practice responses. The new terminology signalled a break with the past; renegotiation of the concept symbolised the changing composition and relationships in the policy community around alcohol, and the impact of the new concept lay as much in the way it was taken up and used in policy and practice as in the 'proof' that it offered anything radically new. Within the mental handicap division of the DHSS, the section dealing with alcohol was renamed the 'social handicap section' reflecting, according to one account, the influence of civil servants who supported a broader view of 'alcoholism' and the beginnings of the influence of social work perspectives on medical understanding of the problem (Rutherford, interview). Most importantly, the new thinking fitted well within other conceptual changes which were altering perspectives on the nature of the alcohol problem and drawing attention away from those most severely affected by their drinking towards the consumption patterns of the population as a whole and the harms which were now believed to be associated with consumption levels.[2]

Alcohol Consumption and Alcohol Related Harm: The New Vision

The move away from a policy focus on alcoholism and alcoholism treatment to a concern with alcohol consumption can be traced back to 1956 when Sully Ledermann, a French demographer and statistician, published a study which suggested that there was a relationship between the average per capita level of alcohol consumption and the level of alcohol misuse in a population (Ledermann 1956). The theory was briefly noticed in the British medical press, but it aroused little interest in professional or government circles in England and there is no evidence to suggest that, if it was known to Ministry of Health officials, it was given any consideration at all. As noted in an earlier chapter, the Ministry's view throughout the 1950s was that alcohol posed little threat to the health of the nation and, as evidence, the Ministry quoted the results of Parr's survey of 400 GPs (Parr 1957).

The reason why Parr's research was accepted as legitimate 'evidence' and other research findings were ignored or missed, lies in the specific policy context and historic situation which influenced the selective use of research in policy debate. For a start, Parr's study fitted snugly within the boundaries of departmental responsibilities. The Ledermann hypothesis, bringing together consumption (Home Office business) and excessive consumption, (alcoholism and, therefore, Ministry of Health business) could not easily be incorporated within existing areas of responsibility for purposes of policy formation and implementation. An even more serious barrier to Ledermann's work was that it went against the tide of prevailing concepts and prevailing perceptions of the nature of the problem. Ledermann's theory encouraged an epidemiological and social-structural approach which had undertones of 'temperance' rather than of 'science'. This was the era of the rebirth of the disease concept of alcoholism which was seen to affect a minority of excessive drinkers and to be a separate issue from general consumption by ordinary people. Moreover, towards the end of the 1950s the medical profession, psychiatrists in particular, were beginning to form a 'policy community' with Ministry of Health officials and were seeking consensus to unite the field in a drive to activate policy. Consumption of alcohol in the population as a whole simply seemed irrelevant to the major issues of providing a humane and appropriate response to alcoholism. Thus, while the Parr survey could be used to legitimate existing ideology, departmental boundaries and existing policy, Ledermann's hypothesis demanded a radical rethinking of current orthodox views likely to challenge the legitimacy of the government approach and its associated medical experts, rather than to support it.

An International Policy Community Issue

More than twenty years later, by the end of the 1970s, there had been a crucial 'frame shift' in alcohol policy towards a general population, prevention oriented approach. Ledermann's theories, although still hotly debated (Duffy 1980; 1982; Tuck 1980) and modified by subsequent theorists (Skog 1981; 1985) had won acceptance by a powerful section of the policy community and helped to legitimate the change of policy focus. The story of how research interacted with policy underscores the changing ideology of alcohol and its associated 'policy community'.

The initial response came from the Canadian policy–research nexus. Ledermann's basic premise, that total per capita consumption was related to alcohol misuse was taken on board by a group of scientists from the Addiction Research Foundation (ARF) in Ontario (Room 1991). Their original report, submitted in 1968, drew cautiously on Ledermann's theory in analysing data on the distribution of consumption in Ontario but refrained from mentioning any policy implications. This was augmented by some 'conservative policy-oriented speculations' by the director of the ARF in the 1967 ARF Annual Report; but in 1969 a review of the research by the director of the ARF contained 'a blunt statement of policy advocacy'. Commenting on the use of research findings in this instance, Room argues that:

> This documentary history suggests strongly that modestly presented research analysis was seized upon by the policy-making level of ARF as an organising tool for a coherent alcohol policy position. (Room 1991, p. 325)

By 1971, the researchers themselves were presenting their work much less cautiously and linking consumption levels to 'alcoholism' in general. The importance of this body of work appears, once again, to be the fact that it was taken up at policy level and given visibility because the policy climate was changing rather than because it contained anything particularly new.

Support for the 'consumptionist' perspective came from the WHO as early as 1967, when the World Health Assembly adopted a resolution basically concerned with levels of alcohol consumption and their health implications. The report from the 14th Expert Committee on Mental Health acknowledged the shift away from alcoholism treatment and argued 'the need for a complementary approach – that any alcoholism programme must have a preventive as well as a curative component, that alcoholism or alcohol dependence is only a part of alcohol-related problems and that alcohol problems and alcoholism cannot be tackled without a policy towards the agent, alcohol' (WHO 1967). The shift towards prevention opened the way to debate on preventive strategy and consideration of control of alcohol consumption as one way forward. The WHO report marked the start of collaborative work between a number of key European institutions and personalities, initially the Finnish Foundation for Alcohol Studies under its Director, Kettil Bruun, and the Addiction Research Foundation in Ontario. Both these institutions played a prominent part in the collection of empirical evidence on the relationship between alcohol consumption and a range of harms, and came to act as advocates for the theory of the link between per capita alcohol consumption and the level of alcohol-related harm in the population. By 1980, in the report *Problems Related to Alcohol Consumption*, the WHO position favoured legislative and fiscal control on alcohol consumption (WHO 1980).

How did the English situation develop? Here, as Baggott (1990, p. 30) has pointed out, the Ledermann hypothesis provided a rallying point for the more diverse 'policy community' developing round alcohol in the early 1970s. The limitation of alcohol availability and consequent harm became a unifying concept for a coalition of revisionist 'alcohol doctors', civil servants, the alcohol voluntary sector, the police and the law, groups with otherwise quite different objectives. As discussed above, disease theories were modified; the concepts of dependence and alcohol-related disabilities were being promoted, and a 'social' alliance emerged which included elements of the old temperance position. The English debate on the Ledermann hypothesis also took place against a general background of a greater emphasis in government policy making on prevention and the role of personal behaviour. Again, international influence was a feature of broader policy directions, illustrated by the reception given to the publication of the 1974 Lalonde report in Canada. Hailed by Sir George Godber as 'one of the great moments in health care' (Godber interview), and described by Klein (1983, p. 171) in his analysis of the National Health Service as the future 'manifesto of the preventionists', the report set out the changes in environmental conditions and individual lifestyles required to promote good health. Undoubtedly, it influenced the discussion document *Prevention and Health: Everybody's Business* issued in 1976 by the British Government (DHSS 1976a). Internal pressures on government were also important. Webster documents how,

> The pressure to give greater attention to prevention by the mid-seventies became impossible to resist, partly because of the growing effectiveness of pressure groups concerned with issues such as smoking, alcohol and diet.

Many of these groups had either been founded or resuscitated in the
mid-sixties, and were reaching their maturity as political forces in the
mid-seventies. (Webster 1996, p. 660)

Other aspects of prevention – for instance, legislation on health
and safety at work, and environmental concerns such as the
health effects of high levels of lead in the atmosphere – added to
an expanding range of inter-connected issues relating to prevention
policy and forced the Labour administration of the 1970s to take
action. An investigation into preventive medicine, undertaken by
the Social Services and Employment Sub-Committee of the
Expenditure Committee between November 1975 and July 1976,
resulted in a substantial report with fifty-eight recommendations
including the need to control alcohol abuse. According to Webster,
the report had an immediate effect, influencing the hasty
production of the consultative document *Prevention and Health:
Everybody's Business*; this was seen as heralding the Health
Department's commitment to prevention and the shift towards
greater personal responsibility for health, trends which were
confirmed in the White Paper, *Prevention and Health*, published
in 1977 (Webster 1996, pp. 674–6).

The alcohol debate was part of this paradigm shift. It was
specifically stimulated both by the work at the Addiction Research
Foundation in Ontario and by the publication in 1975 of the report
Alcohol Control Policies in Public Health Perspective presenting
cross-national evidence on the relationship between consumption and
alcohol-related harm in society. The report based its argument firmly
on the premise that 'changes in the overall consumption of alcoholic
beverages have a bearing on the health of the people in any society.
Alcohol control measures can be used to limit consumption: thus,
control of alcohol availability becomes a public health issue' (Bruun *et
al.* 1975, p. 13).

Public health doctors, as a profession, had little to say specifically
on alcohol, although some individual doctors (such as Dr Herbert
Chalke, public health physician for Camberwell) became involved in
alcohol concerns. The profession was, itself, in a state of confusion
over its role in relation to other branches of medicine (Lewis 1991)
and it was not until 1991 that a professional viewpoint on the
prevention of harm related to the use of alcohol was issued (Faculty
of Public Health 1991). Policy sponsors for the public health view of
alcoholism came from psychiatry and from the new professions
entering the alcohol arena as well as from the traditional
temperance organisations. The adoption of a 'public health'

perspective served to mark out the 'new alcohol doctors' as sponsors of a public health approach to alcoholism and, once again, to unite different interest groups to push for policy action.

The 'New Alcohol Doctors' as Policy Sponsors

Although a broad alliance supported the consumption–harm view, the role of doctors as experts was central in bringing the new thinking into governmental circles both nationally and at the international level. One of the international collaborators was Griffith Edwards, by this time a leading figure in the alcohol field. As discussed in previous chapters, Edwards had gained considerable credibility as a policy advocate for public health approaches to the alcohol problem through his work in the Camberwell area of London and through publications which pressed a 'public health view rather than a clinical view' (Edwards, interview). However, Edwards attributed the international lead in promoting the public health perspective to Kettil Bruun, the Finnish social scientist, 'a man who inspired great affection'. He remembered being asked to join what was largely a social science group because he was known to be interested, although he had no technical competence in the statistical issues. According to Edwards, it was 'the same cast of actors, same group of friends' who were responsible for the influential WHO reports which affirmed a public health concern with a wider target group by shifting the problem definition away from 'alcoholism' towards the broader concept of 'alcohol related disabilities' (Edwards, interview). In the UK, it was Edwards who persuaded the Royal College of Psychiatrists to set up a special committee to 'develop a perspective on alcohol and alcoholism' based on the available evidence. Under Edwards as chairman, the committee included some of the most influential figures in the substance misuse field and its establishment marks the first interest shown in the topic by the Royal Colleges. The report, *Alcohol and Alcoholism*, published in 1979, accepted that 'consumption of alcohol per head of the population and the damage to health caused by alcohol are closely associated, though in ways that are poorly understood' (The Royal College of Psychiatrists 1979, p. viii). The report also contained a succinct statement on the relationship between research evidence and policy action in the acknowledgement that, 'This report is in the best traditions of the public health movement in this country which has in the past so often anticipated by its actions the stringent scientific testimony that later provided the rationale for them' (p. viii). Edwards was also a member of the Advisory Committee on Alcoholism set up by the Department of Health and Social Security in 1975 under the chairmanship of Professor Neil Kessel to advise on services relating to alcoholism. The report on prevention, one of the three reports issued by the Advisory Committee in 1978/79, has been described as an important catalyst in the development of alcohol policy in the 1970s (Baggott 1990, p. 37). This, too, endorsed the consumption theory of alcohol misuse. The Kessel Committee will be discussed more fully below.

Credit for 'rediscovering' Ledermann in England has also been attributed to D.L. Davies, Dean of the Institute of Psychiatry. Davies had never entirely espoused the disease view of alcoholism or the specialist approach to treatment (Edwards, interview; Edwards 1991, pp. 189–205). It was, perhaps, a measure of his interest in the broader aspects of alcohol issues and alcohol policy that he took the lead in starting the annual summer school (described in Chapter 4) and later established the Alcohol Education Centre (AEC). Both the summer schools and the AEC provided a forum for discussion of the consumption–harm theories and their implications. Under the auspices of the AEC, Davies held a symposium in January 1977 on the topic of the Ledermann curve. The symposium was supported by the DHSS so that the problematic aspects of the Ledermann theory could be critically examined. Contributions to the seminar came from Jan de Lint, one of the original Canadian researchers, and from two of the Scandinavians, Skog and Sulkunen, who had been involved in the 1975 Bruun report, *Alcohol Control Policies in Public Health Perspective*. Participants included statisticians from the Office of Population Censuses and Surveys, four representatives from the Department of Health and Social Security and one from the Scottish Home and Health Department, as well as national and international participants who were leading researchers and practitioners in the alcohol field (Alcohol Education Centre 1977). This was the first major national discussion of the Ledermann curve and the first public show of interest by policy makers.

In the foreword to the report of the meeting, Davies recognised the fact that Ledermann's theory and methodology had been criticised on a number of accounts but that the hypothesis had important implications for preventive strategies and 'almost decisive, consequences for theories about causes of excessive drinking, and whether these be largely determined by constitutional or environmental factors'. Whatever the finer points of the debate, Davies appeared to be anxious that any conclusions or recommendations from the seminar should seek to unite rather than split the alcohol field. His final address to the meeting highlighted the need for cohesion and more specifically addressed the difficulty of balancing the differing aims of research and policy:

> What happens, in effect, is that some of us have been going round saying that the Ledermann type of curve is another bit of evidence to support our hypothesis. If it goes out from a group like this that the Ledermann type of curve is wrong, or a myth or something of that sort, that would be used by people who do not understand the refinements of our discussions as saying, 'well, this extra cornerstone that you are looking for to fit your hypothesis does not fit your hypothesis, therefore to that extent, your hypothesis is weakened. (Davies in Alcohol Education Centre, 1977)

This was a central dilemma in using the results of research and theoretical debate, however fascinating in themselves, to inform and advance a coherent policy position.

The Role of the Civil Servant

A detailed analysis of the process by which civil servants in the UK became sensitised to consumption–harm theory in the early 1970s must wait until official documents become publicly available. It is clear, however, that perspectives on alcohol issues were beginning to change at least among medical civil servants, a crucial link with the emergent medical policy community. As psychiatrists, their links with colleagues in the alcohol field had been strengthening throughout the 1960s. In particular, from the time of Richard Phillipson, there were strong ties with psychiatrists working at, or trained at, the Institute of Psychiatry in London and, through them, to the group of internationally active Canadian, Scandinavian and British collaborators whose views on the policy implications of Ledermann's work became a dominant force in the alcohol field. Writing in 1973, Alan Sippert, a senior medical officer at the DHSS, noted that, 'The wider matter of monitoring alcohol consumption and its relation to public health is under consideration' (Sippert 1975),[3] and by 1977, David Ennals, the then Secretary of State for Social Services, could speak publicly of the relationship between alcohol consumption and harm and invite debate on the best measures for combating the problem.[4]

There were also pressures arising from the increasing visibility of the alcohol problem and propelled by the publication of three reports in 1970 – from the National Council on Alcoholism, from the Office of Health Economics and from the Medical Council on Alcoholism – all urging action on the alcohol problem which by now was seen as a social rather than a purely medical problem. As Baggott mentions, around this time, the constituency of support for further government intervention was spreading; groups such as the Howard League for Penal Reform, the Campaign for Homeless and Rootless, and the National Society for the Prevention of Cruelty to Children were concerned about the association between alcohol use and other social problems (Baggott 1990, p. 17). Alcohol issues were given more time on the media and in Parliament, and ministerial initiative played a significant role in prompting action. The late 1960s and early 1970s was, according to one civil servant who had been an assistant secretary at the time, 'a period of government activism' with Ministers such as Sir Keith Joseph and David Owen taking a keen interest in alcohol policy (Lee, interview).[5] Indeed, Baggott argues that the personal interest of Sir Keith Joseph, then Secretary of State, was the key factor behind the higher priority given to alcohol in the early 1970s (Baggott 1990, p. 20).

Another factor which undoubtedly drew attention in the DHSS to the wider issues of alcohol consumption and control, was the conflict surrounding the 1972 report from the Erroll Committee and a subsequent Bill in 1976 to put into effect measures to relax the licensing laws (Home Office 1972). The Erroll Committee, appointed in 1971 by the Home Secretary to review the liquor licensing system in England and Wales, aroused strong feelings from different interest groups, including the alcohol industry, the temperance movement and the medical lobby. The committee recommended a relaxation of the rules governing the granting of liquor licences, an extension of drinking hours at on-licensed premises, and that children under fourteen years old should be allowed in licensed premises under certain conditions. The report's recommendations were strongly opposed by the medical lobby and by the Standing Medical Advisory Committee which urged rejection of the proposed measures. David Robinson, a political scientist who had joined Edwards' Addiction Research Unit (ARU) at the Institute of Psychiatry in 1971, recalled the ARU's involvement in producing a critique of the Erroll report as, 'A time when we were explicitly political' (Robinson, interview). The report produced by the ARU, was sent to every Member of Parliament and 'became the bible' for those who opposed the measures (Rutherford, interview), serving to unite groups within the alcohol arena against the common 'enemy', the alcohol industry and its parliamentary allies. Clearly, the earlier consensus between the alcohol industry and the alcohol 'health lobby' based on a treatment response to alcohol misuse at the individual level was at an end.

Within Parliament, opposition to Erroll was led by Sir Bernard Braine MP, chairman of the National Council on Alcoholism (NCA). The DHSS was not represented on the Committee; but, according to Derek Rutherford, who had been a member of the NCA delegation giving evidence to the Erroll Committee, the DHSS had been active in stimulating opposition to Erroll's recommendations. Rutherford, who was appointed as director of the NCA in 1973, recalled that DHSS officials encouraged the NCA to become more politically active and throughout the 1970s gave Rutherford and the NCA a number of 'prods' to take up control issues on their behalf. This enabled the department to remain in the political background because, as Rutherford noted, 'the drinks industry thought it was me very often, because I am an abstainer ... but it wasn't'. David Robinson, too, recalled that, 'the DOH tried very hard to get the consumption issue brought to the fore'. Here, we see how the policy community was activated by government officials to serve their interests, just as in other instances official action was stimulated by policy activists outside official circles.

In 1976, following the defeat of Erroll and subsequently Kenneth Clarke's Licensing Amendment Bill, DHSS and Home Office attitudes towards liberalisation hardened and appeared to accept that licensing reform was off the political agenda for a time. Inter-departmental interests were, however, far from consensual. As later discussion will show, officials in the DHSS, interested in adopting a prevention approach to alcohol consumption, were to experience difficulty in devising a prevention strategy which was acceptable to other government departments concerned with the economic aspects of alcohol control policies, to Ministers subject to pressures from the industry and the public, and to the alcohol health lobby, campaigning quite strongly by the end of the 1970s for greater control over the price and availability of alcohol as a means of lowering per capita consumption. Ministerial commitment and leadership within the DHSS remained indecisive throughout the 1970s (Webster 1996, pp. 683–6). It is clear, however, that over the course of the decade civil servants in the DHSS became increasingly sensitised to the alcohol prevention debate and were probably active in supporting a comprehensive policy on alcohol misuse, including the use of control policies to reduce consumption. Baggott notes that a sub-committee of the House of Commons Select Committee on Expenditure (1976), which considered alcohol misuse as one of several public health issues, concluded that alcohol consumption was related to the level of alcohol misuse and implicitly recognised the importance of control measures as a prevention response (Baggott 1990, pp. 38–41).

In particular, the contribution made by Alan Sippert (as senior medical officer) and Chris Ralph (a civil servant who remained involved in the alcohol policy division for nearly a decade) has been recognised by others active in the core of the policy community during the 1970s. Both men were closely in touch with the field. Sippert was an observer on committees such as the Special Committee of the Royal College of Psychiatrists, and the Advisory Committee on

Alcoholism and attended conferences such as Davies' Ledermann symposium. He was described by some who knew him as widely liked and trusted and, together with Chris Ralph, influential in the field. Chris Ralph, although a relatively junior civil servant, was undoubtedly a powerful figure. Described by one colleague as 'the most influential in the country as a whole'; Ralph had a very clear vision of policy and was 'good at finding the levers of power'; he excelled at writing speeches and was a master of the art of influencing ministers (Wawman, interview). An example of the method which Ralph and others used to influence ministers and 'promote' policy issues, given by one department official, typifies the way in which civil servants operate to influence policy (Walt 1994, pp. 80–8).

> Patrick Jenkin ... he was made to say things like 'Alcohol abuse is of epidemic proportions'. Him having said that, we were thereafter able to say, whenever you wrote or said anything, 'The Minister said that ...'. So, you get them to say it and you quote it ad lib over and over again .... When Ministers will not do this, it takes away your ability to influence official policy. (Wawman, interview)

Sippert and Ralph were also the linchpins between the wider alcohol policy community and the alcohol policy development group within the DHSS which met regularly to formulate policy. The indications are that both Sippert and Ralph favoured the new thinking on alcohol consumption and supported WHO pressures to set goals to reduce harmful alcohol consumption by the year 2000. By the 1980s the European Economic Community was also prompting Member States to examine the association between rising consumption and alcohol-related problems (Webster 1996, p. 684). But there were tensions between government departments concerning the resource implications of the new perspective (Cartwright, interview; Robinson, interview) and pressures to take on board a 'consumption' strategy were strongly resisted at ministerial level. The emphasis on prevention and control inflamed existing inter-departmental conflicts and more than ever cut across departmental boundaries and responsibilities so that the publication of alcohol policy statements was impeded by the need for inter-departmental agreement (Baggott 1990, pp. 38–43).

The effect of inter-departmental conflict, and of wider political and policy change, is illustrated by the rejection of the report from the Central Policy Review Staff, the Think Tank report (Bruun 1982; CPRS 1982), and the subsequent issue of the DHSS report, *Drinking Sensibly* (DHSS 1981b). According to Webster, in an attempt to handle the problems arising from differences in inter-departmental interests, consideration of alcohol issues was delegated to the CPRS. A brief review was produced in 1977, impressive enough to convince Ministers that action on alcohol was necessary. But disagreement between Ministers and the proximity of a general election sealed the fate of subsequent action (Webster 1996, pp. 684–5). The final Think Tank report, produced in 1979, documented the evidence for the consumption–harm theory and used it to argue the case for the stabilisation of per capita consumption achieved by a range of control approaches (for example price or availability of alcohol). In the view of the CPRS, health education was unlikely to be effective in the short term. The report was never officially published possibly, as one editorial commentary maintained, because the Think Tank, which was set up under a Labour government but completed its report at the time of a general election and an incoming Conservative government, fell foul of 'bare-faced political expedience' (editorial, *British Journal of Addiction* 1981, 76, pp. 1–2). By this time the evidence on which the theory was based, fed by an expanding body of research from different countries, tended to be widely accepted by groups concerned with issues of alcohol misuse. The consensus was illustrated by the reactions to a Home Office publication which questioned the connection between the rates of alcohol consumption and harm (Tuck 1980). This report was severely criticised and dismissed as part of a 'disquieting lack of even-handedness' in the government's presentation of evidence on the issues.[6] The report, according to one account, caused some irritation in the DHSS because civil servants there did not know it was being published; it was 'a case of the Home Office not telling the DHSS what it was doing and what she was saying was not in line with thinking in the Department' (Wawman, interview).

But the alcohol 'health lobby' were equally unhappy with the later production of the DHSS discussion paper *Drinking Sensibly* which was rejected by one reviewer as 'facile and inadequate' when compared to the Think Tank report (Plant 1982). Nevertheless, the analysis of alcohol problems contained in *Drinking Sensibly* shows that the consumption–harm hypothesis had made some inroads into official thinking despite the watering down of strategic approaches to lowering alcohol-related problems, a result of the compromise needed to secure the agreement of the different government departments involved in the discussion and writing of the document. The difficulties in producing the document were commented on by Dr Ron Wawman, the senior medical officer involved in the writing:

large chunks of some particular chapters were actually written by other departments. So the Home Office and the Ministry of Agriculture, Fisheries and Food and particularly the Treasury, all had an input into what was written. Then we found ourselves commenting and challenging their statements. So this went on back and forth for months ... and in the end, the decision to publish was taken by a cabinet committee – I knew that for a fact. So, we are talking about a statement of government policy. (Wawman, interview)

While acknowledging that the policy statement was the result of compromise, Wawman felt that its virtual rejection by the policy community represented a lost opportunity to debate important issues raised in acknowledged government policy.

The response by the policy community to *Drinking Sensibly* indicates the extent to which the consumption–harm theory had acquired support within professional circles and there seems little doubt that the civil servants who were closely linked with the alcohol arena shared the views of their fellow professionals, although this isolated them from colleagues in other government departments. Acceptance of the new, broader vision of the alcohol problem which emerged in the 1970s was undoubtedly enhanced by the findings of the Advisory Committee on Alcoholism or the Kessel Committee, as it became known after its chairman, Professor Neil Kessel. This committee occupies a central position in the history of alcohol treatment policy and is generally regarded as marking the shift from service provision for 'alcoholics' to service provision for 'problem drinkers', based on the idea that services had to respond to a much wider target group of drinkers than had previously been the case. In particular, the report *The Pattern and Range of Services for Problem Drinkers*, published in 1978, was significant in consolidating and legitimising the direction of existing policy trends and in setting the agenda for service implementation throughout the 1980s.

The Advisory Committee on Alcoholism (the Kessel Committee)

The Advisory Committee on Alcoholism was established in 1975 to

Advise the Secretaries of State for Social Services and for Wales, the Central Health Services Council and the Personal Social Services Council on services relating to alcoholism and where appropriate to promote their development. (Advisory Committee on Alcoholism 1978b, p. ii)

The reasons behind the establishment of a committee at this particular time are not entirely clear. In a letter of invitation to join the committee, David Owen (then Minister of State for Health) suggested that it was in response to changing ideas on the way in which treatment and community services should develop, and to mounting pressure to consider questions of prevention. The existing advisory machinery – the Standing Mental Health Advisory Committee of the Central Health Services Council was no longer seen as sufficient, and a new source of advice specifically on alcoholism and services for alcoholics was required.[7]

The appointed chairman was a former senior registrar of D.L. Davies, Neil Kessel, who had spent some time working in Edinburgh before obtaining the Chair of Psychiatry at Manchester University where he built up alcohol treatment services, training and research, and become the DHSS consultant adviser on alcohol in the mid-1960s (Kessel, interview). Again, the Institute of Psychiatry/Maudsley presence on the committee was strong; the committee membership included D.L. Davies, Griffith Edwards and Timothy Cook, and representation was greater from medicine than from other professional groups. But the background of committee members also reflected the DHSS's broadening consultative base and the diversity of professions and institutions now having an interest in the alcohol field; the committee included psychiatrists and physicians, psychologists, social workers, nurses, educationalists, individuals from the church, from the temperance movement, and from legal institutions. The DHSS and the Home Office were represented as advisers, with Chris Ralph as secretary to the committee. In later commentaries, the membership was criticised as still unrepresentative of the range of skilled individuals working in alcoholism treatment in ATUs – 'it was thought curious in many quarters that the Committee had among its members not a single representative from among the several well qualified and experienced (but yet relatively young) consultants who had been in charge of such units since the early or mid-sixties' (Glatt 1979b).

However, membership had been chosen in consultation with a wide range of organisations and a primary concern was to avoid an imbalance towards psychiatry (Kessel, interview). When the committee met for the first time on 23 April, David Owen opened the meeting by expressing the hope that it would make a positive contribution to preventive medicine and take a more active role in promoting services than had hitherto been usual for advisory committees.[8] But the terms of reference for the committee were not specified and the guidelines were too vague to prevent discord among members about what the focus of their discussions should be.[9] Some debate arose among committee members over whether their prime concern should be services for alcoholics including homeless alcoholics, or whether they should conduct a more fundamental examination of the nature and causes of alcoholism – a focus more in line with the growing emphasis on alcohol consumption and prevention. It was pointed out to the committee that the DHSS was directly responsible only for policies on the provision of services for alcoholics and that Ministers looked to the committee to review these and advise on improvements.[10] It was agreed, then, that the committee's prime task was to consider the development of services for alcoholics, including preventive services, and that early consideration should be given to the following areas:

- methods of persuading alcoholics to use the available services; the education of professional workers and of the public to secure a better understanding of the problem of alcoholism

- co-ordination of medical, local authority and voluntary services for alcoholics

- encouragement of experimentation in the provision of services for alcoholics

- preventive services (on which, it was noted, they were likely to be asked for advice by the DHSS in the near future), and

- examining the pattern of drinking among the young.[11]

Over the course of the first two meetings, three sub-groups were set up, one on homeless alcoholics, one on prevention, and one on education and training. Two of the sub-groups, prevention, and education and training, produced reports in addition to the main report *The Pattern and Range of Services for Problem Drinkers*. It is indicative of changing perspectives on the nature of the problem, and the strength of the lobby within the committee pressing to examine approaches relevant to a broader spectrum of drinkers, that the committee's terms of reference and early discussions spoke of 'alcoholism' and 'alcoholics' while the final reports used the terms 'problem drinking' and 'problem drinkers'. This shift was welcomed by commentators at the time and in retrospect as legitimising the policy relevance of a wider brief for health services and as symbolising the shift in responses to drinking in the UK. Other, less obvious, shifts emerged from 'negotiated settlements' which attempted to reconcile the differing ideological positions of committee members. There was, for instance, disagreement about whether service provision should be co-ordinated around a hospital or a non-hospital base. This was resolved in the report by stating the need for a 'place' which would act as a centre of activity and provide a focus for primary and secondary workers.[12]

The committee was wound up at the end of its appointed three year period in 'a perfunctory fashion' under conditions of some discontent among committee members[13] and, according to some sources (Baggott 1990, p. 22), on the explicit initiative of the Minister of Health.

According to the chairman, Professor Kessel, knowing that the DHSS was trying to economise, the committee members had agreed that the committee should not continue but that a nucleus group should be retained to monitor progress in implementing the committee's recommendations. This was conveyed to the DHSS and a meeting arranged between Kessel and the Secretary of State. At that meeting the Secretary of State announced that a decision had already been taken to close the committee. A request to attend the committee's last meeting to thank members for their work and explain the reasons for its discontinuance was agreed but in the event did not take place. No explanation was provided to committee members. Webster (1996, p. 685), however, links the abrupt ending of the committee to the looming general election and to the fact that, like the Select Committee on Expenditure and the CPRS, 'the Advisory Committee was inclined to make recommendations unacceptable to Ministers. Its elimination therefore removed a potential source of embarrassment.'

The report concerned with treatment services, *The Pattern and Range of Services for Problem Drinkers*, published in 1978, recommended a strategy for the delivery of locally based alcohol services which required a co-ordinated response from statutory and voluntary services. It was hailed in retrospect as a landmark which provided a strategy for future service delivery,[14] but immediate reactions within the alcohol field were far more critical and less inclined to see the report as proposing anything new. Alcohol policy had been moving towards a community-based response for at least a decade. A boost to the development of community-based alcohol services had come in 1970 when Sir Keith Joseph, the then Secretary of State for Social Services, granted £2 million for the development of both statutory and voluntary services for alcoholics The role of the Kessel reports was seen to provide confirmation of the government's strategy rather than to turn it in any new direction (commentaries in the *British Journal of Addiction* 1979, 74, pp. 118–32). In particular, the report *The Pattern and Range of Services for Problem Drinkers*, was significant in consolidating and legitimising the direction of existing trends in treatment policy and in setting the agenda for service implementation throughout the 1980s.

But there were other criticisms. To some, the report, perhaps inadvertently, seemed to enshrine the 'medical model', which many people on the committee believed they had cast out, in that it appeared to endorse the expansion of 'treatment' to enormous numbers of people in a situation where the lack of skills and interest among other primary care workers inevitably threw the onus for a treatment response on to the GP.[15] Another contentious issue was whether the committee had misunderstood the functions and role of ATUs. Glatt, for instance, argued that ATUs were a necessary part of a comprehensive plan of services for all types of problem drinker (Glatt 1979a). The move to district level services was also opposed on the grounds that the larger regional facilities brought together a range of treatment, training and research expertise which would be lost. Here debate was fed both by ideological differences in the field and by professional and personal vested interests in service developments.[16]

But the main critique centred on the problems of policy implementation, noting that the report did not provide a sufficiently rigorous analysis of the implementation difficulties nor suggest guidelines for putting the recommendations into effect. Critics felt that the committee had avoided the question of effectiveness of the proposed strategy. The report's recommendations were challenged on the grounds that it provided no evidence for its conclusions and that they were based on the experience and knowledge of committee members with only limited evidence taken from other sources (Hodgson 1979; O'Leary 1979; Thorley 1979). It was not unusual for advisory bodies to make proposals which were 'ahead of research evaluation' (Advisory Committee on Alcoholism 1978b, p. 2) and as one commentator observed, the style of the committee was clearly in keeping with a tradition of British policy making, in that it avoided or was suspicious of research evaluation (Thorley 1979). But there is no doubt that the Advisory Committee had been influenced by research. The Maudsley Alcohol Pilot Project (MAPP) which will be discussed in more detail in Chapter 9, had undoubtedly informed the Committee's deliberations, and provided the model for the suggestion that service delivery should be based on multi-disciplinary 'community alcohol teams' (Advisory Committee on Alcoholism 1978b, p. 25). However, the MAPP project was not referenced in the report. Thorley, noting that the MAPP team had been 'a highly trained, energetic and most gifted band of individuals' used the project as further evidence for the *difficulty* of mobilising primary care workers. The lack of appropriately trained professionals at all levels of service delivery was compounded, Thorley argued, by 'insufficient professional interest and commitment' (Thorley 1979). A related criticism was that the report must have been produced by 'thoroughly optimistic chaps' who had disregarded the mismatch between the enormous size of the target population as defined in the report and the limited resources available to provide an appropriate response (Grant 1979).

Such critiques of the Advisory Committee's report highlighted difficulties arising from the historical and social context and the administrative structures within which treatment services had developed. Particularly important was the failure to address the lack of co-ordination and collaboration between services. Statutory and voluntary services continued to develop separately and despite discussion of the reasons for this, for example, the fact that voluntary organisations feared loss of autonomy,[17] the Kessel Committee did not suggest any solution. A related difficulty was that at local as well as national level, alcohol services straddled different administrative and professional boundaries. The recognition that alcohol problems had a social as well as a health dimension, and the emphasis on community-based provision, merely exacerbated the struggle between central and local government and between local health and social care authorities over who was responsible for funding alcohol services (O'Leary 1979). The 1974 reorganisation of the health services had transferred responsibility for community health care to the NHS from local government but the latter retained their responsibility for social care. A system of joint planning, introduced to encourage collaboration between NHS and local authority agencies and the 1976 financial incentives to encourage Joint Health Care Planning Teams to promote collaborative projects did not work well, either in the alcohol field, or in other specialist areas (O'Leary 1979; Baggott 1990, p. 85–90).

Looking at the failure of the report to address implementation, the most damning criticism was one which challenged the whole *raison d'être* of the committee by claiming that it provided yet another example of the government's 'lack of intent' with regard to implementing alcohol policy; in other words, 'that successive governments and their civil servants have deliberately avoided a full and proper implementation of various proposals and recommendations that have received official endorsement' (O'Leary 1979). As other policy analysts have pointed out, the use of committees and of research as a delaying tactic or as a political device to replace action is commonplace (Weiss 1986). Certainly, issues such as service co-ordination prominent in the debate at this time were not resolved and have remained pertinent into the 1990s. But as it turned out, there was no lack of intent to move service delivery into the community. What financial resources were available to the DHSS were used to this purpose, openly acknowledged in documents on priorities in research and service development.[18] Issues of service delivery will be discussed in more detail in Chapter 9. The need to develop and deliver a wide range of services became particularly pressing as the emergence of an epidemiological perspective and attempts to provide more accurate measures of the size and seriousness of the alcohol problem confirmed the 'common wisdom' that rising consumption was accompanied by a rise in alcohol-related problems.

The Size of the Problem

A further important development which confirmed perceptions of
the extent of the alcohol problem, the diversity of the potential
'clients' of treatment, and the need for a community-based
treatment response was the acquisition of a better picture of the
nation's drinking habits. Developments here have to be seen
within the framework of the evolution of epidemiological
approaches and the growing importance of epidemiology as part of
the 'tool kit' of public health (Berridge 1996).

Epidemiology has a long history. In its modern form, its origins
are generally traced to the work of the English sanitary reformers
and French scientists in the first half of the nineteenth century; but
it was the shift from the dominance of an infectious disease
paradigm towards an epidemiology of non-communicable disease
which laid the foundations for epidemiological theory and methods
after the Second World War. In their examination of the evolution
of epidemiology, Beaglehole and Bonita (1997) describe the distin-
guishing features of the new epidemiological paradigm as, 'the
systematisation of the epidemiological literature, the concentration
in wealthy countries on non-communicable diseases, the development of graduate training programmes, and the availability of
research funds' along with the search for multiple causes (pp. 96–7).
The outcomes of case control studies on cigarette smoking and
cancer and of cohort studies on heart disease, helped to establish
the emergence of the new epidemiology in the 1950s. Subsequent
developments in epidemiology have been divided into three phases.
The first, from the mid-1940s to the mid-1960s, saw the creation of
methods and measures necessary for the study of non-communicable diseases, the elaboration of theories of multi-causation, and a
focus on the agent, host and environment as the principle
determinants of disease. The latter emphasis, as Beaglehole and
Bonita point out, largely 'sidelined' the social system, which, in the
alcohol field, was to remain a feature of problem explanation and
response until the 1990s. The second evolutionary phase, lasting
until the early 1980s, saw the development of more sophisticated
methods of data collection and an ability to handle and analyse
large-scale data sets using computers and the increasingly specialised
software packages. It was only towards the end of this phase that
epidemiological studies became a significant feature of alcohol policy
at national level. Over the last decade, within the developing 'public
health epidemiology', attention has turned to the measurement of
exposure, which has included aspects of diet, use of tobacco, alcohol

and medication, and a concern with risk groups and risk behaviours (Rose 1992; Beaglehole and Bonita 1997, pp. 85–111).

In an examination of AIDS policy in the UK, Berridge (1996) has traced the role of epidemiology in the formation of health policy in the post-war period, noting the contribution of epidemiology to the redefinition of public health around an individual rather than a collective or environmental focus. Similarly in alcohol, the use of epidemiological perspectives and methods to examine and explain alcohol consumption and alcohol-related harms has paralleled the evolutionary phases outlined above. By the 1970s, it was commonly accepted that the size of the alcohol problem had grown since the 1950s, was continuing to grow, and involved a high cost – economic, social and personal – to the community. Estimates of the number of people with 'a serious drinking problem' stood at around half a million (or 13 in every 1000 adults) in 1977 (Advisory Committee on Alcoholism 1978a) compared to the 1950s figure, based on the WHO formula, which estimated around 350,000 alcoholics of whom 86,000 were chronic – 1 in 1000 (Glatt 1982). But these figures were based on customs and excise data and on formulae such as Jellinek's (Glatt 1982, pp. 135–7). Estimates were criticised on methodological grounds and on the grounds that they did not adequately reflect national drinking patterns. Survey data was equally inadequate. Prior to the 1980s, local epidemiological studies had provided a partial view of population consumption patterns; but it was not until the 1970s that epidemiology was employed as a means of obtaining a more comprehensive picture and informing national policy on the prevention and treatment of alcohol problems. By this time, the focus in public health approaches was on individual lifestyles and, as in AIDS policy, epidemiology had become the bedfellow of public health. The earlier clinical focus on identifying individuals who were drinking harmfully or were in need of treatment had broadened to include 'risk groups' and subsequently, in the late 1980s and 1990s, 'risk behaviours' associated with alcohol use within the general population. The first national survey in England and Wales was conducted in 1978 by the OPCS on behalf of the DHSS (Wilson 1980). The idea was to obtain baseline data and repeat the surveys every ten years (Wawman, interview). It was followed by two other national general population surveys within the next decade (Goddard and Iken 1988; Goddard 1991) and a number of other surveys designed to obtain information on specific 'risk' groups, such as women (Breeze 1985).

While the new focus on alcohol consumption underlined the need for a better empirical base for policy and service planning, the measurement of consumption to examine trends over time proved problematic. Precisely how estimates of alcohol consumption are arrived at – both at individual level and at aggregate national level – their accuracy, and their usefulness as a basis for the establishment of a treatment system has been the subject of much academic debate (Room 1980; Gusfield 1982; Levine 1984). Those who have cast a critical eye on the scientific underpinnings of the estimates contained in policy statements, have drawn attention to the interactive relationship between information and 'facts' which define the nature and size of a problem, and the systems established to respond to the problem. The question 'How many alcoholics are there?' has no straight answer. Surveys and research studies have employed a wide variety of criteria and measures for deciding who should count as an 'alcoholic' or 'problem drinker' or as 'at risk' of problem drinking. One researcher illustrated the difficulties by showing how his estimate of the number of problem drinkers in the US could swing from 5.7 million men and 2.5 million women to 3.7 million men and 1.5 million women depending on the method of estimation he used (Hilton 1989).

An important feature of surveys carried out in the 1980s and 1990s was the standardisation of the measurement of alcohol consumption and the application of the units system for the assignment of individuals to drinking categories. A 'unit' of alcohol is 8 grammes which is contained in half a pint of normal strength (4 per cent abv) beer, a standard glass of wine, or a standard pub measure of spirits (UK measures). Since the 1980s, the adoption of the units system of measurement has been instrumental in building a high degree of consensus in the UK regarding not only the size of the problem but also the measurement of alcohol consumption and harmful drinking. The way in which agreement was reached and the way in which the measures adopted affected the potential target group for intervention, provides a good example of the interactive relationship between problem definition and the interest constituency around alcohol. It indicates also ways in which the alcohol policy community was striving to unite different interest groups around a new consensus of the alcohol problem.

In 1979, the report *Alcohol and Alcoholism* from the Royal College of Psychiatrists claimed that 'solid evidence indicates that if someone drinks regularly the equivalent of between five and ten pints of beer or more each day, (10–20 units) he increases his risk of contracting cirrhosis' (p.79). Cirrhosis was chosen as an indicator 'not so much because of the importance of the condition in its own right, but because scientific evidence points to its value as a general indication of the level of alcohol-related disabilities' (p. 141). Four pints of beer a day, or equivalent (approximately 56 units a week) was suggested as an upper limit of 'safe' daily drinking. The 'solid evidence' for the recommendation was not documented or referenced, and possible differences between men and women were not addressed although the report recognised that 'different people react differently'. The questionable nature of the evidence was recognised by policy makers at the time but concern to unite and produce an 'expert' consensus was high.[19]

In the mid-1980s the three Royal Colleges all produced reports on alcohol, initiated, it was claimed, by their concern about the alcohol-related problems seen increasingly by their members and by the rising per capita consumption of alcohol and alcohol-related harms, which constituted 'an endemic disorder of frightening magnitude' (Royal College of General Practitioners 1986; Royal College of Physicians 1987, p. 2, pp. 108–9; Royal College of Psychiatrists 1986, foreword, p. 3). The Royal College of Psychiatrists now stated that continuing research had confirmed a greater risk for women who drank heavily, and that different guidelines were needed for each sex. All three reports contained the same advice regarding levels of alcohol consumption and risk to health. The recommendations stated that up to 21 units a week for men and up to 14 units a week for women were 'sensible'; drinking became hazardous at 21–49 units a week for men and 14–35 units a week for women, and dangerous at levels above 49 units for men and 35 units for women per week. All three reports drew heavily on research and 'science' to legitimate their conclusions and recommendations but again, there was no clear description of the research basis for the units guidelines. Many years later, in an interview to the *Guardian*, Richard Smith, one of the medical experts from the Royal College of Surgeons involved in setting the unit recommendations, had this to say:

> A number of reports had been produced and we were told that the public really wanted to know how much was safe ... The answer is, of course, that we don't know. One strand of thought on the committee said that we should say so and another strand said that we shouldn't confuse people. So we plucked a figure out of the air and in some ways that belongs to the paternalistic tradition. (*Guardian* 20 July, 1996).

Consensus, it appears, eventually rested on the belief that the health lobby should present a consistent message regarding the unit guidelines in an attempt to combat the alcohol industry's advertising strength and to unite prevention efforts within the alcohol arena (Morgan, interview; Wawman, interview). Each report from the Royal Colleges was, in effect, another 'rallying cry' depending for its impact more on its prestigious institutional base than on documented evidence. The uncertain scientific basis of the units measures was never resolved; as we shall see in the last chapter, criticism and discussion rumbled below the surface of consensus, emerging again in the 1990s as research on the benefits of alcohol reawakened the debate and fuelled a move towards re-evaluation of the evidence on 'sensible' levels of consumption (DoH 1995).

The adoption of the units system of measuring alcohol consumption meant that individuals could more easily be located along a continuum from non-harmful to harmful drinking and the size and degree of problem drinking in the population more precisely calculated. The first survey of drinking in England and Wales carried out at the end of the 1970s used the levels recommended for men in the 1979 report from the Royal College of Psychiatrists and calculated a lower level for women. According to this survey, 6 per cent of men and 1 per cent of women were in the heaviest category (Wilson 1980). Subsequent surveys of alcohol consumption used the unit guidelines to define groups whose drinking put them 'at risk' of developing problem drinking as well as those already within the harmful drinking category. Ten years later, figures given in the OPCS survey *Drinking in England and Wales in the late 1980s* indicated that 23 per cent of men and 8 per cent of women were drinking over the recommended sensible weekly amounts and 6 per cent of men and 1 per cent of women were drinking more than the maximum 'safe' amounts (Goddard 1991). By now, nearly a quarter of the male population and a considerable number of women had become the target group for both preventive approaches and early intervention although the numbers of individuals in the heaviest drinking category had not increased greatly over the decade. Identification and 'screening' of individuals 'at risk' became an important aspect of intervention activity and service development included attempts to attract such drinkers into the helping services (Wallace and Haines 1985; Anderson 1987).

But by the 1970s, attention was being drawn not only to the numbers of people drinking harmfully but to the seriousness of the social as well as individual consequences of problem drinking. The costs to the nation were being calculated, resulting in a 'guestimate' that alcohol generated social costs of around £2 million a year (Maynard 1989). The power of the epidemiological-economic view of the alcohol problem was to strengthen throughout the 1980s and, as we shall see in Chapter 9, commissioning research to underpin the economic basis for strategies to address the problem was an important element in DHSS tactics and inter-departmental negotiations.

Thus, despite the acknowledged difficulty of agreeing on the size of the alcohol problem and despite lack of consensus or consistency over the years on how the problem should be measured, epidemiology assisted, in Wiener's terms, to 'demonstrate' the size and policy salience of the alcohol problem (Wiener 1981). The argument since the 1960s has been that the problem is growing, that there is a hidden pool of unmet need, and that there are insufficient or inappropriate resources to respond to those in need of help. This argument has helped to lay the foundations for the development of services supplied by the very same organisations and individuals who are prominent in defining the problem. To suggest, for example, that the development of Councils on Alcoholism represented partly 'a response to the growing need for services, given the increasing incidence of problem drinking, but also to the redefinition of alcoholism as problem drinking' (Collins 1990, p. 24) is still only part of the picture. As Gusfield has noted in the case of the 'troubled person's professions' in the US, the activity of professional groups in activating and mobilising support for a social problem also influences the construction of the problem, its theory of explanation and its policies to alleviate the problem (Gusfield 1982). In the UK also, 'caring professionals', voluntary workers, researchers and other groups involved in the 'alcoholism industry' create and generate needs as much as respond to them. (This will be illustrated further in two case studies in Chapters 7 and 8.) According to this perspective, the actual size of the problem is less important than the consensus that it is 'a great and growing evil' (Royal College of Physicians 1987). As in the earlier situation when efforts to win acceptance for the disease concept generated different levels of discourse for professional, policy and public consumption, so the use of the 'sensible drinking' measures differed in discussion in the academic, policy and practice arenas. The methodology used in epidemiological research, the definition of drinking categories and the terminology used to describe different levels of consumption as 'safe' or 'at risk' or 'harmful' were criticised and debated within academic circles and within the specialist alcohol world; but in wider circles and for media dissemination, what mattered was the 'proof' that large numbers of people were drinking harmfully and that it was a government responsibility to address the alcohol problem. The fact that very few of the large number of people defined in surveys as drinking harmfully would share that definition of their behaviour or ever be prepared to accept intervention or treatment was taken up as a challenge to service providers to devise more attractive and suitable services rather than seen as a challenge to the appropriateness of an intervention and treatment response.

Re-conceptualising the Problem of Alcohol

This chapter has concentrated on an examination of change in the conceptualisation of the alcohol problem which took place over the course of the 1970s and resulted in a new policy consensus within the core of the policy community. But examples of apparent consensus have already been shown, on closer inspection, to mask considerable doubts and disagreements in the field and to derive, very often, from factors extraneous to the research evidence. It is debatable how much initial acceptance of the consumption–harm theory owed to the accumulation of research evidence and the demonstration of scientific 'progress'. Rather, the response to available evidence depended on the selection and interpretation of facts within an ideological frame and within political and administrative structures; as ideologies and structures changed – or evolved through the efforts of leaders in the field, professional institutions and international exchange, and the composition and interests of the policy community – so perspectives on the nature of the alcohol problem changed. There continued to be a 'dissident' lobby of experts who questioned the hypotheses, the epidemiological evidence and the interpretation of data which supported the new public health approach to alcohol policy (Heath 1988; Anderson 1989; Duffy 1993) and, as we shall see in the final chapter, perspectives of the problem began to be modified again in the 1990s. Moreover, therapeutic practice, while gradually coming to adopt the new language of 'alcohol misuse' or 'problem drinking' continued, into the 1980s, to provide services influenced predominantly by 'disease' theory.

The conceptual shift which took place would have been incomplete without the influence of parallel developments which not only fuelled the new 'movement' with a further rationale for replacing the disease model of treatment but also provided a theoretical framework more suited to implementing a prevention and early intervention philosophy. A focus on the drinking habits of the population as a whole and on the harms accrued by individuals who could not be categorised as 'alcoholics' opened the doors to including new groups of drinkers as appropriate targets for intervention and new groups of professionals offering therapeutic approaches which would formerly have been regarded as inappropriate for the clients of alcohol treatment services. Chapter 7 outlines the emergence of clinical psychologists as part of the expanding policy network around alcohol. In Chapter 8, women's drinking is used as a case study of the process whereby the 'expanded vision' of the alcohol problem drew new target groups within the intervention orbit.

The forces which resulted in changing conceptions of the alcohol problem have to be seen also in conjunction with parallel trends towards implementing a community-based treatment delivery system. By the 1970s, both ideological and budgetary considerations were pushing policy makers towards the adoption of community rather than hospital based health services, a trend which attracted powerful support within the alcohol arena as early as the 1960s. Again, the Kessel Committee's endorsement of the shift towards a primary care response to intervention in alcohol problems served to legitimate a process already underway. Chapter 9 examines moves to establish a co-ordinated structure of community-based services to address problem drinking.

As we shall see, the rationale for these shifts drew increasingly on research evidence; the policy community both increased and became more diffuse over the course of the 1980s as policy networks evolved new understandings of the nature of the problem and the necessary response; and the public health model began to influence not only the selection of populations and groups for intervention but also the contexts and settings within which intervention should take place and the types of interventions deemed suitable.

The demand for partnership approaches in the delivery of health and social care services was also to press for alliances between health, social services and the criminal justice system, further reflecting the shift from the treatment of alcoholism towards the management of a wide range of alcohol-related harms.

Thus, the wider policy and political background sketched out in this chapter – the move towards health prevention and personal responsibility for health – continued to strengthen under Conservative government in the 1980s and set boundaries on what could be achieved by the DHSS and the alcohol policy community. Equally, although it is beyond the scope of the present study, issues of illicit drug use, and the crisis response to the problem of AIDS/HIV drew ministerial attention, resources and, to some extent, wider medical concern away from alcohol issues. In short, the trends discussed in this chapter put an end to alcohol *treatment* policy and shifted the focus to policy concerning the management of alcohol problems and alcohol consumption within the general population.

7 New Professions in Alcohol Problems Treatment: A Case Study of Clinical Psychology

Overview

The swing in policy statements towards prevention and the early identification of problem drinking which accompanied the 'consumption–harm' conceptualisation of the alcohol problem inevitably required an evaluation of the appropriateness of treatment approaches and treatment services. Treatment could no longer concentrate on helping the 'alcoholic'; it had to address the drinking habits of a much wider spectrum of people, some of whom would not previously have been considered as 'suitable cases for treatment'. In tandem with the growth of the treatment population, went an expansion of the professions and voluntary workers providing alcohol treatment and a drive to diversify the types of services for problem drinkers. This chapter begins with a brief outline of changes in treatment approaches as revealed in published literature reviews. The chapter then presents a case study of the emergence of clinical psychology to illustrate the accommodation of new professions and new treatment approaches within the alcohol arena and the conflicts which arose as different professional groups began to colonise the new territory opened up by a prevention and early intervention approach to alcohol problems.

New Treatment Approaches

By the 1980s, 'alcoholism' and the 'alcoholic' had become aspects of a much larger problem. Policy concern within the DHSS now rested on the relationship between alcohol consumption and harm – measured in terms of harm to the individual and to society – and on tackling harmful drinking at all points along a continuum from non-harmful drinking (appropriate response primary prevention), to 'risky' drinking (requiring early intervention), to harmful and dependent drinking (requiring a variety of brief or intensive treatment approaches). In short, the new conceptualisation of the problem expanded enormously the target group for interventions of different kinds and the disease concept of alcoholism was no longer a sufficient theoretical base for the development of treatment services or 'intervention' approaches.

Changes in treatment approaches had been happening, of course, since before the 1950s. Using a quantitative analysis of the alcoholism treatment literature published between 1940 and 1972, Giesbrecht and Pernanen (1987) provide some indication of changes in treatment modalities, and consequently in the range of approaches available to practitioners prior to 1970. The seven categories of treatment and the frequency with which they appeared in the published literature at different periods is shown in Table 7.1, overleaf, adapted from Giesbrecht and Pernanen's review. Changes within each of the seven categories were also examined in the study and provided examples of the rise and fall in the popularity of different treatment techniques over the thirty-year period. For instance, papers on behavioural techniques in the 1940s reported mainly on the use of aversive conditioning (e.g., with apomorphine or later, disulfiram), whereas in the 1960s new behavioural approaches such as sensitisation, desensitisation, social skills training and assertiveness training were being described. As mentioned in an earlier chapter, 'tea and a chat' – as a way of providing advice in the 1960s – was later to develop into a more structured 'counselling' approach.

Giesbrecht and Pernanen recognise that what is published does not necessarily reflect what happens in practice and the range of treatment modalities described in the international literature may not be found in the practice of any one country. Many of the professionals interviewed for this study were prepared to admit that, even into the 1970s, they had little idea how to treat alcoholism and felt that they had few 'treatments' at their disposal. But many factors determine the adoption of treatment approaches and treatment techniques at particular moments in time. Discussing the results of their review, Giesbrecht and Pernanen concluded that changes they had found in the alcohol treatment modalities reported in the literature could not be explained by theoretical advances or accumulated knowledge from scientific research studies. They argued that,

the changes that have occurred are much more the result of changes in activity and application rather than outcomes of theoretical analyses or empirical findings. Furthermore, it appears that they are caused less by accumulating scientific knowledge than by changes in conceptions and structurings of research and knowledge. (Giesbrecht and Pernanen 1987, p. 193)

Table 7.1 The Share of Different Modalities Discussed in Alcoholism Treatment Publications during the Period 1940–72

Modality	1940–54	1955–64	1965–72	Total
Biochemical therapy Treatment procedures involving use of drugs, other chemicals, nutrients or bodily supplements.	47% (358)	62% (242)	65% (189)	59% (789)
Individual psychotherapy Treatments utilising a psychological approach that included reference to interviewing psychic or cognitive processes; one-to-one client–therapist treatments which stressed the importance of the relationship.	16% (75)	29% (68)	52% (39)	25% (182)
Group therapies Treatments where several patients were engaged in treatment activity at same time, in a group, with therapist leader(s); partially using group processes for the attainment of therapeutic goals.	35%[a] (26)	32% (44)	54% (59)	43% (129)
Community and social approaches Publications on government and other civic policies regarding treatment of alcoholics. Studies/descriptions of special programmes for alcoholics; Alcoholics Anonymous, if seen as an adjunct or referral resource for other services.	21% (38)	24%[a] (25)	43%[a] (21)	27% (84)
Behavioural therapy Behaviour modification techniques in all forms: aversive conditioning, desensitisation, assertiveness, social skills learning, relaxation therapy; any treatment utilising principles of reinforcement and conditioning.	36%[a] (28)	42%[a] (12)	64% (42)	51% (82)
Milieu and family therapy Treatment of the alcoholic's family members; the alcoholic together with family, or in relation to the family role. Treatment environment, or activities in the treatment environment were manipulated or examined with regard to their therapeutic effects. Studies/descriptions of special programmes e.g. religious-based helping agencies.	36%[a] (28)	35%[a] (20)	40%[a] (25)	37% (59)
Other therapies Transactional analysis, hypnotherapy, Alcoholics Anonymous when not used as a community-based adjunct to other treatment.	24% (110)	27% (75)	43% (76)	30% (261)
Total	37% (649)	45% (486)	55% (451)	44% (1586)[b]

Notes: a Size of sub-sample is less than 30. b Excluded abstracts where a modality could not be ascertained. Many therapeutic approaches reported in the literature used more than one modality. The data in the table are based on the modality which was ranked first on a set of criteria established for coding. Table adapted from Table IV (p.186) and description of coding on pp.184–5. The influence of research on practice – as on policy – is only one element in the process of change or the emergence of new trends.

Source: CAAAL 'Treatment' File in Giesbrecht and Pernanen (1987); base figures in parentheses.

The influence of research on practice – as on policy – is only one element in the process of change or the emergence of new trends. To take an example, as we saw in the case of disulfiram discussed in Chapter 2, a new discovery or advance in technology can lead to a surge of enthusiasm and a spate of publications until the new therapy finds its place in the treatment repertoire or falls out of favour. After an initial 'honeymoon' period, disulfiram became unpopular with many therapists in the UK. By the late 1970s, Ettorre's survey of alcoholism treatment units found that only eleven of the thirty units reported using disulfiram and most prescribed it for less than half of their patients (Ettorre 1984). Belief in the effectiveness of an approach and observation of the effects – and side-effects – on patients are obvious elements in decisions whether or not to adopt a treatment. Earlier discussion has shown, however, that changes in therapeutic practice and in the popularity of treatment approaches can be explained only partially by new discoveries and technological advances or by proof of effectiveness. The diverse interests of individual therapists and professional groups, differing beliefs in the causes of alcoholism – emphasising the physiological or psychosocial dimensions of the problem – and differences in institutional settings, local circumstances and administrative structures are also factors which affect the content and delivery of treatment programmes. Since, as Giesbrecht and Pernanen among others have found, many commonly used treatments have not been proven to be effective (Miller and Hester 1986; Heather 1993), considerations other than 'proof' of effectiveness, appear to explain continuing allegiance to some treatment approaches and the comparative neglect of others. This is illustrated in analyses of the fate of disulfiram. Reasons offered for the rejection of disulfiram in the UK treatment context have included, among other things:

- the influence of AA who regard disulfiram pejoratively as a 'crutch',

- the influence of psychoanalysis and the search for underlying psychodynamic mechanisms,

- professional rivalries in the alcohol problems field and anti-medical sentiment,

- vested financial interests in long-term in-patient treatment for alcoholism which are incompatible with the out-patient use of disulfiram (Heather 1993).

While the history of the evolution of treatment approaches to alcoholism remains to be written, it is clear that change in therapy 'fashions' and the growth of professional and voluntary groups working in alcoholism treatment in the UK were closely inter-linked. Within the broader view of alcohol problems, perspectives other than medical and psychiatric assumed greater salience in the development of interventions suited to a more heterogeneous target population. Indeed, it can be argued that without the inclusion of treatment models drawn from disciplines other than medicine, it would have been impossible to offer the range of interventions needed to meet policy demands to lower the number of individuals drinking above the 'sensible' limits recommended by the three Royal Colleges. Furthermore, as we shall see in Chapter 9, the policy drive to deliver treatment in primary care and community settings added to the need for interventions which could be incorporated into existing practice in generic health and social services and delivered by non-specialists. Thus, the input from disciplines and professions other than medicine was crucial in expanding the range of treatment theories and methods and in opening up a more optimistic therapeutic role for non-specialist, primary care workers. In the sections below, the role of clinical psychology is examined as an example of how non-medical professionals began to penetrate the alcohol arena, became increasingly influential on treatment approaches and began to carve out a position within the policy community.

Widening Professional Networks

Within the NHS and social services, the 1960s and 1970s was a period when the professions were 'in flux' (Webster 1996, p. 443). GPs were striving to improve their professional status and remuneration; nurses were similarly engaged in battles over their pay and conditions; community medicine and the role of public health doctors was under review and the personal social services were undergoing reorganisation (Webster 1996, pp. 296–310, 431–50). Hospital scientific and techni-cal services also came under scrutiny, the concern being the haphazard and unco-ordinated way in which an increasing range of professional groups had evolved within the NHS. Clinical psychologists were one such group. According to Webster, disappointed with the outcome of a review of the situation by an expert committee under Sir Solly Zuckerman and with subsequent action to amalgamate and co-ordinate the hospital scientific and technical services, the British Psychological Society pressed for consideration of their professional status. A sub-committee of the Mental Health Standing Advisory Committee under the chairmanship of Professor Trethowan was set up, amid considerable conflict, to consider the position of clinical psychologists within the mental health services. In particular the position of psychiatry in relation to clinical psychology was a source of tension, and negotiations were drawn out for nearly a decade. Finally, in 1977, the publication of the report from the Trethowan Committee recommended greater professional autonomy for clinical psychologists and predicted a sharp increase in the demand for their services. At that time, 600 clinical psychologists were scattered throughout the mental health services and it was estimated that the number would rise to 2320 (Webster 1996, pp. 314–18, 444–7). The increasing importance of clinical psychologists as a professional group in alcoholism treatment has to be seen, therefore, against the background of a more general rise to greater professional prominence within the mental health services as a whole.

Clinical psychologists were not the only professional group to become more prominent in alcoholism treatment from the 1970s. Nurses, especially psychiatric nurses, social workers, counsellors and trained voluntary workers, began to find career opportunities in alcoholism treatment, although their numbers remained small.[1] But psychologists, in particular clinical psychologists, present the clearest example of an emerging professional group which had an important impact on alcohol treatment approaches and policies since the 1970s. This was the first professional group to win a hearing in the treatment community for alternative ways of explaining and managing alcohol problems and is, possibly, the professional group which, along with psychiatry, had the greatest impact on the development of treatment theory. It was not until the 1980s that generic health workers, social workers and counsellors, as professional groups, began to assume a more prominent role in alcohol treatment. Prior to the 1980s, their contribution was limited by the prevailing approach in treatment agencies based on the disease concept of alcoholism. Until that time, treatment agencies focused predominantly on helping 'alcoholics' or 'dependent' drinkers and many agency workers based their interventions on the notion of alcohol dependence as a progressive disease. The goal of treatment was abstinence and clients' 'denial' of the problem, or lack of motivation to change was seen as a major barrier to 'recovery'. Many generic health and social workers still regarded 'alcoholism' as a specialist treatment field where they had a minor, if any, role to play (Shaw et al. 1978). Psychology was to furnish the therapeutic tools by which, at least in theory, the prevailing treatment culture might be changed and policy objectives to encourage 'sensible drinking' and reduce alcohol related harms put into practice.

The Growth of Psychological Perspectives

Examination of the role of psychology in the alcohol field has been at least partially covered elsewhere. Berridge (1990) has sketched the development of psychological treatments in her history of the Society for the Study of Addiction; Heather and Robertson (1985), among others, have provided an analysis of the factors influencing the shift in emphasis from a disease perspective of alcoholism to an alcohol problems approach; Roizen (1987) has examined in detail the genesis and significance of the debate on controlled drinking as a goal of therapy; and Tober (1991) has provided a brief outline of the 'New Directions' group which facilitated the spread of debate in the UK on controlled drinking approaches and adopted social learning theory as the basis for understanding problematic drinking and providing a therapeutic response.

The input from clinical psychology has to be seen against the background of the development of psychology itself as a new disci- pline, separating from its roots in philosophy in the late nineteenth century. Wundt, who opened the first psychology laboratory in Germany in 1879, is generally taken to be the founder of modern psychology. Wundt and his colleagues were attempting to investigate 'the mind' through introspection, recording and measuring the results of their introspections under controlled conditions. It was this emphasis on measurement and control which is taken to mark the separation of the 'new psychology' from its parent discipline of philosophy. Clinical psychology as a profession emerged from the scientific discipline a few years later in 1896. Its beginnings have been attributed to Lightner Witmer, an American professor at the Univer- sity of Pennsylvania who first presented his ideas at a meeting of the American Psychological Association. Whereas the psychologist was concerned with assessment and measurement, the clinical psycholo- gist argued that the academic discipline could have treatment applica- tion and that treatment could be carried out by psychologists. Witmer's theories were not well received at first. But during the first half of the twentieth century, through a process of 'professionalisation' strategies which included the establishment of professional organisa- tions and later certification and training, clinical psychologists began to carve out a treatment role. Psychological approaches to the treatment of shell shock in the First World War gained the discipline a firmer footing within psychiatry while in the inter-war years, the role of psychology was further advanced by increasing discussion of the treatment of drug addicts, most of whom, at that time, were middle class. A further boost to the profession came in the course of the

Second World War when a demand for short-term, cost-effective treatments to return soldiers to the battlefields involved psychologists working closely with psychiatrists in the use of group and individual therapies. As a result, Walker (1991) concludes, in his account of the emergence of clinical psychology, 'by the end of World War II, the clinical psychologist had clearly established a new identity as a mental health professional with treatment as well as assessment skills'. However, there was still debate about the function of clinical psychology and during the 1940s and 1950s the role of the clinical psychologist was still largely confined to assessment (diagnostic testing and interviewing) rather than treatment.[2]

Psychological explanations for habitual drunkenness had been implicit in the terminology and concepts used by alcohol doctors in the early nineteenth century (Edwards 1992); but psychological approaches to the treatment of inebriety were not introduced until the beginning of the twentieth century when they provided an alternative, and often conflicting, strategy to the dominant physicalist and biochemical models. At that time, psychological treatment, in the form of psychotherapy using hypnosis and 'therapeutic suggestion', aimed to replace 'the erroneous ideas and auto-suggestions impelling the patient consciously or unconsciously towards relapse' with 'normal and reasonable ideas' concerning the use of alcohol (Berridge 1990, p. 1015). Although psychological approaches remained a minor part of alcohol treatment strategy throughout the first half of the century, psychology was important in widening the treatment population to include voluntary, middle-class groups of patients, and in steering psychiatry away from the compulsory, institutional solution to the treatment of inebriety towards out-patient care. Later, in the 1970s, psychological theory was to play a similar role in underpinning moves away from in-patient and hospital-based treatment towards community care approaches. By the 1950s, the dominant psychological approach 'behaviourism', with its emphasis on the role of learning and on the measurement of behaviour, was just starting to be refined through the work of cognitive psychologists interested in mental processes (Micale and Porter 1994). But in alcoholism treatment, the physicalist challenge to the psychotherapeutic treatment methods which had developed in the inter-war years, continued, and possibly strengthened, into the 1950s, advanced by leading practitioners such as Yerbury Dent, who were openly hostile to psychological theories of alcoholism (Berridge 1990). Despite this, a degree of rapprochement between biochemistry and psychology occurred post-Second World War, strengthened with the adoption by the WHO in the 1950s and 1970s of definitions of alcoholism and addiction which incorporated both physical and psychological elements. This was embodied later in the 'alcohol dependence syndrome' and in the 'disabilities' approach to alcohol problems, discussed in Chapter 6, which further legitimised the psychosocial elements of the definition of the alcohol problem. Thus, it was not until the 1970s that psychology was able to influence alcohol policy and treatment practice in any decisive way. It was during this period that clinical psychologists in the UK achieved their emancipation from psychiatry and secured their position as a high status profession within the health services in general as well as in the alcohol field. As mentioned earlier, by the 1970s considerable tensions existed between the dominant treatment model based on the disease concept with its goal of lifelong abstinence, and developing psychological perspectives and approaches which posed a challenge to existing therapeutic beliefs and practices. Psychological theory suggested that alcoholism was a learned behaviour and that techniques could be developed to help people change; psychological theories allowed the possibility that the goal of treatment could be variable and that some people could practise 'controlled' drinking. It was a challenge which culminated in public debate in the US (Roizen 1987). It could be argued, then, that the impact of psychological theory was due, in part, to the absorption of psychological insights into psychiatry, in part to the *Zeitgeist* which provided an opening in a changing field, and in part to expansion and change in clinical psychology as a discipline and in its changing position within the mental health services. That therapeutic approaches drawing on psychological insights were seen as a challenge, rather than merely an alternative or an adjunct to existing treatment practice, emerges clearly from analyses of the debates on the question of whether the goal of treatment might be 'controlled drinking' rather than lifelong abstinence.

The Treatment Goal

As we saw in the last chapter, there had never been consensus within the medical profession regarding the nature of the problem and its treatment. Commenting in his autobiography on discussions at meetings of the Society for the Study of Addiction, Barry Richards wrote of one occasion when Francis Camps, Professor of Forensic Medicine at the University of London Hospital Medical School,

> delivered an unorthodox address in which he announced himself as highly sceptical about treatment in general and psychiatrists in particular. Such is the controversy surrounding this subject that subsequent meetings were invariably distinguished by the appalling rows that used to take place ... Given a dozen medical experts on alcoholism in the room at the same

time, I guarantee that as far as methods of treatment go, ten entirely different viewpoints would be expressed.[3]

The ambivalence within psychiatry itself and within the medical profession as a whole regarding aspects of the disease concept was provoked in the early 1960s by controversy over the aim of treatment.

The debate began with the publication in 1962 of a paper by D.L. Davies in which he described a follow-up study of ninety-three alcoholic patients who had received treatment at the Maudsley hospital; of the ninety-three, Davies found seven who were judged to have resumed normal drinking. The observation that excessive or 'alcoholic' drinkers could return to normal drinking had been made long before 1962; but Davies' paper, published at a time when the new alcohol field was still rallying around the disease concept, was interpreted as constituting a challenge to the biochemical and psychological irreversibility of alcoholic drinking. In the debate which followed, Davies' work was criticised on methodological grounds, principally that the diagnostic criteria used were unsound and the 'normal drinkers' were not 'real' alcoholics. More important, perhaps, the controversy revealed conflict, openly expressed by those concerned, between the interests of research, and the perceived interests of clients of alcoholism treatment. Although from the start, Davies was careful to stress that his findings did not imply abandonment of the abstinence goal in the treatment of alcoholism, fears were expressed concerning the therapeutic consequences of his findings; commentators advised keeping quiet about the research and that it should not be acted on because of the risk to alcoholics. But despite the critiques it attracted, overall, as Edwards (1985) noted, the work was dismissed at the time as of little clinical value. Subsequent evaluation of Davies' study, indicates that it provides yet another example of how the scientific basis of research is less important than the interplay of competing interests in the field, the social-historical context from which the research emerged and in which it was judged (Edwards 1994, pp. 349–59). In this case, research emanating from a highly respected source was later shown to be based on substantially flawed data. But as the review by Edwards points out, Davies' paper served to catalyse ideas and activity; it challenged the entrenched 'disease concept' (and, possibly, served to expose underlying tensions and disagreements in the field), and achieved fruitful consequences despite unintentionally placing faulty information into the public arena. In the UK, Davies' work was followed by a few papers, also published by psychiatrists, questioning orthodox views on concepts such as 'loss of control' which were central to the disease model of alcoholism

(Kendell and Staton 1966; Merry 1966). All the same, there was little critical debate and the questions raised did not present any serious challenge to the prevailing treatment culture at that time.

Throughout the 1960s there was little direct input from psychologists. Jim Orford, one of the first research psychologists to enter the alcohol field, remembered the controversy and angry reactions he received at a conference in the late 1960s when he raised the question of whether alcoholic drinking was learned behaviour and whether people could learn to drink less harmfully (Orford, interview). In the course of the 1970s, however, an important alliance was to emerge between a group of psychiatrists who were critical of the dominant models of practice and clinical psychologists who provided the conceptual, theoretical framework for the development of new perspectives on treatment. By then, research from the US and Australia had begun to provide a stronger framework of theory and empirical support from which to challenge treatment practice.

The involvement of clinical psychology in alcoholism treatment was evident in the US from the mid-1960s. There, behavioural psychologists began to experiment with controlled drinking using insights from social learning theory to underpin their therapeutic practice and research (Roizen 1987). While debate on Davies' findings was confined to a relatively restricted professional circle and was conducted in a 'gentlemanly' manner, events in the US took a more public, controversial turn. In the US, the focus of the debate moved from the confines of academic and professional discourse into the public arena with the publication of the Rand report in 1976. The report reaffirmed the presence of controlled drinkers in a population followed up for eighteen months after discharge from federally funded alcohol treatment centres (Armor et al. 1976). Further, contrary to Davies' approach, the authors took the view that a controlled drinking outcome was a legitimate aim of treatment. Dismissed by one UK commentator as 'much ado about nothing much' (Hodgson 1979), the report nevertheless inflamed existing tensions between abstentionists and non-abstentionists and called into question the scientific validity of research methodologies. One of the report's critics later led an attack on the controlled drinking treatment goal by criticising the work of the Sobells, clinical psychologists working in California who, since the beginning of the 1970s, had reported on experimental controlled drinking trials (Pendery, discussed in Roizen 1987, pp. 264–6). This proved to be the most fiercely and publicly conducted exchange in the controversy adding to the earlier fears and methodological critiques a challenge to the integrity of the researchers, from which they were later cleared.

However, according to some accounts, the watershed for clinical psychologists working in the UK, came not from the US but from work in Australia (Tober 1991, p. xiii; Heather, interview; Orford, interview). This was the publication in 1976 of a study by Caddy and Lovibond reporting on controlled drinking trials. By this time, a considerable body of research had accumulated which adopted a behaviourist approach to the treatment of alcoholism and an increasing number of studies were reporting some resumed normal drinkers in treatment populations (Roizen 1987, p. 256). Nick Heather, a British clinical psychologist, became a leading figure in the 'controlled drinking' debate. His interest was aroused while he was working as a junior clinical psychologist in the NHS in the early 1970s. By the end of the decade, he was fully involved in alcohol problems treatment and at the forefront of developments in psychological approaches to problem drinking. Reflecting on the importance of a controlled drinking lobby for the development of clinical psychology as a profession, he argued that

> It was obvious that here was a principle to which psychologists could contribute. In a model where abstinence was the only solution, psychologists might play some part but the notion of controlled drinking rejected the disease model in the strict sense – the AA notion – and psychologists became more relevant to the field than before. That was the crucial point. (Heather, interview)

Clinical psychologists could, in other words, claim ownership of the new ideas and open the door to a new range of therapeutic techniques based on psychological theories and principles.

The accumulation of research evidence for a more flexible treatment goal and the increasing importance of clinical psychology as a profession took place in the face of growth in the corps of traditionally orientated treatment paraprofessionals in the US and continuing dominance of the disease and AA view of alcoholism both in the US and in the UK. In the UK, despite refinements of the concept in academic debate, most treatment services still operated largely on a disease, AA, abstinence model. There were, therefore, considerable tensions within the treatment field. Debates of this period highlight not only tensions between different disciplinary perspectives on treatment but also differences in the ethical positions adopted by researcher-clinicians and by other groups of lay and professional workers concerned with problem drinkers. Roizen's (1987) analysis of the controlled drinking debate highlights a number of these issues and tensions, most notably, strains in the underlying value systems of institutions involved in the treatment of alcoholism. Thorley, a

Maudsley-trained psychiatrist working in the field at that time, noted the links with the UK policy response. He felt that,

> in the context of this semi-ideological tension – it wasn't exactly a battle but it was an ideological tension between the empirical control drinkers and the abstinence only brigade – was the formation in 1975 of the government committee on Alcoholism .... (Thorley, interview)

As we saw in Chapter 6, however, the Advisory Committee on Alcoholism (the Kessel Committee) was a response related as much to the concurrent move towards community-based services as to tensions arising from changing perspectives of the nature of the problem. Indeed, as we saw earlier, tensions in the field were reflected in the committee's debates. A more visible and immediate manifestation of tensions in the UK was the 'breakaway' coalition of psychiatrists and psychologists who formed the 'New Directions in the Study of Alcohol' group.

'New Directions in the Study of Alcohol':
Disseminating Psychological Perspectives

Soon after the publication of the paper by Caddy and Lovibond in 1976, D.L. Davies gathered 'the more liberal wing of alcohol studies' to discuss his work on return to normal drinking (Heather, interview). A year later, at a second meeting in Dumfries, a proposal was adopted to form the 'New Directions in the Study of Alcohol Group' with George Gawlinski, a social worker, as the first chairman and Nick Heather (who took over the chair around 1981) as an active member. In taking up the controlled drinking approach, the group was 'taking on a paradigm shift which had already happened' (Heather, interview) but the UK still had no 'lobby' to advocate treatment or policy change. The New Directions group was to provide this focus and support for the development of ideas. Davies, it appears, felt upset by his loss of control of the group which no longer came under the aegis of the Alcohol Education Centre which he had set up in 1972. But he had no objection to the swing of interest towards examination of the implications of social learning theory and the controlled drinking experiments for treatment approaches. The group united representatives from medicine, psychology and other disciplines through its opposition to the traditional disease view of alcoholism and to the argument that alcoholism was essentially a part of medical thought and practice. On the other hand, some psychiatrists, at least, felt that the major contribution of psychology had been to give expression to existing good practice in the treatment field by couching ideas in more scientific language. Anthony Thorley, a member of the New Directions group almost from its inception, explained that,

> Things like drinking diaries, goal setting, cognitive shaping, motivational interviewing, all the jargonised process would have been there in good practice but not particularised into these terminologies that we now use ... When I contemplate the way clinical psychologists and social psychologists have pulled these ideas out from what in a sense is very obvious. (Thorley, interview)

It is possible that the ease with which existing 'good practice' could be fitted into the new perspectives helped to recruit interested psychiatrists. Parallels can also be drawn to the dissemination of the 'disease concept' in the 1950s when new terminology had a part to play in rallying support for change in policy and practice. Certainly, within a few years, psychological theories and approaches were being incorporated more directly than previously into psychiatric practice. Anthony Thorley recalled that when he joined the Maudsley alcohol unit in 1975, 'it was an abstinence only unit; there was no concept of controlled drinking around'. He remembered suggesting to the consultant Griffith Edwards that behavioural techniques derived from clinical psychology could be incorporated into treatment practice. Edwards was, apparently, dismissive of the idea but, at the same time was beginning to employ clinical psychologists in his research unit. The result, according to Thorley, was that, 'Within about a couple of years, there was a revolution and this kind of approach, certainly in terms of clinical ideas, was being experimented with.'

Hostility to the 'controlled drinking' goal was not confined to the specialist psychiatric units. Thorley also reflected on the reactions within Councils on Alcoholism, where

> staff wanted to counsel people to aim for controlled drinking as a goal. They were virtually sacked, or marginalised or kicked out. And those of us who were interested in this kind of technique and methods of achieving this goal with certain clients, we found ourselves very much in the minority ... and we were hounded in all sorts of ways. (Thorley, interview)

Although psychologists were becoming more influential, they, themselves, realised that 'they probably still needed a medical benefactor in order to give psychologists the ability to do things'. Medical benefactors came from among those psychiatrists who 'tended to be more radical and more free thinking'; 'Other psychiatrists were extremely hostile' (Heather, interview). Some, at least, were also interested in challenging 'the establishment', which, at the time, meant the

Maudsley Hospital, the Institute of Psychiatry and the London base. Earlier chapters have described how the Institute of Psychiatry and the Maudsley Hospital provided a strong, academic training base which gave rise to an influential network of psychiatrists and psychologists, well connected to DHSS officials and at the heart of the policy community. Discussing individuals who were not part of that network, Heather explained that,

> A lot of these psychiatrists ... were fed up with the domination of the Institute of Psychiatry and they wanted to do their own thing. The Institute had links with the Ministry of Health, had the ears of ministers and were responsible for formulating policy and so on. So I think it was a reaction against that – simply London versus the rest ... There's no place for us in the British scene, so we'll form our own little group and challenge the power base in London. You can not discount the fact that there were motivations at that kind of level. (Heather, interview)

To some extent, exclusion from the core of the policy community and the radical 'label' became part of the identity of the New Directions group. The opportunity to become more centrally involved in the policy process was offered in the early 1980s when the group was invited to accept official designation as a kind of DHSS 'think tank'. The offer was turned down, according to Heather, 'because we did not want to be stuck or labelled in that way as an official generator of new ideas. It was regarded as a kind of invidious position to be in. We certainly did not take anybody's money' (Heather, interview).

The view from outside the New Directions group endorsed that decision and used the preservation of 'autonomy' as a reason for not recommending government funding. A report from an enquiry into the role of voluntary organisations and their funding discussed the role of the New Directions group and noted that:

> From the comments of some of its members and reports from elsewhere, it would seem that the group has the potential to provide opportunities for exchanges of views and, in particular, new initiatives. We should not wish to see such a forum compromised in any sense and would therefore hope that it can grow and flourish independently of any government financial support. (DHSS/NCVO 1982)

The dilemmas posed by concerns to avoid 'de-politicisation' without closing the networks and routes to influencing policy are common to activist groups in the alcohol field as elsewhere (Coxall 1985). The next chapter will describe how a similar decision to remain on the margins of the policy community was taken by a group of activists concerned to improve responses to women with drinking problems.

The New Directions in the Study of Alcohol Group went on to take up issues other than controlled drinking, its intention being, 'vigorously to pursue the investigation and implementation of new interventions for problem drinkers'. Tober writes that, 'There was a feeling implicit in the name of the group, that these would be endlessly forthcoming: such was the optimism generated in this new era in the alcohol field' (Tober 1991, p. xiii). The group continued to function as a vehicle for discussion into the 1990s, but as the 'controlled drinking' controversy faded, the group's image as a radical debating ground became more quiescent.

Perhaps because of its chosen 'outsider' status, the New Directions group did not function as a vehicle for individual psychologists to gain a foothold at the centre of policy making; this was retained by psychiatry which had professional representatives strategically placed within the civil service and in dominant positions within advisory committees at national and international levels. Nevertheless, psychological approaches and techniques were to play a vital role in implementing the new vision of the alcohol problem by offering a more diverse range of intervention responses to suit a treatment population expanding beyond 'alcoholics'.

Thus, despite the contribution of psychology to the changing conceptualisation of the alcohol problem and despite the involvement of a few social scientists, at policy-making levels, there was no dramatic change in the power structure of the alcohol policy community during the 1970s. Rather it was a period of expansion of spheres of activity at the level of treatment provision, service implementation, and research initiation which resulted, initially, in broadening the periphery of the policy community and widening policy networks but left the seat of power with a central core of psychiatrists and their service/research teams. However, there were increasing opportunities for psychology and other disciplines such as social work and counselling to gain a slice of the cake as claims that the alcohol problem was growing became underpinned with empirical data and statistical 'proof', and as new measurement techniques helped to carve up the target group into different types of 'problem drinkers'.

Alcohol Consumption and Problem Drinking:
The Contribution of Psychology

It is important to emphasise the concurrent nature of events described in Chapters 6 to 9. Changes in the conceptualisation of the problem, the growing input from clinical psychologists and other professionals, the expansion of treatment populations, and changes in treatment approaches and service delivery developed interactively. The personalities involved moved within overlapping professional networks and within the same – although expanding – policy community; the 'facts' which underpinned the debates were often drawn from the same pool of research; and the perspectives and models of treatment which emerged were not always conceptually distinct.

It would be misleading to suggest that psychological perspectives replaced the disease view of alcoholism in the emerging paradigm of 'problem drinking'. Rather the input from psychology to treatment theory and practice took place over a long period of time during which aspects of psychological theory and treatment techniques became absorbed into existing treatment approaches, including psychiatric practice. As Thorley's observation indicated, behavioural techniques had long been a component of psychiatric treatment approaches but in the 1970s, psychology furnished a new conceptualisation and provided a new language which helped to reframe understanding of the problem and open up alternative forms of treatment response both within psychiatry and for a wider spectrum of professions and voluntary workers. Moreover, an increasing emphasis on 'risk factors' in health, allied to the strengthening epidemiological perspective of health problems, drew attention to the existence of 'risk' in alcohol consumption and to the need to manage risk rather than to treat alcoholism (or dependence) as an actual disorder existing in the community (Falner *et al.* 1991). This, too, influenced alcoholism treatment and treatment research and was conducive to the incorporation of psychological theories and approaches in prevention and treatment strategies. As we have seen, the psychiatric management of alcoholism was, itself, still evolving; psychiatrists were still adapting their theories and, by the 1970s, in many cases psychiatrists and psychologists were working in the same institutions. The process of change was an interactive one – which later came to include other professional perspectives although these have not been included in this account. Change was accompanied by conflict and debate in the field which triggered existing tensions and sparked professional rivalries. But in an expanding arena, there was leeway to accommodate the growth of professional groups and alternative theoretical perspectives. Thus, despite the increasing strength of psychological approaches and the adoption of a 'problem drinking' perspective (rather than a disease perspective) by many therapists and treatment agencies, different treatment models continued to co-exist; Alcoholics Anonymous groups, for instance, grew in number and some agencies, influenced by developments in the US, began to offer 'Minnesota Model' approaches to treatment (based on AA's Twelve Steps recovery programme).[4]

It could be argued, as Gusfield (1982) does that the growth of the 'troubled persons' professions (or the 'caring' professions) is not a simple result of a greater need to provide treatment for more people; rather it is part of a dynamic relationship between a client group and the professionals or volunteers who seek to serve the group and promote their interests. Certainly, in emphasising the size and diversity of the alcohol problem and in opening out the definition of who needs help for drinking, the alcohol community itself helped to create both a wider target group for intervention and expanded opportunities for professional and voluntary activity in responding to the problem. Psychologists were a part of this expansionist activity. The process by which this could occur is illustrated further in the second case study of the development of services for women. The effect of shifting perceptions of the alcohol problem and the interaction of problem perception, professional activity and the use of research in 'animating', 'legitimising' and 'demonstrating' an area of concern, is illustrated in the emergence of concern over women's alcohol consumption where the activities of a small 'policy advocacy group' promoted the needs of women drinkers as a policy issue.

8 New Target Groups: A Case Study of Women and Alcoholism Treatment

Overview

This case study illustrates the symbiotic relationship between the emergence of new target groups for intervention and the growth of professional groups, treatment theories and therapeutic approaches typical of the alcohol arena since the mid 1970s. It highlights how grass-roots activity within the expanding alcohol arena was able to carve out and develop a new target group for intervention in the face of policy indifference and a low policy profile on women's drinking for most of the period studied. Previous chapters have already provided examples of the social and cultural bases of problem definition in the alcohol arena. At different historical moments, and in cultural contexts as diverse as the Roman Empire and Victorian England, women's alcohol use has emerged, disappeared and re-emerged as a focus of public concern. This chapter examines the shift which took place between 1970 and 1990 in perceptions of women's drinking from low risk to high risk and argues that it owed more to a combination of social and political factors allied with developments in the alcohol arena than to 'scientific' evidence or research findings. Women's alcohol use became defined as problematic and attempts were made to place women's issues on the policy agenda before there was much research on the topic. The chapter examines the process by which a 'policy advocacy group' emerged and, over two decades, developed into an 'interest constituency' around women's drinking; it considers specifically the influence of perspectives stemming from the women's health movement and from feminist theory, and it locates the shifting policy relevance of women's alcohol consumption within the wider changes in the alcohol arena discussed in the last two chapters.

Women's Drinking: From Eugenic Concern to Feminist Action

In most cultures, women's use of alcoholic beverages has generally been subject to greater social control and restriction than that of men and problem drinking by women has usually incurred greater condemnation and greater punitive sanctions (Waterson 1996; Plant 1997). Perhaps as a result of this, women in most societies have tended to consume less alcohol and have suffered fewer problems related to their own drinking than have men (Moira Plant 1990). Nevertheless, from time to time, women's alcohol consumption has become the focus of policy attention. In the UK, this has happened at times of high or rising consumption of alcohol. But examination of the history of public concern with women's drinking indicates clearly that level of consumption is only one factor – possibly a minor one – in defining women's drinking as an issue which warrants a policy response. An analysis of the processes by which women's use of alcohol has found a place on the policy agenda at different historical periods, highlights, as in other areas of alcohol policy, the complex interaction between the activities of interest groups, the production and dissemination of information and the social and political context of policy making and policy implementation. This was clearly the case in the nineteenth century as much as in more recent times.

For the good of the nation:
responses to women's alcohol use in the nineteenth century

In England, debate over women's drinking was prominent in scientific journals, popular literature and temperance tracts during the second half of the nineteenth century and into the early years of the twentieth. It was linked with the major concerns of that era – a declining rate of population growth, high infant mortality and an unhealthy working class all of which were believed to threaten both the quality of the national 'stock' and the supremacy of the English abroad. In seeking explanations and solutions, women became a focal point for many of the proposed measures to counteract the increasing 'degeneracy of the race'. Women's drinking habits, along with a whole range of female behaviours and working-class lifestyles, became the object of reforming zeal among the emerging groups of health professionals, charitable societies and ladies' organisations. The promotion of temperance took its place in a long list of reforms targeted at women – on infant feeding, hygiene, physical education, cookery, the provision of clean milk and involvement in paid employment (Davin 1978; Lewis 1980; Gutzke 1984).

Members of the Society for the Study of Inebriety, founded in 1884, were prominent in bringing alcohol to the fore in discussions of national efficiency, providing evidence of the degenerative effects of alcohol to the 1904 Interdepartmental Committee on Physical

Deterioration and, in accordance with prevailing ideologies, focusing attention on the relationship between female inebriety, child welfare and racial degeneration (Berridge 1990).

Academic and medical papers written at the turn of the century claimed 'strong evidence to show that alcoholism is spreading at an alarming rate among females' (Kelynack 1902). Typically, no figures were offered in support of the contention; rather observations of changing patterns of social behaviour were provided as evidence. The following quotation provides a glimpse of how changes in women's drinking habits were viewed during this period:

> Girls and women of the labouring classes now openly throng our public houses and drinking saloons. The 'ladies bar' is becoming a recognised resort ... it is quite customary for women to meet in the afternoons for beer and gossip. Confectioner's shops, restaurants and various so-called refreshment houses offer ready means whereby women of the well-to-do class may obtain limited supplies of alcohol. (Kelynack 1902, p. 196)

Young girls were alleged to be indulging in drinking and smoking[1] and there was a continuing outcry over the employment of young women as barmaids and the subsequent decline of many into alcoholism (Scharlieb 1907). Women were regarded as being particularly at risk of succumbing to temptation and of drinking immoderately because they suffered from 'an inherent vulnerability of the nervous tissues' which lowered their resistance to alcohol, and because alcohol provided a support in 'these days of incessant activity' when girls and women were 'subjected to the strain of competitive examinations, the excitement of society life or the worries of domestic duties' (Kelynack 1902, pp. 199–200).

There were close links between members of the Society for the Study of Inebriety, members of the temperance movement, the eugenic movement and the infant welfare movement. Many of the doctors, medical officers of health, health visitors and philanthropic gentry who presided over the voluntary societies, belonged to more than one group within the different movements. Dr Kelynack, a prominent medical practitioner, editor of *Child Welfare Annual* (1916) and a leading figure in the Society for the Study of Inebriety, couched his arguments in familiar eugenic terms when he stated that 'among the agencies making for physical decay, mental retrogression and national enfeeblement, the use of alcohol by women stands prominent' (Kelynack 1902).

Women professionals were no exception in laying responsibility for racial degeneration on females. Mary Scharlieb, an eminent eugenist doctor and writer, president of the Society for the Study of Inebriety (1912–16) and a consultant gynaecologist, also stressed the role of the individual drinking mother as nationally harmful. Mrs Scharlieb was not lacking in humanitarian sentiments about women's drinking. She was well aware that environmental or social factors played an important part in women's health and felt that much of women's alcoholism was due to 'misery drinking' because of the poverty and joylessness of their lives. Nevertheless, like most of her medical colleagues and the infant welfare movement of her time, Mrs Scharlieb believed that 'it depends on the mothers of the nation what the future men and women of the nation shall be' and she supported solutions aimed at changing individual behaviour, notably education, as the most promising way to address the problem (Scharlieb 1907).

The women's temperance movement (although concentrating largely on the evils of male drinking) shared much the same view of women alcoholics as the medical profession. Writing in the late 1870s, Mary Bayly, a gospel temperance advocate, expressed the view that, 'Women quickly pass beyond the range of moderate drinking. They have less power than men to resist temptation, and if the home life of our country is to be saved, temptation, to a great extent, must be removed out of the way' (Bayly 1878, cited in Kitze 1986). The British Women's Temperance Association (BWTA), while concerned about women alcoholics and involved in the provision of inebriate homes, clubs and activities for women, did not take on board an obviously 'feminist' approach nor espouse women's suffrage issues as did their American counterpart, the Women's Christian Temperance Union (Kitze 1986). Despite the many links and cross-membership between the British Women's Temperance Association and other organisations more closely allied to emancipation issues (e.g. the Independent Labour Party, which supported both female suffrage and temperance), the BWTA limited its campaigning to temperance issues and did not challenge prevailing conceptions of either the nature of womankind or of her place in society (Banks 1981).[2] On the other hand, movements concerned with women's suffrage and emancipation showed little interest specifically in the question of women's drinking and appear to have had little influence on discussion in this sphere (Banks 1981).

In short, the emergence of concern over women's drinking in Victorian England was a secondary, if powerful, element in the politics of imperialism and in the creation of a new ideology of motherhood, a trend which minimised the contribution of environmental factors and maximised the role of female attitudes and behaviour in the creation of social problems. This interpretation of the problem was supported by different interest networks within the policy community around alcohol at that time. But by the beginning of the 1920s, with changing social circumstances and a fall in the rate of alcohol consumption by men and women alike, the question of women's drinking ceased to have any political significance and faded from public consciousness.

The rediscovery of female alcoholism – a feminist concern

By the late 1950s, when a new wave of concern over alcohol misuse arose, the focus was firmly on male drinking and in particular on the group of men whose drinking was clearly defined as 'alcoholic'. Women were much less visible in the treatment services and featured little in discussion of treatment approaches or in research studies (Vannicelli and Nash 1984). The female alcoholic, as she emerges from the clinical literature of the period, is a stereotypical figure suffering from greater pathology than the male alcoholic and having a poorer prognosis (Clemmons 1985; Waterson 1996). For example, writing in the 1950s, Lincoln Williams described the

> immature female psychopathic addict, often emotionally labile and a possible suicide risk, perhaps sexually frigid, perverse or promiscuous ... the woman patient so vulnerable to emotional disturbances finds it more difficult to readjust her life and to make a successful recovery than the male. (Williams 1956)

It was not until the mid 1970s that the 'female alcoholic', as a subject of research and treatment concern, was rediscovered in the UK – some years later than the revival of interest in the US where research and discussion had been growing steadily for almost a decade (Committee on Labor and Public Welfare 1976). The new wave of anxiety over women's drinking culminated in the publication of a WHO report entitled *Alcohol Related Problems in High Risk Groups* in 1990, in which each of six European countries considered women as a group at high risk of developing alcohol related problems (Martin Plant 1990). Again, an examination of the rationale for the emergence and continuing status of women's drinking as a policy concern reveals that research or 'scientific' evidence played a relatively minor part in bringing the issue to the fore. Invariably countries reported much lower rates of alcohol consumption and alcohol related problems among women compared to men (Roman 1988; Moira Plant 1990) and although women's alcohol consumption in the UK, as elsewhere, rose between 1950 and 1990, the validity of categorising women as 'high risk' on the basis of consumption figures and rates of alcohol-related harm was challenged (Ahlstrom 1983; Fillmore 1984; Vogt 1984). Theories that changes in the drinking habits of women were leading to a convergence between male and female consumption patterns and a rise in alcohol-related problems found little support in an international review which concluded that:

> On the contrary, major gender differences appear to be evident and to be persisting in a large number of varied national and cultural contexts. Evidence from countries in which several surveys have been conducted at different times did not suggest that the overall pattern of alcohol use amongst women has changed very greatly during the past twenty years. (Moira Plant 1990, p. 7)[3]

Physiological research, which indicated that women may be more at risk than men of developing alcohol-related health problems appeared to carry more weight but the findings were still often unclear and disputed. Throughout the centuries and across cultures, the possible damage to the foetus from alcohol has always been recognised; but even in this case where there was greater research effort, the results were not always conclusive (Plant 1985). In short, it is clear that neither the reality of how much alcohol women were consuming nor the possibility that women are more vulnerable than men to the effects of alcohol are sufficient to explain why, at a particular point in time, women's alcohol use became defined as a social problem. It is more likely, as Weiss (1991) argues in her examination of the uses of research in public policy, that 'in some settings research has greater impact when it becomes part of advocacy for a preferred position'. This was the case in bringing women's alcoholism to public notice. An emergent 'policy advocacy' group forming around issues of women's drinking used available research from both the alcohol field and from the wider literature on women's health to build an argument for the policy salience of women's alcoholism treatment.

Undoubtedly, as in the case of nineteenth century alarm over women's drinking, many factors contributed to the renewal of interest in women's use of alcohol and to the reformulation of the problem which was to take place over subsequent years. But there is no doubt that the women's movement was an important element in the equation. The new feminism of the 1960s challenged existing orthodoxies on women's health status and the quality of health care they received, provided a critique of medical practices and medical relationships with women, and framed women's health issues in political and economic terms. The new movement was activist as well as ideological, campaigning for women's right to take control over their bodies and over the processes of medical care, supporting the development of alternative approaches to health care and the formation of new forms of health care organisation (Ruzek 1978; Doyal 1979). It was the women's movement which provided the ideological motivation and the theoretical foundations for explanations of women's use and misuse of alcohol and for the development of a critique of social responses to the female alcoholic (Ettorre 1989; 1992; 1997).

Against the background of the renewed vigour of feminism, developments in the alcohol field were also important in bringing questions of women's alcohol use to the fore and it is these developments which will be examined below.

The first was the emergence of a 'policy advocacy group', drawn from among the new recruits to the growing field of alcohol research and service provision, a group of mainly female workers influenced indirectly, if not directly, by feminist ideology.

The second factor was the development of a rationale which provided the theoretical and 'scientific' basis for analyses of women's drinking and which was necessary to gain recognition and legitimation of the new concern.

Finally, as discussed in the two previous chapters, changes in the concept of the problem, from 'alcoholism' to 'problem drinking', developments in ways of measuring harmful drinking, linked to developments in research and service provision were influential factors in the emergence of women's drinking as a concern meriting national and international policy attention.

The Emergence of a 'Policy Advocacy' Group

The impetus for action came from people working at grassroots in the services, many of them women, many from backgrounds in psychology and social work rather than medicine. A key role was played by female researchers and service providers allied to the Camberwell Council on Alcoholism which has been discussed in an earlier chapter.

Around 1973, the number of requests for information on women alcoholics received in the Camberwell Council's office increased notably and Council members realised that there were considerable gaps in existing knowledge about women's alcohol consumption and their needs for help.[4] Discussions with local agencies revealed that there had been recent changes in the number of women being referred to the services and that service providers were concerned because so little was understood about how best to meet the needs of women alcoholics. As a result, a series of seminars for local lay and professional people was arranged, covering a wide range of topics and addressed by a variety of speakers including a local police constable and a consultant psychiatrist. Most of the seminars concluded with a general discussion of women's role in society.[5] The success of the seminars led to the establishment of an action group with a brief to collect information, promote the study of women's alcoholism and arrange further seminars and events. The group met, almost every week, for four years from 1974 to 1978, the members amounting over time to some thirty people with a regular core of twelve (Camberwell Council on Alcoholism 1980).

The action group quickly gained recognition as an effective and prestigious section of the Camberwell Council on Alcoholism. Representatives of the group were regularly invited to address conferences and lead seminars at national and international level. Information supplied by the group formed the pivot of newspaper features and radio programmes and a slot for women was secured in the programme of the Advanced School on Alcoholism run by the Alcohol Education Centre.[6] Less academic methods, drama and folk songs, were also used to arouse awareness. By 1978 the work of the group had expanded to encompass international projects with attempts to set up an international information exchange network on women and alcohol.[7] At that point the group began to question its ability to continue the work on such a scale and whether it was still appropriate to remain under the auspices of a local Council on Alcoholism.[8] The idea for a new national organisation – DAWN (Drugs, Alcohol, Women Nationally) to take over the work of the Camberwell group was born during a train journey on the way to a conference. The outcome was the formation of a Steering Committee in 1979 and the first DAWN symposium in November 1980. DAWN, staffed at various times by one or two paid workers with voluntary help, became a pressure group and a co-ordinating body linking a growing, but increasingly diffuse network of individuals with an interest in women's alcohol use. The Camberwell Council Women's Group brought ongoing projects to completion and wound up its initiative with the publication of a book *Women and Alcohol* (Camberwell Council on Alcoholism 1980).

Throughout the seven years of its existence, the Camberwell Group had retained an informal structure relying on a network of friends and committed colleagues to forward the work in their own time. Women involved in the group recalled that little help was forthcoming from their institutions, although for the most part it seems, 'they did not block the work – it was just seen as our hobby' (Otto, interview). The group failed to attract substantial, long-term funding possibly because of its reluctance to jeopardise its autonomy by becoming integrated into a more structured and powerful organisation (Litman, interview). In this respect, the group shared the concern of the New Directions group, discussed in the previous chapter, to preserve its autonomy and freedom to challenge prevailing notions of appropriate treatment approaches. Although it failed to establish itself as mainstream, nevertheless, by the time it disbanded the Camberwell Women's Group had created a new awareness of women's drinking and through contacts with workers in other parts of the country, had established the basis for an 'interest constituency' among service providers and research workers which ensured a continuing commitment to working with women alcoholics.

The Rationale for Action

Early efforts to bring the question of women's alcoholism to the notice of colleagues and the public at large were undoubtedly as much campaigns of conviction as the presentation of 'facts' and reveal the tenuous role of research in policy action. Knowledge culled from feminist thought, from work on homeless women and from American research on women and alcohol gradually evolved into a rationale which quickly became a 'set piece' as the Camberwell Group gave talks and wrote articles. The rationale for action was based on the argument that women with alcohol problems were both quantitively and qualitatively underserved by existing treatment services. As in the case of male drinkers, the concern initially was very firmly with 'alcoholic women' both with the visible woman who came for help and with the assumed pool of secret or 'lace curtain' drinkers (Litman 1975).

The arguments rested on two main observations. First, people working within the services had reported an increase in the number of women presenting for help. A report from Helping Hand in 1976 stated that thirteen years previously there had been one female for every seven to eight male alcoholics approaching Helping Hand services with a request for hostel accommodation, whereas by 1976 the figures indicated one female to three males presenting themselves for help (Helping Hand Organization 1976). Alcoholics Anonymous reported a large increase in female membership in the ten years prior to 1976 from a ratio of two women to seven men, to a ratio of one to one.[9] Some councils on alcoholism similarly reported rising numbers of female clients (Sclare 1970). Figures for alcohol-related harms – liver cirrhosis, arrests for drunkenness and admittance to psychiatric hospitals – were shown to be increasing among women, leading to the conclusion that, 'Female alcohol rates in Great Britain are increasing per se and seem to be increasing at a faster rate than male alcoholism' (Litman and Wilson 1978). The second observation was that existing facilities were unable to meet the needs of women coming forward for help, possibly because the services had been developed with male alcoholics in mind. Women, it was argued, had specific and different needs for help, some of these arising from their traditional gender roles and relationships to men (e.g. low self-esteem; self-loathing; sexual problems; abuse in childhood and adulthood). Service providers, most of whom were thought to hold traditional views and values about women's role, were seen as reluctant to face change in their methods of working and it was argued that there were too few women workers in the services, particularly in policy-making positions (Litman 1975; Helping Hand Organization 1976).

The truth or otherwise of this 'rhetoric of woe', as it has been called elsewhere (Roizen and Weisner, cited in Fillmore 1984), was immaterial. What was important was the building of a credible argument as the basis of claims for support and funding. Those writing at the time acknowledged that interpreting the increase in women coming for help was problematic. Sclare (1970), for example, pointed out that the rise in incidence rates could have been accounted for by social changes which made women's alcoholism more visible: 'Are more lonely, shame-ridden women drinkers now coming to attention in the new climate of female emancipation? Or is there a true increase in the incidence of alcoholism in women?' The critique of the quality of service provision was largely ideological for it rested on an acceptance of underlying feminist principles which linked women's alcoholism with the position of women in society in general and in particular, with the dependence of female identity on male-defined role expectations. Explanations for women's drinking did not ignore physiological vulnerability but the emphasis was placed on psychological factors, on the social context of drinking, and on the influence of social change on women's alcohol consumption. The problem of women's alcoholism was seen to require services which would 'help women to value themselves in whatever way they chose to, not in traditional ways', a treatment approach which was 'underpinned by feminist ideology' (Richmond, interview).

It was this feminist interpretation of female alcoholism, rather than the fact that there were women alcoholics or the evidence of increasing alcoholism and harm among women since the 1950s, which was truly new in the field.

Legitimating the Concern

Gaining legitimation for the 'new' problem of women's alcoholism was not easy. For many people it was a matter of indifference, for others it was still too sensitive a topic. A member of the Camberwell Women's Group remembered how she had found herself talking at meetings only to people who were already aware, or to supportive friends, while at conferences the sessions on prostitution were more popular (Otto, interview).

Committed women working within the services had a difficult task to convince colleagues to their view that women clients required special consideration and that changes were necessary in the structure of services as well as in treatment approaches if they were to provide appropriate help for female drinkers. In the case of ARP (Alcoholics Recovery Project), one of the first services to raise the question of separate facilities for women, the suggestion was considered as outrageous at first because 'Nobody had ever been singled out to be treated differently' (Graham, interview). Opposition to the proposal was possibly due as much to the apparent feminist perspective underlying the suggestion as to the perceived deviation from normal practice. Male staff, in particular, appeared to be suspicious and to feel threatened by the move towards separate provision for women. When the issue first arose at a staff conference in the summer of 1979, it led to 'some classic debates where colleagues would say, "What do you mean there are differences, women are just men with no penises"' (Richmond, interview). Even after a Women's Alcohol Centre had opened – as late as 1984 – with a female staff, including one worker who 'came in apologising for not being a feminist', they still had to combat the attitude that, 'this is a lesbian house and the buzz went around ARP that strange things went on' (MacIntyre, interview). Strategies to legitimate the proposals for women's services included 'talking about it endlessly' and writing numerous reports for staff meetings so that eventually, 'the impetus to go for a women's centre became almost logical because it had been talked about so much' (Richmond, interview). By now, the time was right politically. The establishment of the Greater London Council Women's Committee provided a sympathetic power base from which ARP eventually secured funding for a women's centre.

According to some accounts, the need for legitimisation posed a particularly important dilemma in relation to the psychiatric profession. On the one hand, the support of psychiatrists was vital because it provided credibility and 'respectability' to the women researchers and service providers who campaigned for change. One researcher maintained that when addressing an audience in the early days it was helpful to have a supportive psychiatrist on the platform nodding agreement in the background. Audiences, including professionals such as social workers, invariably looked to the psychiatrist to legitimate what the speaker was saying (Otto, interview). On the other hand, some of the women activists believed that the feminist critique of prevailing treatment approaches posed a threat to orthodox psychiatry by suggesting that psychiatrists were not handling women's problems properly. It was, therefore, important to present women's alcoholism as a new problem, rather than as an old problem with a new interpretation, if psychiatric support was to be retained (Otto, interview). A different perspective of the critique of psychiatry was offered in hindsight by Gloria Litman, a psychologist and researcher involved in the field in the 1970s. She suggested that psychiatrists were too powerful to feel threatened; but as a largely male, medical group they presented a useful 'common enemy' and a focus for critiques of treatment approaches (Litman, interview). Furthermore, the women involved both at the core and on the periphery of the activist group were largely social workers, psychologists or social researchers, and it is possible that the professional tensions between psychiatry and other professions emerging in the alcohol treatment arena – touched on in the last chapter – may have spilled over into the advocacy of women's treatment. Opposition to perceived psychiatric control of treatment services thus served to unite the emerging interest constituency around issues of women's drinking.

From Female Alcoholic to Women's Drinking

If the epidemiological and 'scientific' evidence was a somewhat shaky reason for the initial prominence bestowed on women's alcoholism, broader developments and change within the alcohol field soon provided a firmer theoretical base from which to argue the case for special consideration for women. As discussed in Chapter 6, concurrent with shifting definitions of the problem, the 1970s and 1980s witnessed the awakening of a new public health approach to alcohol problems with an emphasis on community care, individual responsibility and lifestyle, and the importance of prevention. The creation of public and professional awareness was fostered by the establishment of new organisations whose primary aim was public education and professional training.[10] Alcohol problems, as with health matters in general, became 'everybody's business' (DHSS 1976a) and everyone who drank was at risk of developing problematic drinking at some time in the life cycle.

Greater acceptance of consumption–harm theory, the fact that female alcohol consumption had risen since the 1950s and the lower 'safe' levels of drinking applied to women meant that greater numbers of women could be considered as 'at risk'.[11] The expanding alcohol research industry fed additional fuel to the notion that women ran a greater risk than men of developing alcohol-related problems by reporting that physiological differences between the sexes made women more vulnerable to the harmful effects of alcohol. Differences in the rate of alcohol metabolism, in the development of alcohol-related liver disease as well as research on the relationship between drinking and the menstrual cycle were three of the more soundly documented areas of vulnerability (Camberwell Council on Alcoholism 1980; Roman 1988). As in former periods of anxiety over female drinking, women's reproductive role received particular attention. Interest in the effects of alcohol on the foetus was rekindled by research from the US by Jones and Smith (1973) who, in a publication appearing in the British medical press, coined the phrase 'foetal alcohol syndrome'.

These changes in the alcohol field as a whole provided a legitimate basis for concern to stretch beyond the small number of alcoholic women coming for help in the 1970s to women's alcohol consumption per se. Whole new groups of women became potential clients of the helping services and by the 1980s the services were beginning to reach out to women still in employment, with intact relationships, less physically and psychologically damaged, more middle class. Special efforts were also being made to address the needs of lesbian women, ethnic minority women and women with children (DAWN 1981).

The number of services paying specific attention to women's needs increased, although the expansion was largely confined to London and the south-east. In London, in 1974, there were twenty-one agencies providing some form of help for women but many of these were non-specialist or had a main focus other than alcohol. By 1984 a DAWN report found sixty specialist agencies and ten non-specialist agencies in London providing help for women with alcohol problems (DAWN 1984).

Talks and workshops on women and alcohol brought new recruits to the ranks of enthusiastic workers keen to further services for women, sometimes in the face of an apparent lack of demand for existing provision.[12] Thus, although it was argued that adaptations in the services and the promotion of services for women was a necessary response to the unmet pool of need in the community, service expansion could also be seen as a result of the creation of demand by the efforts of committed workers and the growing 'interest constituency' which they initiated, to sell the services they offered and safeguard their interests in women and alcohol (Gusfield 1982).

Responses to Women's Drinking: A Policy Dilemma

The ideological basis of concern over women's drinking in the Victorian era differed markedly from that of the 1970s. In the earlier period, with responsibility for 'racial degeneracy' ascribed to individualist rather than environmental causes, women's drinking became linked to major issues of national well-being and women were allocated a central role in securing a healthy population. To do this, required an improvement in women's performance of domestic and child-rearing roles and a strong ideology of womanhood and motherhood, supported by the policy community around alcohol, emerged around these aims. Turn-of-the-century campaigners promoted educational efforts which concentrated on improving women's skills as housewives and mothers and on inculcating the dominant ideology of motherhood. Temperance teaching generally formed a part of the general educational approach and temperance leaders were frequently to be found among the supporters and initiators of educational projects (Davin 1978; Lewis 1980). Treatment and rehabilitation aims for women alcoholics stressed control measures designed to reform women and return them to their expected roles as mothers and the nation's housekeepers. The majority of inmates consigned to the state inebriate reformatories between 1899 and 1914, the whole period of their existence, were women and failure to reform was regarded as an individual problem rather than due to inappropriate or inadequate institutional provision (Hunt *et al.* 1987). Thus measures to address the problem of women's drinking supported rather than threatened prevailing notions of women's place in society.

By contrast, in contemporary Britain the issue of women's drinking emerged from a feminist perspective of women's health which was concerned with the well-being of women rather than the good of the nation and which located harmful drinking primarily within a social and economic context, explaining women's drinking habits as related to their dependent positions in society. This presented difficulties in negotiations with policy makers.

There were two important strands to the policy demands put forward by the original group of women activists. First, there was a demand to stimulate forms of service provision which were more appropriate to women's needs, which might encourage women with alcohol problems to come forward for help, and which would provide the support they needed to cope with their lives without alcohol. In other words, it was recognised that women wanted to carry out their responsibilities as mothers, partners, or employees – they did not necessarily want to relinquish these roles. Services it was argued, had to help women examine the causes of their drinking and provide a forum where women could discuss issues such as low self-esteem and self-loathing, abuse in childhood and adulthood, incest and rape, and feelings about motherhood, without the presence of men. At a basic level this may be regarded as helping women overcome problems which hindered them in the performance of their traditional roles. But second, there were the less precise 'feminist' demands, to locate the problem of women's drinking within a critique of gender relationships and societal expectations of women's roles, and to empower women within the treatment setting so that they might gain control over their lives.

This dual aim in policy demands has been noted by Moser (1989), in an examination of gender planning in the Third World. Moser makes a distinction between 'practical' gender needs which arise from the concrete conditions of women's lives, and 'strategic' gender needs which arise from women's position in relation to men, in particular their social position of subordination and dependence. Policy and planning to meet practical gender needs is a response to an immediate perceived necessity and is aimed at helping women to cope with and to carry out expected roles and duties. It does not challenge prevailing forms of gender relationships. Policy and planning to address strategic gender needs poses a threat to prevailing social norms and relationships.

As in other areas of health and social welfare, policy responses to women's alcohol problems have largely concentrated on meeting practical gender needs. For instance, one of the few policy statements in the early 1980s regarding women and alcohol was a statement in 1983 concerned with drinking during pregnancy.[13] Certainly, women involved in the early 'activist' group felt that interest in foetal health gained greater policy attention than the treatment needs of women alcoholics. Comments from Shirley Otto, a research psychologist, give some insight into their thinking at that time:

> We drew our ideas from feminist thought and from the work on homeless women. We were guilty of ending up talking about 'empty nest' syndrome and such like but it was all we knew at the time ... We were also caught up fighting off the foetal alcohol stuff. That just gave the boys such fun. As soon as they got hold of it they ran with it. Because it was such a lovely stick to beat women with. But it didn't come off – it hasn't come off. They were less interested in women, more interested in foetal alcohol syndrome. At first it was not too difficult to stave it off, because it was unclear what it was and how it applied. And people were using very different definitions of it. But it's something that gets money. It implied the idea of the degeneration of the race although they did not use these terms. Very, very occasionally they could think of providing provision for mothers and babies which was an acknowledgement that woman had children, but they wouldn't provide creches that gave women fuller lives. (Otto, interview)

At the same time, it is important to note the contrast between the high profile, 'alarmist' American response to issues of foetal harm and the policy attention it received in the UK.[14] In the UK, there was a degree of media coverage, some research interest and the incorporation of the issue in health promotion material. Officials in the DHSS were concerned about claims that women who drank very little during pregnancy nevertheless ran a significant risk of foetal abnormality and feared that advice based on such a view would lead to levels of anxiety and guilt in some women which would far outweigh any benefits from the advice. Following a review of the literature and ongoing research in the US, and wide consultation with groups such as the medical Royal Colleges, a statement was delivered in the Commons by John Patten. The statement said that there was no evidence of serious damage to the foetus from drinking within 'sensible' limits but that it was advisable to drink as little as possible.[15]

Again, as in perceptions of psychiatric responses to activists' arguments, women activists' perceptions of the policy response could be seen as rooted in their particular social context. Fighting off the male establishment concerned with women's reproductive functions afforded another element in formulating a cohesive ideology with which to define the position of the activist group in relation to (and in opposition to) the medical and policy establishment. But whatever the differences in perceptions, in considering policy responses to demands for improved services for women alcoholics, the two strands of action identified by Moser are important. The first opens up the possibility of a non-threatening relationship with policy makers at the service provision level. The second may be seen as a threat to existing social values and relationships unlikely to be acceptable in a largely male-dominated policy arena, and, at a practical level, to present much greater problems for policy implementation. Stedward (1987) has documented a similar difficulty in securing policy action on battered women.

Activating policy presented, therefore, dilemmas at several levels. For the core of policy 'campaigners', the dilemma arose because workers committed to improving services for women based their arguments on the specific gender-based conditions of women's lives to gain recognition of women's alcohol problems and support for an improved response. At the same time, they challenged gender-based relationships and male-dominated structures as one of the causes of women's harmful drinking and a barrier to rehabilitation. As the comment quoted above from Shirley Otto indicated, the difficulty was recognised by women activists and felt most keenly in issues touching on women's roles as mothers.

In the course of the 1980s greater diversity of opinion appeared within the widening circle of concerned women in the services and in research. Not everyone was comfortable with what seemed to be an extreme feminist ideology and with their observations that women with alcohol problems did not all respond well to overt feminist approaches. As one service worker put it:

> Although the ideology is around in my head, it tends not to come out of my mouth ... In terms of the women who came to the centre, the younger women were lesbian, lots of them, talked about themselves and women, using feminist language – more as an attack on society. Many of the older women found the terminology alienating. In terms of what we did in practice, it must have been underpinned by feminist ideology because it was different from what we would do with men in terms of how we helped women to value themselves in whatever way they chose to, not in traditional ways. (Richmond, interview)

However, there appears to have been a high measure of consensus within the core of women with closest access to policy makers. For that group, the greater part of the educational and service response to women's alcohol problems was seen as still 'on the level of attempting to relieve symptoms and no more'. Primary care workers, it was claimed, acted more often as vehicles for social control rather than social change, helping women 'to deal with the symptoms and their frustration rather than helping them to realise their potential to change the situation' (DAWN 1980). Policy continued to support women's traditional roles and the implementation of measures to realise a more radical treatment approach to women's alcoholism were, from an activist point of view, slow to develop.

Activating a Policy Response

From the point of view of the policy maker, both financial and ideological considerations underpinned the more cautious approach to declaring a commitment to issues of women's drinking and treatment needs. Even as late as the mid-1980s, evidence for the policy salience of women's consumption and women's treatment needs was seen as insufficient. The Breeze report, a national survey of women's drinking and attitudes towards alcohol use, had been commissioned by the Department of Health and Social Security as one of a series of surveys to provide a better picture of the nation's alcohol consumption. The findings from the report, published in 1986, were widely quoted by service providers and researchers as evidence of the need for prevention and intervention efforts directed towards women. The report's recommendations were received more sceptically by some officials in the DHSS. Contrary to expectations, the survey had identified a very small number of heavy drinking women, too few, it was felt, to provide significant information on their problems and needs. As a result the survey was not considered strong enough to draw good conclusions for policy action (Wawman, interview). Nevertheless, as one senior medical officer remarked, it 'provided the people who wanted to do something with evidence to back up their perception' (anonymous, interview). Demands from activist groups to provide separate treatment provision for women were never favoured. At a time when central funding for service development was restricted, the bias of the department was, in the first place, to improve generic services rather than support separate treatment approaches and facilities, and again, there were doubts regarding the evidence on which arguments for separate treatment approaches were advanced. A third important factor was the initial lack of an institutionalised channel of communication between women activists and department officials and the unfamiliar approaches and methods adopted by women in presenting their case to policy makers. Both the ideology and the negotiating strategies of the early activist group were at odds with bureaucratic culture. As one department official observed,

> We met DAWN members. They came to give us their views. In fact, if I am not mistaken, at one point they would only meet female members of the department. It was interesting and quite a challenge to us which we did our best to rise to. But they presented a very different method of working from what the department was used to. (anonymous, interview)

Thus, while interest in the epidemiology of women's drinking attracted some attention in the early 1980s, there was initially very little response to issues of service needs.

It was, however, impossible for the department to ignore the issue of women and alcohol and the need to take women's drinking seriously entered official thinking 'in dribs and drabs' (anonymous, interview). A number of factors were instrumental in raising the profile of women's drinking on the policy agenda. For one thing, following the United Nations 'Decade for Women' in 1985, the government had set up a Ministerial Group on Women's Issues (MIGWI) in May 1986 to 'provide a co-ordinated examination of policy issues of special concern to women'.[16] Although women's alcohol use was not its primary concern, the Ministerial Group provided a climate of opinion conducive to the consideration of women's needs which was supported further through the active interest in women's health issues shown by Edwina Currie, the Health

Minister at that time (anonymous, interview). Second, the gradual increase in research helped to build a case for the policy-relevance of women's alcohol consumption and treatment requirements. But more important, perhaps, was the influence of the wider policy community developing around the issue.

The establishment of Alcohol Concern in 1984, funded by the government to co-ordinate services and awareness activities formerly managed by the voluntary sector, provided an initial institutional channel for filtering pressure into policy-making circles. This was strengthened when Alcohol Concern and the Health Education Authority (HEA) initiated activities to promote service and prevention activity targeted at women (Baker, interview). For example, funding provided by the DHSS and administered through Alcohol Concern, was allocated with the guidance ' that services should give special priority to provision solely for women and where provision was not solely for women, the application for funds must show clearly that women were not going to be discriminated against' (anonymous, interview; Baker, interview). The growth of the alcohol treatment arena in the 1980s brought many more women into service provision and both Alcohol Concern and the HEA came under pressure from workers in the field to activate policy responses to women's drinking and service needs. The DAWN campaign to raise the profile of women and alcohol and secure funds for service development was remembered by one Department of Health official as very effective, 'not necessarily immediately on government but on the other agencies. DAWN hit Alcohol Concern very hard and the department got hit after that' (anonymous, interview).

One example of how organisations representing the wider policy community exercised their influence is provided by a flurry of activity on issues of women's alcohol use around the late 1980s and early 1990s. The first initiative, a national conference entitled, 'A Women Centred Approach: Planning and Practice in Alcohol and Drug Services', attempted to represent a broad range of interests and included alcohol, prescribed drugs and illicit drugs. The background paper to the conference stated that, 'In 1988 the Department of Health identified the need for a conference on Women and substance use'.[17] How that need was identified was described by a civil servant working in the department at the time. He remembered that the impetus to take action came from a joint approach from Alcohol Concern, DAWN and SCODA (Standing Conference on Drug Abuse), another government-funded organisation concerned with drugs, and together, these organisations had persuaded the DHSS to provide £5000 to fund a conference (anonymous, interview).

Preparation for the conference included consultation with the department to identify issues of concern to them. These were clearly related to the department's wider considerations in alcohol service provision, in particular the concern to support the provision of care within the generic health services and to approach issues of separate women-only facilities with caution. At the same time, the conference themes suggested by the department showed an awareness of research findings – for instance, on the barriers to help-seeking for women with alcohol problems – and of the main concerns of workers in alcohol treatment facilities. The planning process also included a pre-conference meeting with groups of women working in the services and in research who met to discuss the issues and set the agenda for the conference. In this way, through the new institutional channels, the views of individuals on the periphery of the policy community were channelled into policy making and the influence of the wider arena of alcohol workers filtered indirectly into policy-making circles.

By this time, however, it was clear that there was no longer a strong core 'policy advocacy' group. The growth of the alcohol treatment arena and the 'institutionalisation' of women's alcohol issues within Alcohol Concern and the HEA marked the end of the early activist phase and the apparent consensus which had united the relatively small group of people working to gain recognition of the special needs of women drinkers. Early research-based arguments, used to build a 'rationale' for action, were reviewed as new research became available; institutional concerns influenced the policy stances of individuals more overtly than formerly, and perceptions of the problem and of the appropriate response began to diversify within the alcohol field itself. For instance, one member of staff at the Health Education Authority remembered that alcohol service workers had pressurised the HEA to target specifically pregnancy and alcohol issues whereas within the HEA opinion favoured the integration of information on alcohol and pregnancy within a holistic model of health care, believed to be more suited to women's needs (anonymous, interview). DAWN, although still in existence, suffered from funding problems by the late 1980s and was unable to sustain its role as a national campaigning body. Thus, although there was a larger 'interest constituency' of researchers and workers in treatment services throughout the country, they lacked the cohesion and unity of purpose which had distinguished the early activist group. These trends became visible in the steering group appointed by the Department of Health in 1991 to advise on strategy regarding women and alcohol.

Re-Conceptualising the Issues: Women Take the Lead

The rationale for the initiative, given in a press release (undated), drew largely on the now familiar arguments that,

> Alcohol consumption amongst women is increasing and women are more vulnerable than men to alcohol's effects. The financial costs of alcohol misuse among women are high, but the personal and social costs are a great deal higher, which is why the government is committed to addressing the problem.

In addition, Baroness Hooper, Parliamentary Under-Secretary of State, in launching the steering group, announced her concern, 'about women drinking heavily during pregnancy, because of the risk to the unborn child' (press release). In short, the public message at this point emphasised physiological vulnerability, the role of motherhood and the personal and social costs of alcohol misuse, arguments akin to the eugenic concerns of earlier times although couched in terminology appropriate to the late twentieth century. However, responses to the initiative and to a subsequent conference organised by the Department of Health and the Royal College of General Practitioners in 1990 made it clear that there was again a discrepancy between official thinking and the perceptions of workers and researchers in the field. For one thing, the definition of women's consumption as a matter of public concern was not entirely welcomed by some members of the working party who were able to support their disquiet with the findings from a WHO study indicating sensible drinking patterns among women as a whole (Moira Plant 1990). An 'alarmist' approach, it was suggested, could do more harm than good. One member of the group representing service providers expressed her reservations:

> What we were particularly worried about was that by making too much of a song and a dance about it you would actually create a sort of backlash where it would be even harder for women to approach us for help ... You have to be very careful how you handle the media because the media are going to jump on the main fact that women are drinking more and say they cannot cope with their dual roles of work and mothers etc. ... for which there is not the evidence for a start. (Baker, interview)

At the same time, the earlier consensus and shared understanding of the issues which had marked the discourse and activities of women activists was no longer evident among representatives on the Steering Group. The group brought together researchers, service providers, representatives of the alcohol industry and public personalities such as Esther Rantzen, Claire Rayner and Jancis Robinson, presenting diverse views which represented different institutional and interest group priorities. The lack of a shared discourse – in terms not only of ideas but of the language used to convey ideas – was evident in a comment from Sue Baker, Director of Services at Alcohol Concern. She felt that,

> there were quite a lot of academics and you wondered whether they were having a kind of argument between themselves which had very little to do with – I do not know the dynamics and I do not know the research ....

The potential for conflict in a group of 'stakeholders' with divergent interests and ideologies was high. Reflecting on official attitudes and policy objectives at the start of the Department of Health's Steering Group on women and alcohol, Baker felt that what policy makers were fumbling for was:

> a sensible line that nobody was going to radically disagree with afterwards. There was a lot of strong opinion but they did not want to say anything that the academics would argue with and hence calmed down about the actual figures quite substantially and also changed tack on the moral argument, which again, was there at the beginning.

Possibly, as the 'interest constituency' around issues of women's alcohol use grew larger and more diverse and as the research informing the rationale for action became more complex and 'scientific', it became more difficult to reconcile the language of 'advocacy' with the languages of research, practice and policy.

Despite these difficulties, a consensus appears to have emerged from the Steering Group which presented a challenge to the assumptions underlying the initial government message. It was symbolised in the theme – 'Women take the Lead' – of a conference with which the working group ended. The report of the conference stressed the fact that the majority of women drank within the 'sensible' limits recommended by the three Royal Colleges, that prevention efforts should seek to support women's 'sensible' drinking, while at the same time acknowledging the need for appropriate forms of intervention and services for women with alcohol-related problems (Department of Health and Royal College of General Practitioners 1992). There were, however, pointers in the document to new dilemmas for policy on women and alcohol in the 1990s.

The keynote address to the conference, given by John MacGregor, at the time Lord president of the Council and Leader of the

House of Commons, ended by emphasising three messages which indicated the possible direction of policy for the 1990s.

The first of these was: 'Women *take the Lead* in encouraging sensible drinking in their families and in their communities. We want to do what we can to strengthen their hand.'

The second message delivered was: 'Women *take the Lead* in drinking sensibly themselves. We want to support them, and do what we can to ensure that this common sense approach is not eroded by external pressures.' This statement was supported by earlier reference to increasing pressures on women to 'keep up with the boys' in their drinking, to drink in response to heavy social and domestic pressures, and to expected erosion of differences between men and women in their patterns of alcohol consumption.

The final message was: 'Women *take the Lead* in asking that the sort of help provided be more sensitive, not just to their own needs, but also to the needs of each individual, male or female. It is crucially important, when encouraging women who want help, not to fall victim to society's attitudes, because guilt and shame can stand in the way of a person's benefiting from help.'

While the conference report symbolised the important part women had played in redefining official concerns and approaches to issues of women's alcohol consumption and service needs, it remained at the level of a potential statement of policy. There was no indication of how the three messages might be implemented other than that delegates to the conference should 'return to their organisations and encourage *them* to take the lead in encouraging and helping *women to take the lead* in this important area' (italics in the original). Moreover, the statements contained the seeds of continuing dilemmas for women. For one thing, they are reminiscent of age-old expectations that women should act as the 'moral guardians' of their families and of society as a whole. The possible association between harmful alcohol use and expectations of women's social and domestic roles ('misery drinking') is recognised, but there is no attempt to address the challenge of reconciling 'strategic' gender needs with 'practical' gender needs in responding to women's problem drinking. More specifically, the report did not take on board the possible need for far-reaching reforms in social policy and social welfare which might ensue from any long-term strategy to support women's role as the advocates of 'sensible drinking'. In short, despite attempts at re-conceptualising the issue of women's alcohol use, these messages contained overtones of the response to women's drinking, dominant at the turn of the century.

Thus, despite gaining a tenuous place on the policy agenda, as the interest constituency grew larger, early consensus was fragmented and became coloured by professional and institutional interests and priorities. The outcome, as indicated in the report of the conference was, perhaps, a more diffuse message easier to assimilate into official trends and policy approaches than the arguments and demands of the original activist group had been. Furthermore, the emphasis on prevention and support for women was acceptable to the many different professional groups which had become 'stakeholders' in the alcohol treatment and prevention arenas. Not surprisingly, as policy attention turned to issues of prevention and early intervention as a more appropriate response to the needs of most women, the concerns of the original 'policy advocacy' group with the need for special treatment approaches and facilities remained at the level of grassroots initiatives. It would appear that having campaigned for many years to put women and alcohol on to the political agenda, and, even if modestly, having succeeded, service workers in the 1990s inherited the unresolved dilemma of counteracting any tendency to 'moral panic' over women's alcohol consumption, preserving a feminist (or women-centred) analysis of women's problem drinking and, at the same time, retaining government support and funding for the provision of appropriate treatment and rehabilitation services.

Targeting Women: A 'Grassroots' Initiative

The growth of the interest constituency around issues of women's alcohol consumption, the shift away from the 1970s focus on the need for specialist service provision for women with alcohol problems, and the emergence of a more 'institutionalised' channel of communication with government undoubtedly served to move concern over women's drinking from an 'outsider' to a 'threshold' position in relation to negotiations with policy makers. But there is no doubt that, in contrast to the late Victorian era, the issue remained marginal to the major policy debates and concerns of the post-war period. Women's drinking entered the margins of policy consideration only when epidemiological and economic perspectives of drinking problems indicated the need for a preventive approach directed towards the population as a whole.

Examination of efforts to place women's alcoholism treatment on the policy agenda illustrates the place of active grassroots advocacy of an issue in expanding the alcohol treatment arena. But it also highlights the difficulty of securing policy salience for issues which are not already identified as priorities, especially when the policy advocates are 'outsiders' or marginal to the core of the 'policy community'. Quite the reverse is seen in the next chapter. Here an

analysis of the shift in service delivery from specialist inpatient care
to primary care shows how policy makers, in a 'top-down' initiative,
used the resources at their disposal to encourage the involvement of
general practitioners and primary care workers despite the reluctance
of primary care professionals to accept an expanded role in
responding to alcohol problems.

9 Implementing Policy: An Integrated, Co-ordinated Network of Services

Overview

Discussion in Chapter 6 showed how the new, broader vision of the alcohol problem which emerged in the 1970s found expression in three reports from the Advisory Committee on Alcoholism (the Kessel Committee) and how the report *The Pattern and Range of Services for Problem Drinkers*, which recommended a strategy for the delivery of locally based alcohol services, was significant in setting the agenda for service implementation throughout the 1980s. This chapter traces efforts to implement the Kessel recommendations. Three parallel approaches to securing an integrated network of services, are examined.

First of all, the chapter examines the drive to encourage the primary care team, and in particular general practitioners, to identify and respond to problem drinking in their patients. Previous case studies have indicated how individuals from different professional groups and different disciplines began to enter the alcohol field, and were able to influence treatment theories and approaches from within a specialist base. The situation was quite different in attempting to encourage generalist workers to incorporate alcohol problems within their therapeutic frameworks and treatment settings. Attitudes within general practice were strongly resistant towards taking patients' drinking habits on board. The motivation to mobilise the primary care team came from policy makers and from advocates of community-based care working within the alcohol arena. Examination of the primary care response to alcoholism treatment provides a good case study of the gap between policy intent and policy implementation.

The second important trend of activity throughout the 1970s and 1980s was the attempt to secure collaboration between health and social services, and between the statutory and voluntary sectors. DHSS activity aimed to solve some of the tensions in the field; problems arising from the different administrative organisation of services and the different disciplinary approaches which hindered collaboration between health and social services; tensions between different organisations in the voluntary sector which made communication between the department and voluntary organisations difficult; problems of departmental control over an increasingly large and fragmented arena. Through the use of financial resources and research, the department aimed to stimulate service developments in the desired direction – towards community-based provision.

The third trend examined in this chapter is the increasing use of research to underpin policy decisions. The complex relationship between research and policy is highlighted by changes in that relationship occurring in the 1970s as the DHSS became more proactive than in earlier decades in commissioning and using research in the formulation and implementation of policy. Securing an integrated, co-ordinated network of services and shifting service delivery into the community constituted the major thrust behind DHSS activity in the 1970s and 1980s and actions taken by the department illustrate the determination with which policy implementation was pushed in that direction.

The GP and the Primary Care Team

As in other chapters, it is important to look back to the 1950s to set the context for many of the problems and dilemmas which beset the translation of policy intent into practice. Throughout the whole of the post-war period, GPs were regarded as important agents in the identification of alcohol problems and in the delivery of treatment services. Over that time, perceptions of the specific role GPs might play in diagnosing and managing alcohol problems changed, influenced as much by developments in the structure and philosophy of general practice and by changing ideas about the nature of health and health care, as by trends in the alcohol field itself. However, while policy statements increasingly laid great emphasis on the role of primary care workers, the workers themselves were less willing to become more involved in interventions or treatment responses. As with public health doctors, individual GPs had been active in issues of alcoholism treatment since the 1950s; but it was difficult to stimulate interest within the professional group as a whole. Policy 'sponsors' or leaders did not emerge and there was little expression of interest in alcoholism from GPs as a professional body until the 1980s. The publication of the report *Alcohol: A Balanced View* from the Royal College of General Practitioners in 1986, marked a degree of acceptance among leaders of the profession that alcohol was an important issue in general practice; but the problem of expanding the role of primary care workers in alcohol intervention was far from solved.

Starting with the 1950s, subsequent sections trace the pressures and persuasions which have accompanied attempts to place policy into practice.

The GP 1950–70: A peripheral role

Several factors combined to make it unlikely that, in the early years of the National Health Service, the GP would play a role in alcoholism treatment. Although already beginning to rise slowly, alcohol consumption was comparatively low; public lack of awareness and knowledge about alcoholism extended to the medical profession and there was virtually no training in the recognition and management of the problem. The focus on 'alcoholism' drew attention only to the most severely affected patients and both professional and public attitudes towards 'alcoholics' were unlikely to encourage patients to disclose drinking problems at an earlier stage. Although there were pronouncements about the importance of early diagnosis, few attempts were made to define what was meant by this or how GPs might go about the task. There was a lack of specialist facilities and referring patients to mental hospitals was not easy both because beds could not always be found and because patients were often reluctant to attend a mental hospital. Alcoholics Anonymous was not yet widespread or well known and private treatment was restricted to the few who could afford it. As previous chapters have shown, with the exception of a few charitable hostels and shelters, there were virtually no rehabilitation or aftercare facilities for alcoholics. There was, therefore, little incentive for the GP to identify cases of alcoholism and it seems that few went out of their way to do so (Parr 1957).

But the emergence of the alcohol arena was accompanied by a slow growth of interest in research and a focus on general practice was one of the research areas to develop. With the exception of the survey of health visitors and probation officers carried out in 1960–63 by the Rowntree Steering Group on Alcoholism, research interest centred for many years on the GP rather than on other health, social or community workers as possible sources of information on alcoholism. Much of the early interest was epidemiological and stemmed from the activities of interested individuals who based their case for the research on the WHO report which claimed that the extent of alcoholism was unknown and possibly much greater than acknowledged at government level (WHO 1951).

The earliest survey of the prevalence of alcoholism in general practice, undertaken by Dr Denis Parr, at the time a senior registrar at St George's Hospital in London, has already been mentioned in Chapter 2. Parr's interest in alcoholism was initially stimulated by the

1951 WHO report and around 1953 he joined the Society for the Study of Addiction, which, looking back, he characterised as 'a club for eccentrics' (Parr, interview). In 1954, Dr Walter Maclay (MoH), a friend of Parr's professor at St George's Hospital, London, offered to nominate a senior registrar to represent England at a WHO European Conference on Alcohol Prevention and Treatment. Parr won the nomination from a fellow senior registrar on the toss of a coin and attended the meeting. On his return, Parr secured the co-operation of the College of General Practitioners and in 1956 conducted a survey of 480 members of the Research Panel of the College to ascertain the prevalence of alcoholism seen in general practice. The results from the 369 useful replies, indicated a relatively low figure of 1.1 per 1000 patients aged sixteen or over. It was calculated that, irrespective of the size of the practice, the average GP was aware of two and a half to three chronic alcoholics on the practice list (Parr 1957). Despite methodological limitations of which Parr was fully aware and which others voiced at the time (Parr, interview; Glatt, interview), the survey became the 'bible' in official discussions of alcoholism prevalence for some time to come. Parr himself was not involved in policy circles and did not continue to work in the alcohol field for very long.

Later studies continued to base prevalence estimates on general practice populations and to consider the extent to which GPs might be expected to function as primary agents in the identification of alcoholism (Grant and Boyd 1962; Shepherd et al. 1966; Hensman et al. 1968; Patterson 1972; Edwards et al. 1973; Wilkins and Hore 1977). The studies produced varying figures, due in part to differences in the methods of collecting the information and in the definitions of alcoholism used by researchers. Hensman et al. (1968), for instance, used the same definition as Parr but also asked GPs to comment on the numbers of 'problem drinkers' and chose an age of twenty years and over rather than sixteen plus. Most surveys relied on GPs' recall of patients with alcoholism except later studies in the 1970s, which used methods of questioning patients directly about their alcohol consumption (Patterson 1972; Wilkins 1974).

Despite such differences in approach and the varying results produced, the overall consensus was that GPs consistently underestimated the numbers of people with drinking problems in their practices. Several articles in the medical press during this period tried to arouse GPs' awareness of alcohol problems by emphasising the valuable role they had to play, especially in diagnosis of the problem, and by providing information about treatments available for the 'disease'. Some of these writers, like Glatt, were psychiatrists; a few, like Basil Merriman, were GPs (Glatt 1960; Merriman 1960b; Folkson

1965; Gardiner 1971; Parry 1971; Wilkins 1971). As noted in Chapter 4, both Glatt and Merriman were in touch with the Rowntree Trust Alcohol Advisory Group which encouraged the dissemination of information to GPs. A few organisations, such as the Medical Council on Alcoholism and the Camberwell Council on Alcoholism also attempted to reach GPs and other community workers, but the impact of such efforts appears to have been minimal at the time.

One of the GPs approached in the course of research for this book was Dr Benno Pollak, a south London doctor, whose surgery was in the proximity of the Maudsley Hospital. He recalled clearly the state of his own knowledge on alcoholism in the days before his interest was captured and he became active in local initiatives in the alcohol field:

> During the early 1960s there was very little information about alcoholism available to GPs. You didn't know where you were; you couldn't read anything up about alcoholism. There were only a few bizarre organisations existing at the time ... I had no ideas about drink problems at all ... What annoyed me was when the researcher asked me how many alcoholics we had, I had no idea and I felt frightfully embarrassed. I could only think of about three out of the 4000 patients in the practice. (Pollak, interview)

Expectations within and outside the profession tended to assign a supportive, peripheral role to the GP with respect to alcoholism treatment. Parr, for instance, in his 1954 report of the WHO seminar to the MoH, stated that in his opinion the GP had an indispensable part to play in the detection of early cases of the disease, in the after-care of patients who have received specialised treatment and in dealing with relapses.[1] A few people, like Glatt, acknowledged that in many cases the GP 'may be the only medical man needed to help in the recovery programme, in particular if he is prepared to enlist the co-operation of Alcoholics Anonymous' (Glatt 1960). Yerbury Dent's view was that GPs might play a bigger role in treatment once they realised that addiction to alcohol was a disease (Berridge 1990, p. 8) and Hobson, also a 'specialist' in alcoholism, felt that GPs were quite capable of adopting psychotherapeutic methods of treatment.[2] As early as the 1950s, ideas were floated on the GP's role in home detoxification and on their potential to use apomorphine or antabuse where there was adequate home supervision (ideas which came to the fore again much later in the 1980s); and on the possible advantages of having GP beds in local hospitals where family doctors could treat their own patients.[3] Interestingly, few of the voices speculating on the role of the GP in alcoholism treatment belonged to GPs themselves and pronouncements were more of a rallying cry than a reflection of what was actually going on in general practice. Dr Pollak, quoted above, provides a more typical example of the experiences and feelings of GPs at the time.

More commonly, treatment was expected to be undertaken by specialists. This is, perhaps, not surprising in an era when, within medicine as a whole, specialisation in medicine was increasing (Godber 1961) and when the dominant policy drive in the alcohol field (as in drug treatment) was towards providing specialist hospital-based treatment for the severest end of the drinking spectrum (MoH 1962; Glanz 1994). Added to that, as was recognised in the first annual Report of the Medical Council on Alcoholism (1970), most GPs were 'unable to diagnose and treat the disease because they have not received responsible advice and training'. In short, it would not have been difficult to find supporters for the view expressed by one GP that, 'the GP is not by disposition, character or activity, suited to an interest in alcoholism' (Nicholas 1970, cited in Wilkins 1974, p. 24). However, changes within general practice in the 1960s, allied to changing demands for treatment in the alcohol field, were to alter the position of the GP.

The changing face of general practice

Over the course of the 1960s, primary health care services had already begun to change in ways which, in theory, opened up possibilities for the care of people with alcohol problems within the primary sector. By the 1960s, the appropriateness of the existing structure and organisation of medical services, particularly the division between the hospital and general practice sectors, was being questioned. Policy makers, noting with concern the continuing escalation in the cost of hospital medicine, declared their support for the expansion of health and social services designed to enable people to be treated on a domiciliary basis (Baggott 1994, pp. 87–9; 219–21) and the argument for strengthening community care was reinforced by the publication of a number of studies describing the detrimental effects of institutionalisation (MoH 1960; Townsend 1962).

GPs themselves, engaged in negotiations over remuneration for their services and concerned with the status of their profession, had begun to scrutinise the state of general practice and to consider their role in the provision of health services. Since the establishment of the NHS, their separation from hospitals and their lack of a specialised field of medicine, had resulted, it was believed, in an under-evaluation of their services and skills, lower pay and poorer career prospects than their hospital colleagues, and difficulties in recruiting the best young doctors into general practice. At the same time, GPs contended that they had gradually extended their responsibilities for health beyond purely clinical concerns to embrace preventive health care and the psychosocial care of their patients. The two-year training course in practical psychiatry offered by Dr Michael Balint at the Tavistock Clinic in London and the publication of his influential book, *The Doctor, his Patient and the Illness* in 1964[4] opened psychological and psychiatric treatment approaches to GPs and provided a high-status career option within general practice. GPs were able to claim that 'whole person' care (the synthesis of physical and mental health) was an area of specialisation unique to general practice (BMA 1970; Honigsbaum 1979). The attention of policy makers and the leaders of the profession turned, then, to proposals for change in the structure and philosophy of general practice which would enable it to become the centre of community-based health and social services.

GPs were urged to form partnerships and to work in groups, they were given financial incentives to attach health and social workers to their practices and develop a primary care team; they were encouraged to improve practice premises and facilities and work in health centres; they were given greater access to hospital diagnostic facilities; opportunities to form links with hospital colleagues were opened up; and training for entry to general practice was recommended (Honigsbaum 1979). These measures, it was hoped, would not only improve the status and quality of primary care but would also enable GPs to contain the care of patients to a much greater extent within their practices and relieve the pressure on overburdened and costly hospital services.

A spate of government-initiated pamphlets and reports reflected what was already taking place and further legitimated the move to community-based health and social services (DHSS 1975; DHSS 1976b; Shepherd 1980). In theory, therefore, measures taken over the course of the 1960s and 1970s to establish the multi-disciplinary primary care team, concerned with the psychosocial as well as physiological aspects of health, provided an ideal base from which to deliver a service aimed at problem drinkers. By the 1970s, the needs of problem drinkers for a social and psychological treatment approach were considered to be at least as great as the need for physical care.

As we have seen in earlier chapters, trends in the alcohol field in the 1960s and 1970s, also had a bearing on the role of the primary care team. The new concern was with people with 'drinking problems', who could not be dismissed as requiring specialist help and for whom the case for preventive and early intervention measures could be argued strongly. Further, the growth of a wider range of community-based facilities, notably Councils on Alcoholism, Alcoholics Anonymous groups and a variety of hostel provision – although slower to develop than some had hoped – had increased the potential for responding to alcohol problems at primary care level. In practice, however, securing the commitment of primary care workers to respond to demands for greater involvement in alcoholism treatment was to prove difficult.

In looking at the problem of encouraging involvement with alcohol problems, it is pertinent to remember that the swing to 'community' was taking place in medical care as a whole and that pressures were coming from other quarters to take on aspects of care which had formerly been considered as specialist. In the 1970s, 'shared care' was becoming a goal in diabetes, hypertension, and a range of other medical specialisms where it was felt that closer collaboration between the specialist and generalist sectors was desirable. In the course of the 1980s, GPs were recruited in the effort to reduce tobacco use and smoking-related harm and by the end of the decade similar demands were being made with regard to the care of illicit drug users (Russell *et al.* 1979; Glanz 1994). By 1990, increasing demands on GPs to provide health promotion services were backed by financial incentives, but the preventive role was unpopular with a large proportion of the profession (Florin 1996). Thus, as Baggott (1994, p. 204) comments, primary care issues 'reached the top of the agenda' in the 1980s, and attempts to devolve some aspects of specialist alcohol care down to the GP must be seen as only a minor part of moves towards the much wider reorganisation of primary care which were to culminate in the issue of the White Paper *Promoting Better Health* in 1987. While pressures to take on an ever-increasing share of health care mounted, the high hopes of the 1970s for what could be achieved by the new structure of general practice – the team, working with group practices, from premises such as health centres which would facilitate the running of clinics and close liaison with social services – were not always realised and frequently brought new tensions and inter-professional difficulties (Jefferys and Sachs 1983). One example of the difficulties in initiating professional change, was the fate of the 1986 report of the Community Nursing Review team (Cumberledge report) which attempted to promote greater autonomy and responsibility for nurses in the organisation of local community nursing. The report was criticised as 'politically unrealistic' since it challenged a GP-centred system of primary care. The government, it has been suggested, did not back the central recommendations of the Cumberledge report because it was not prepared to challenge medical power and instead passed over to health authorities decisions whether to implement recommendations in the light of local needs (Baggott 1994, p. 209). In alcohol treatment as in other spheres of medical care, the power structure encouraged a focus on GPs as the main target of research and of mobilisation efforts throughout the 1980s. But with respect to alcohol, the problem was how to persuade GPs to take on what many viewed as 'dirty work' (Strong 1980). Stimulating collaboration between service agencies and the development of a community-based network of services with primary care services occupying a central role was the ideal on which policy makers rested their hopes.

Expanding Community-based Treatment Approaches: Experiments in Primary Care

Community Alcohol Teams (CATs) were among the first of several experimental projects funded in the 1970s and 1980s. They arose out of a research proposal to the DHSS from Edwards at the Maudsley Hospital. When DHSS money became available in 1970, Edwards wanted to continue with local community survey work started in the 1960s; but the immediate response from department officials was not promising and the money was obtained only after 'a thorough ding-dong' with civil servants (Edwards, interview). The project, which became known as MAPP (Maudsley Alcohol Pilot Project), ran from 1973 to 1977. The objective of the research was to study the situation in Camberwell, to make practical recommendations for an improved local response to problems of alcohol misuse, and to make any recommendations which might have value nationally. The community research comprised four studies conducted between 1973 and 1975 which provided an overview of the range of alcohol problems and service responses in the Camberwell area of London (Cartwright et al. 1975). The report of the initial community surveys, delivered in 1975, appears to have had a mixed reception; Chris Ralph, for one, was remembered for his scathing remarks about the value of the work (Cartwright interview). But, among other things, the research report proposed ways of improving the response to problem drinkers by GPs and a range of other health and local authority workers, and identified problems likely to hinder the more effective involvement of these groups (Cartwright et al. 1975). This aspect of the project grasped policy attention. The research was followed by an experimental 'community alcohol team' to test the hypothesis forwarded in the report that primary care involvement could be improved by increasing 'therapeutic commitment' to working with problem drinkers. A multi-disciplinary team was set up comprising a Maudsley-trained registrar, Terry Spratley, and two medical sociologists, Stan Shaw and Alan Cartwright (the research director), and joined later by Judith

Harwin, a social worker; they formed the action research group which comprised the first 'community alcohol team' (Shaw et al. 1978).

The aim of the CAT was to examine ways in which generic workers might be supported through joint management of patients and clients and through the availability of consultancy with specialists to acquire greater 'therapeutic commitment' to working with people with alcohol problems (see Box 1).

The provision of information, training and joint management support was the function of the Community Alcohol Team. The MAPP model did not envisage the CAT as providing a new specialist, community-based service. There were, however, aspects of the MAPP project which reflected the differing perspectives of the team members and which resulted in later tensions when attempting a more general application of community alcohol teams in other areas of the country. Cartwright explained the tension as arising from the fact that there were 'the two sides of the model'; a practical approach which involved helping to set up community services, and a theoretical approach which attempted further understanding of how change is brought about (Cartwright, interview). In the longer term, the action aspect was to dominate the operation of other CATs.

However, the MAPP team provided the initial model for the development of the Community Alcohol Team which, as mentioned in Chapter 6, influenced the recommendations of the Advisory Committee on Alcoholism and further DHSS-sponsored research on CATs (Stockwell and Clement 1988). Between 1979 and 1982 a series of seminars and consultations were organised by the DHSS and a spate of publications and reports from government and professional sources reinforced the broadening of the alcohol treatment field to include prevention and early intervention, confirmed the commitment to deliver the bulk of interventions within community-based settings organised at district level, and stated the aim of providing cost-effective services.[5] Within the profession, there was continuing resistance to these pressures. Although one study in the Manchester area hinted that younger doctors were showing greater signs of interest in working with problem drinkers and felt better trained to do so (Mowbray and Kessel 1986), other surveys found that, as late as the mid-1980s, GPs were still reporting that they were ill-prepared to deal with drinking problems, lacked effective supportive structures and found the work unrewarding (Shaw et al. 1978; Thom and Tellez 1986; Pollak 1987). By now, efforts to mobilise GPs were more visible in the medical press and organisations such as the British Medical Association and the Royal College of General Practitioners were beginning to take an interest in alcohol treatment issues.

Box 1 THERAPEUTIC COMMITMENT

The MAPP report hypothesised from the study that there were three major factors underlying the inadequate response of primary care workers:

1 Anxieties about *role adequacy* through not having the information and skills necessary to recognise and respond to drinkers.
2 Anxieties about *role legitimacy* through being uncertain as to whether drinking problems come within their sphere of responsibility.
3 Anxieties about *role support* through having nowhere to turn for help and advice when they were unsure how to respond to an alcohol-related problem.

The collective term 'Role Insecurity' was adopted for the net effect of these various sources of anxiety. All three aspects of Role Insecurity were seen as being caused by agents feeling unprepared both intellectually and situationally to respond and ultimately it was manifested by them being unprepared emotionally to respond.

This emotional expression of role insecurity was termed 'low therapeutic commitment'.

In contrast, workers who expressed 'high therapeutic commitment' could be distinguished from others by four positive characteristics:

1 They were experienced in working with drinkers.
2 They were working, or had worked in the past, in a situation in which role support was available.
3 They had received a training in counselling.
4 They had clinical knowledge about alcohol and alcohol-related problems; e.g. how to recognise the likely physical, psychological and social consequences of excessive drinking.

Mobilising the Primary Care Team

The 1980s witnessed a spate of articles in the medical press aimed to encourage GPs to identify and treat drinking problems and providing details of identification methods and treatment approaches (Bligh *et al*. 1982; Wallace and Haines 1985; Stockwell and Clement 1987). Some publications described research which had provided GPs with a 'do-it-yourself kit' (Heather 1987) or had given brief training and advice (Wallace *et al*. 1988) and had monitored the effects on GP behaviour. While the results of such experiments were sometimes hopeful, it was obvious that the provision of better diagnostic tools, knowledge about management techniques or even more focused training sessions were not sufficient to solve the problem of how to implement the new community-based approach. Service co-ordination continued to be a major hurdle as did the reluctance of other health and social service professionals to expand their role in the identification and management of alcohol problems (Lightfoot and Orford 1987; Orford 1987).

Until the mid-1970s, health departments' attempts to stimulate primary care involvement in alcohol problems had rested on the assumption that raising awareness and knowledge of the issues, attacking moralistic attitudes towards problem drinkers and discovering the most effective treatments would secure greater professional commitment and the official message had been delivered via circulars or formally structured academic courses (Shaw et al. 1978). However, the MAPP project proved influential enough to convince the DHSS that former approaches had failed to address GPs' feelings that they lacked the skills and experience they needed, that there was insufficient support from other specialist and community services, and that it was thankless work since 'cure' was seldom possible. This shift from a knowledge-based to a skills-based frame of action for changing professional behaviour informed subsequent attempts to mobilise primary care workers. The MAPP project had also proposed a strategy for encouraging professional change – the Community Alcohol Team – and it was this approach which was now taken up by the DHSS on an experimental basis. Both MAPP and the Advisory Committee on Alcoholism had envisaged CATs as having a dual function, to offer a direct service in the community and, equally importantly, to support and advise other primary level workers on how to identify and manage drinking problems. As mentioned above, it was hoped that the support and consultancy function would strengthen the therapeutic commitment of primary care workers and broaden the base of accessible community care.

By 1986, there were approximately twenty CATs in the UK, eighteen in England, one in Scotland and one in Wales (Stockwell and Clement 1988), but it was clear long before this that hopes for the consultancy function were not to be met. Two of the earliest ventures, at Norwich and Leicester, rejected or were unable to fulfil a supportive or educational role and concentrated on offering a direct treatment service. A review of CATs, carried out on behalf of the DHSS, found that the teams adopted diverse objectives, the priority of some teams being to provide a direct treatment service to clients, whereas other teams placed more emphasis on a consultancy, support and educational role. But teams were under pressure to provide a direct extra service and the review found that the potential of the teams to influence primary care workers' behaviour was modest despite some encouraging results from the Medway, Liverpool and Renfrew teams (Baldwin 1987). Another possible reason for the failure to implement the consultancy function was the difficulty in staffing CATs with well-trained individuals of sufficiently high status to ensure credibility and acceptance by doctors. As in other areas of care where multi-disciplinary collaboration was attempted, traditional professional boundaries, differences in professional knowledge bases and occupational statuses were difficult to bridge.[6] Thus, far from becoming the vehicle for increasing the therapeutic commitment of the GP and other primary level workers, CATs, by and large, became another branch of an increasing range of specialist services delivered outside the hospital sphere.

The difficulties encountered by the CATs, did not stop other experiments which also aimed to increase primary care workers' commitment to working with problem drinkers. 'Facilitator' schemes, initiated in the early 1980s, again with the support of the DHSS, were intended to improve the primary care team's response in particular areas of medical care through joint management of patients. The first of these in the alcohol field was set up in Oxford by Dr Peter Anderson and a second experiment was started in Cornwall under the direction of the Cornwall Council on Alcohol. Again, as well as providing direct intervention within the primary care setting, the aim was to 'educate' the primary care team and provide them with the support necessary to acquire the experience and skills needed to work with problem drinkers. Early results from these experiments seemed to be hopeful – they had taken on board issues of credibility and status – although there were still problems of securing inter-professional collaboration.[7] Other experiments, such as schemes to involve GPs more effectively in the supervision of home detoxification, appeared to have some success in raising the level of awareness and knowledge of GPs. Although the approach itself worked well using community psychiatric nurses (CPNs) in the front line, the extent to which doctors, themselves, were involved was modest, at least in the early years (Stockwell et al. 1986).

Professional reluctance was not overcome by the fact that innovative schemes to gain the involvement of primary care workers were supported by research findings which indicated that primary care workers could intervene successfully in drinking problems.

Since the 1960s, the alcohol research community (many of whom were attached to treatment services) had carried out studies designed to answer questions about the effectiveness of treatment and to investigate the superiority of one type of treatment approach over another. While the results from studies were seldom conclusive – and we have already seen how the selective use of research is frequently used to argue the case for policy action – by 1990 a number of general principles were emerging from the research which could be used to support arguments for shifting a greater share of alcohol intervention into generalist services (Thom *et al.* 1994). It was generally agreed, for instance, that controlled trials had shown no advantage of hospital in-patient over out-patient treatment or of residential over non-residential care (Miller and Hester 1986b; Goodwin 1991). Studies continued to provide evidence that detoxification could be carried out safely in the home or in community settings (Collins *et al.* 1990; Haig and Hibbert 1990; Stockwell *et al.* 1990). Finally, research findings indicated that less intensive treatment, or 'brief interventions' could be as effective as more intensive treatment delivered over a longer period (Bien *et al.* 1993; Nuffield Institute for Health 1993). The latter body of research was particularly important in attempting to attract primary care workers since it indicated that intervention could be incorporated into routine practice without undue expenditure of time or other resources (see Box 2, compiled from various sources).

The reaction of primary care workers to the research 'evidence' for effective primary care intervention in alcohol problems has not been studied. However, by 1990, policy makers, service purchasers and professional leaders were attempting to implement the research. The continuing efforts by purchasers and health authorities to find ways of involving GPs and other primary care workers in providing brief interventions illustrate that translating research into practice is yet another problematic dimension in the dynamics of the policy–research–practice relationship.

The Role of General Practice in the Late 1980s

As discussion so far has indicated, there was little consensus over the years, either within the profession, or between GPs and the 'advocates' of a primary care approach to alcoholism treatment. Rather the situation was conflictual, consisting of a 'them' (the advocates of primary care) and 'us' (the bulk of primary care practitioners) stance which the DHSS was eager to bridge. The general thrust of policy throughout the 1980s towards expanding the preventive role of GPs did not make the situation any easier.

Box 2 BRIEF INTERVENTIONS

May consist of:

- Assessment
- The provision of advice
- Provision of an information booklet
- A few sessions of counselling
- One or any combination of the above

May be delivered:

- By post
- By telephone
- Face-to-face
- By a GP, nurse, counsellor, agency worker, etc.
- In medical or non-medical settings

Have been evaluated to be:

- As effective as more intensive treatments for most people
- Easily integrated into routine care
- Cost effective – cost less than £20 per head

Thus, in contrast to the grassroots efforts to activate policy on women's treatment needs described in the last chapter, the attempt to mobilise primary care workers was a 'top-down' initiative (Walt 1994). The motivation to move alcoholism treatment into the community came from outside the primary care professions, led by policy makers and by advocates of generalist, community-based care working in the alcohol arena. For instance, previous chapters have described how the shift away from hospital inpatient care was supported by 'policy advocates' from within psychiatry as well as other professionals in the specialist treatment agencies. Research and development efforts aimed at general practice reveal the tenacity with which the department, researchers, and leaders in the alcohol arena pursued the aim of implementing community approaches to alcohol intervention. Policy 'sponsors' or leaders within general practice did not emerge until the 1980s when publication of the report *Alcohol: A Balanced View* from the Royal College of General Practitioners in 1986, marked a degree of acceptance among leaders of the profession that alcohol was an important issue in general practice.[8] Even then, despite endorsement from the Royal College, general practice lacked more personalised leadership and a 'model' service such as had been provided by Glatt, Davies and others in the emerging alcohol arena. Similarly, it lacked a strong conceptualisation of the problem as it applied to primary care workers. For the emerging policy community in the 1960s, the disease concept of alcoholism had provided a rallying point. The move towards a broader definition of 'alcohol problems' and towards a prevention approach in the 1970s failed to supply an equally strong, 'marketable' concept which could be 'sold' to GPs.

Examination of the primary care response to alcoholism treatment provides, therefore, a good case study of the gap between statements of policy intent and policy implementation. We turn now to parallel efforts to improve co-ordination between health and social services and to mobilise the non-statutory sector. This, too, was an important part of health department activity in the 1980s, central to the DHSS's goal of reducing harmful drinking and to the success of strategy to deliver integrated, community-based services.

Promoting Integration and Co-operation Between Services

In the chapter entitled 'The way we ought to go', The Advisory Committee on Alcoholism (1978b) spelled out its vision of a co-ordinated network of services which would incorporate preventive measures, primary level services and secondary level services and include the primary care team, the personal social services, the prison and probation services, voluntary agencies, general hospitals, psychiatric hospitals and psychiatric units in general hospitals, and after-care services such as hostels. While specialist, hospital-based care still had an important role to play, the emphasis was on care in community-based settings integrated, as far as possible, into primary level service structures and therapeutic practices. It was an ideal towards which policy had been moving for almost a decade before the committee's recommendations were published in 1978.

The literature on health and social services contains different, sometimes conflicting, explanations for the shift in health and social care away from a hospital and institutionally based service structure towards a community-based approach. There is little doubt, however, that a combination of budgetary and ideological motives, as well as professional interests, lay behind both the rhetoric and the reality of community care policy (Sedgwick 1982; Busfield 1986; Lewis 1987). This was the case in providing an appropriate service response to problem drinking where factors of cost, the availability of services and trained personnel, and varying beliefs about effective and suitable treatment approaches, were some of the factors commonly advanced in support of community-based care. For instance, voluntary (or non-statutory) services had played an increasingly important part in alcoholism treatment since the 1950s; but by the 1970s their role had become crucial with the recognition that statutory services did not have the capacity to respond to the numbers of individuals now identified as appropriate targets for intervention. Furthermore, shifting perceptions of the alcohol problem meant that specialist provision as it had existed in the 1960s was inappropriate for many potential patients or clients of services. As target groups (and professional groups) grew and became more diverse, the appropriate allocation of individuals to suitable treatments and services became an issue of professional and policy interest (Lindstrom 1992). Factors such as competition for professional 'ownership' of new target groups, or a desire to preserve specialisms by ensuring a high level of 'appropriate' referrals, although less likely to appear as a rationale for community-based services, can not be ruled out as a possible influence on those involved in the provision of care. At the same time, the shift was also motivated by concerns centred around the perceived interests of clients. Community-based care was seen to offer a more flexible, responsive approach to clients' needs; it was believed that a community-care response would help to de-stigmatise and normalise problem drinking and thereby encourage problem drinkers to seek help. Securing co-ordination between services in shifting delivery into the community was, then, a recommendation which, in theory, found a high level of agreement among practitioners and policy makers but in practice proved extremely difficult to implement.

Stimulating Collaboration between Health and Social Services: Joint Planning

The shift in general health policy towards the provision of a co-ordinated structure of community-based health and social care had started by the early 1970s, before the Advisory Committee on Alcoholism provided the stamp of approval which escalated policy and professional activity in the alcohol field. In 1974, a system of joint planning was introduced and Joint Care Planning Teams were set up soon after to encourage collaboration between health and local authority officers. Two years later, in 1976, financial incentives were provided to stimulate joint projects. Policy documents issued in the 1980s again pressed for collaboration and steps were taken to include Family Practitioner Committees (later Family Health Service Authorities) and the voluntary sector in the joint planning process (DHSS 1981a; Baggott 1994).

Policy documents on alcoholism treatment, issued in the early 1970s, reflected these general trends. They emphasised the need for a multi-disciplinary approach to problem drinking which was 'both a disease and major social problem' (DHSS 1973), demanded a co-ordinated service response from health and social services and the voluntary sector, and encouraged the development of a range of facilities to support the aim of prevention, early recognition, treatment and rehabilitation in the community (Standing Advisory Medical Committee 1973). Funding was available in these fairly lavish years as a result of £2 million for the development of services for alcoholics announced in 1970 by Sir Keith Joseph, the Secretary of State for Social Services. The details were given in a circular *Community Services for Alcoholics* (1973), which is generally taken to mark the policy shift to planned community provision for alcohol treatment.

The extra funds were used to 'pump-prime' alcohol prevention and treatment services in both the statutory and voluntary sectors. The growth of ATUs in the 1970s has already been discussed in Chapter 3, but it is worth noting again that, at this point in time, an increase in the number of ATUs was still seen as a necessary development in providing an appropriate range of services throughout the regions. Following the circular, the number of ATUs went up from eighteen in 1973 to thirty-four in 1980. The number of Councils on Alcoholism also grew from nine regional councils in 1970 to thirty-five local councils on alcoholism in 1980, and the number of hostels from ten in 1970 to around seventy by the end of the decade (DHSS/NCVO 1982; Baggott 1990). The department's commitment to the development of integrated specialist and community-based alcohol services was, then, clearly stated from the early 1970s.

In general health and social care policy, the failure of the joint planning system to secure collaboration and co-ordination between health and local authority services and to answer the difficulties raised by the ambiguous relationship between statutory and non-statutory services has been well documented in many areas of service provision (Baggott 1994). The Griffiths report (DHSS 1988), for instance, the outcome of a government enquiry into the funding of residential care, and the White Paper which followed (DoH 1989) expanded the role of local authority social service departments in the development of community care strategies and services, but, according to commentators, did not deal adequately with questions of implementation, especially resource allocation (Baggott 1994). In the alcohol treatment field, the final years of the 1980s were riven with dissenting voices over the possible consequences of changes in community care funding. Workers in treatment agencies became increasingly concerned about the implications of the changes on residential facilities. Provision for some individuals, for instance the elderly, and women requiring residential care, was particularly likely to fall between the net of health and social care services with neither side eager to assume the responsibility or the cost of service provision. The suggestion that 'ring-fenced' community care funds should be provided to protect the level of service provision was hotly debated but it was a battle which the alcohol (and drug) field was eventually to lose (Baggott 1994; Harrison et al. 1996). The intention to carry out the reforms went ahead in the NHS and Community Care Act, 1990, although in the end, with the 1992 general election looming on the horizon, implementation did not proceed until 1993.

Within the overall aim of improving the integration and cost-effectiveness of health and social care services, the provision of treatment and rehabilitation for people with drinking problems was a marginal issue. Although guidelines on the responsibilities of health authorities and local authorities were later specified in the 1993 document *Alcohol and Drug Services and Community Care* (DoH 1993), the arrangements were 'permissive rather than prescriptive' (Harrison et al. 1996, p. 249). Again, as was the case with the development of alcoholism treatment units and with councils on alcoholism, authorities at local level responded in very different ways to the implementation of the NHS and Community Care Act. Certainly, at the start of the 1990s, the co-ordination of health and social services for people with drinking problems had not noticeably improved, and according to some assessments, the situation regarding residential care had deteriorated (Harrison et al. 1996, p. 255).

Mobilising the Voluntary Sector: 1970–80

A second strand in developing an integrated service response lay in efforts to mobilise the voluntary sector (or the non-statutory sector as it was increasingly called). This presented two main challenges, the deployment of resources to support community-based service developments, and managing the tensions and rivalries which had emerged as the alcohol field grew larger. Compared to the statutory sector, the problem was not reluctance of agency workers to take on problem drinkers but lack of stable funds, and, as the 1970s progressed, increasing tension between the national voluntary organisations and the DHSS (Lee, interview; Wawman, interview).

In the early 1970s, attempts were made by the DHSS to promote better co-ordination and communication with the voluntary services, for instance through the establishment and funding of new 'umbrella' organisations to represent voluntary agencies and simplify communication with Department of Health officials. One of these was FARE, the Federation of Alcohol Residential (later Rehabilitation) Establishments, set up in 1974 to represent the growing body of after-care and residential facilities. Financial support was given also to existing organisations such as the Medical Council on Alcoholism (MCA) and to the Alcohol Education Centre (AEC) to encourage education and awareness, and training activities. The National Council on Alcoholism (NCA) received grants from 1972 to develop and co-ordinate local councils and liaise with the DHSS.

The acknowledged importance of the voluntary sector in the development of services in the community raised the policy relevance of voluntary organisations and improved their access to the policy making process (Baggott 1990; Finlayson 1994). National organisations, such as the NCA, became more involved in alcohol policy as the decade progressed (Rutherford, interview). But a closer relationship also brought longer-term dilemmas concerning the autonomy of voluntary agencies in receipt of government grants, and issues of control and accountability had to be faced. Joint planning did not solve the problem of providing co-ordinated medical-social care and the system of pump-priming service developments, many of which were run by the non-statutory sector, left the dilemma of responsibility for continuing funding unresolved.

Funding, however, was only one of the problems. The alcohol field was beset with internal conflicts and tensions and these also played a major part in precipitating change. For example, organisations operating hostel provision had long been seen to be overlapping in their functions and closer co-operation might have cut management overheads. But the management committees of different voluntary agencies were fiercely autonomous and had emerged from very different social and ideological roots. Remembering an abortive attempt made by two of the largest voluntary rehabilitation agencies to get together, one assistant secretary at the DHSS described the different ethos of the management teams of two major voluntary agencies.

The first was a traditional charity, successful business men who wanted to do good, and had good advice. They had a lot of good people helping them, and they were running a very professional show where they brought in the experts and said, 'get on with it' – managing it like business people. When we went to their meetings, which we did sometimes, it was all smoked trout and salad and lashings of wine – it had that sort of lifestyle. If you went to talk to them about anything, you had to be prepared for fairly hard drinking of wine or whisky. The second agency on the other hand, their ethos was quite different. They were in what was at that time the fairly new consensus model of management with staff participation and, indeed, patient participation eventually on the committees of the houses. They were all the sort of social workers whose natural drink was beer and whose instinct was to talk about things very deeply, very seriously and for a very, very long time; and at the end they might or might not have reached a decision. They often reached a decision not at the meeting but after it. But they would say after four and a half hours, 'That was a very good discussion'. No obvious outcome but suddenly the next day, they would find they had done something. (Lee, interview)

While the DHSS would probably have welcomed greater co-ordination between agencies, officials did not want to be responsible for a 'forced marriage' (Lee, interview) and did not intervene at first. But it was partly frustration at dealing with a large number of different organisations which led to the formation of FARE in 1974.

The National Council on Alcoholism (NCA) was also struggling with internal rivalries and competition for resources (Rutherford, interview). When the government started to fund the NCA, its aim was to spread money to encourage the development of a network of councils on alcoholism. Their function was to be the provision of information and referral not, primarily, the provision of treatment.[9] One NCA officer recalled the early days as 'an exciting time because the department was extremely helpful' but 'selling' the Department's policy to the larger established Councils on Alcoholism proved difficult and conflicts arose because bigger councils wanted to 'swallow the money' (Rutherford, interview).

Discussion in earlier chapters has indicated that, as with the ATUs in the 1960s, Councils on Alcoholism at first grew according to chance and local initiative rather than according to need or any 'scientific' criteria. Despite these problems, by 1978 when the Advisory Committee on Alcoholism made its recommendations for service development, the voluntary sector was already an important partner in service provision and its leaders were part of the core of the policy community consulted by DHSS officials.

The role of voluntary agencies within a co-ordinated network of services was detailed in the Advisory Committee on Alcoholism's report *The Pattern and Range of Services for Problem Drinkers* (1978b, pp. 22–3). The report mentioned, in particular, the responsibilities of the National Council on Alcoholism, stating that these should be:

(a) to provide a national and public focus for problem drinking;
(b) to act as the national negotiating body for the voluntary counselling services with DHSS;

(c) to evaluate and monitor the quality of its affiliated local councils of
    alcoholism;
(d) to establish new regional councils where appropriate;
(e) to define and help provide the training needs of Directors,
    permanent staff and voluntary counsellors;
(f) to establish minimum standards of competence for permanent staff
    and counsellors.

Expectations of voluntary agencies were not so different from the
role carved out in the early years of the National Health Service.
Provision of an alternative form of treatment, encouraging access
to statutory services, and developing innovative approaches were
central aspects of the role. What was new was an increased
blurring of the boundaries between statutory and 'non-statutory'
services as the voluntary sector 'professionalised' and took on a
larger share of service provision.

But already the policy climate was changing again. The early
1970s revitalisation of policy interest in alcohol – a time when
drugs, which had diverted attention from alcohol in the 1960s,
appeared to be 'out' and alcoholism 'in' (Hore 1974) – did not last.
As Baggott (1990, pp. 40–1) has observed, the allocation of resources
to alcohol and the 'surge of enthusiasm for all matters alcoholic'
during the 1970s are possibly best explained in terms of ministerial
initiative. Following Keith Joseph, ministerial interest in alcohol was
sustained throughout the 1970s by a succession of ministers and
secretaries of state from both Conservative and Labour governments
who seemed to be committed to the prevention of alcohol-related
problems. However, by the end of the 1970s, although the alcohol
question was attracting greater public attention, government action
on alcohol, in line with other aspects of health prevention, was at a
low ebb (Webster 1996, pp. 385–6). Resources were running out and
DHSS officials had less influence over service development and less
ministerial support for the policies they wished to promote
(Wawman, interview). The increasing decentralisation of power over
health care resources which followed the 1982 reorganisation of the
health services, and the lack of continuing funding beyond the
1970s for agencies which had received 'pump-priming' money did
not make efforts to implement policy recommendations any easier.
Moreover, the importance of drug abuse was growing as far as the
department was concerned, and this provided further rationale for
senior officials and ministers to withdraw resources from alcohol
(Wawman, interview). Thus, ministerial commitment, which had
been instrumental in service development, ran out by the 1980s,

and relationships between Ministers, higher officials and DHSS officers, and service providers became less consensual (Wawman, interview).

Consolidation and Control: The Voluntary Sector, 1980–90

Along with problems of securing co-ordination, the lack of stable funding became a constant bone of contention as alcohol treatment services again sank to Cinderella status in the course of the 1980s. Around 1979 to 1980, the NCA was told that funding for local councils on alcoholism would be stopped and FARE was informed that central funding for hostels was to end and be taken over by local authorities (Baggott 1990). Central funding had never been intended as a permanent solution but attempts to cut grants to the voluntary sector met with strong opposition (Rutherford, interview). The issue went to Patrick Jenkin, the Secretary of State, compromises were made and limited funding was promised until 1981. A new principle of a decreasing scale of funding suggested by leaders of the voluntary sector was accepted, apparently without demur from the DHSS, raising conjectures that the threat to cut off funding had been a ruse to get the voluntary organisations to suggest some such system (Rutherford, interview). Questions of funding also raised issues of control and accountability. By now agencies which had started as voluntary, in the sense that they were funded from sources other than government, received at least some of their income from the DHSS and department officials were concerned to ensure value for money.

Within government, at ministerial level as well as among department officials, there was mounting frustration in relationships with the voluntary sector, communication with the 'umbrella' organisations was felt to be inadequate and there were growing doubts about the effectiveness of hostel provision (Baggott 1990; Wawman, interview). As early as 1977, the possibility of a merger between the various voluntary organisations had been suggested without result. Consequently, in March 1981 a study was commissioned by Sir George Young, the Under-Secretary of State for the DHSS,

> in the light of widespread concern about confusion over the roles of the various voluntary bodies operating at national level in the field of alcohol misuse. (DHSS/NCVO 1982)

A working party was formed, comprising two members from a recently established Policy Strategy Unit at the DHSS and two members of the National Council for Voluntary Organisations (NCVO). Their brief was to examine the respective roles of the voluntary organisations which were in receipt of DHSS funds to see if they were providing value for money. This move appears to have taken place at a level above that of the alcohol policy group (the group of relevant DHSS officials) which would normally have expected to be consulted. The impression events made on one senior medical officer in the department was that,

> Things happened over officials' heads. Suddenly we were presented with a fait accompli ... It was done without consultation with the Alcohol Policy Group. So what happened was forced on us. (Wawman, interview)

The evaluation of the voluntary agencies resulted in a reorganisation of the national voluntary organisations and a reassessment of the relationship between the DHSS and the voluntary sector. The Alcohol Education Centre (AEC), NCA and FARE were abolished. The educational function of the AEC was given to the Health Education Authority which had recently been reconstituted out of the ashes of the Health Education Council, according to some accounts, in the hope that the new organisation would prove easier to control than its forerunner (Smith 1987; Wawman, interview). The MCA continued to exist but no longer received a grant from the department. New organisations were formed. In 1983, Action on Alcohol Abuse (AAA) was launched by the conference of Royal Medical Colleges to campaign against alcohol misuse and in the same year the Institute of Alcohol Studies was set up by the United Kingdom Temperance Association (UKTA) as a forum for generating research and debate (Baggott 1990). These organisations did not receive any government funding. The work formerly carried out by FARE and the NCA was to be continued under a new body, Alcohol Concern (at first called NAAM – National Agency on Alcohol Misuse), established with government funding in 1983. An interim executive committee was set up under the chairmanship of Francis Gladstone, one of the NCVO members who had conducted the evaluation and who was subsequently elected to continue in that role (*Alcohol Concern Newsletter* 1984, nos 1 and 2).

The reorganisation of the alcohol voluntary sector attempted, therefore, not only to consolidate and co-ordinate services but also to obtain a greater measure of government control over their activities and use of resources. This appears to be in line with a more general trend in health policy towards a less consultative policy process in the 1980s (Harrison *et al.* 1996). The establishment of Alcohol Concern can be seen as a move in this direction. On the other hand, as we saw in Chapter 8, Alcohol Concern provided an important channel of

two-way communication between DHSS officials and service providers, especially important as the alcohol arena grew larger. Its influence
on service implementation was commented on by a senior medical
officer in the department at the beginning of the 1980s:

> As our ability to influence service provision became less, Alcohol Concern
> became more and more important ... So we began to see that the local
> voluntary agencies had a role which is over and above that of counselling.
> A major role was to stimulate local services. So we pushed very hard and
> got approval from ministers that one of the major roles of Alcohol Concern
> should be the promotion of new Councils on Alcohol throughout the
> country. The Alcohol Policy Group in my time was responsible for making
> sure that the network of councils on alcohol took off. (Wawman,
> interview).

The shifting balance between state and voluntary contribution to
service provision in the alcohol field has to be seen as part of wider
changes in the political climate from the 1970s which 'brought into
sharp focus the "non-statutory" elements in the "mixed economy of
welfare"' (Finlayson 1994, p. 14). Voluntarism, after a period of
political marginality became 'respectable', partly out of economic
necessity but partly also because, by the 1970s, the voluntary sector
had lost much of the evangelical, philanthropic image which had
linked it to its pre-Welfare State image. Acceptance of voluntarism as
an important element in the provision of health and welfare services
was marked in 1973 by the appointment of a minister with responsibility to co-ordinate government support for voluntary organisations,
and by the establishment of a Voluntary Services Unit by the Home
Office. Central government grants to voluntary organisations increased, according to one estimate from £19.2 million in 1974/75 to
£35.4 million in 1976/77 (Finlayson 1994, p. 16). Under Mrs
Thatcher's government from 1979, emphasis on the importance of the
voluntary contribution became more marked to the extent that some
critics argued that the state had been relegated to an enabling role
(Finlayson 1994). These developments underscored the new relationship between statutory and voluntary services. They were visible in the
alcohol field not only in service provision but in changes in the policy
community and in the consultative processes which now incorporated
voluntary organisations to a greater extent, and more centrally, than
had formerly been the case. Possibly, as Harrison et al. (1996, p. 263)
suggest, the consultative process as a whole was becoming less;
certainly it was changing and, as the quotation above indicated,
Health Department officials were beginning to feel increasingly

powerless to influence service developments. Within this framework, the DHSS needed to ensure co-ordination of services, good communication and liaison, and to tackle issues of control and accountability if policy objectives for alcohol treatment services were to be met.

Throughout the 1980s, available resources were, therefore, clearly directed towards stimulating the development of a network of local, community-based services linking statutory and non-statutory agencies. While economic and efficacy issues formed part of the acknowledged reasons for the shift, much of the rationale in policy debates and in the literature rested on the 'evidence' of research findings. The final section in this chapter examines the use of research to further policy objectives in the 1970s and 1980s.

Making Research Policy Relevant 1970–90

Along with the availability of additional funding, research became an important underpinning for alcohol policy shifts over the course of the 1970s. The commissioning of research became more proactive than hitherto and the initiation of research which would provide policy-relevant data to manage moves towards community care became a priority for the next two decades (DHSS Homelessness and Addictions Research and Liaison Group 1984). Again, this was not unique to the alcohol field or to the DHSS. In 1971, a report of the Central Policy Review Staff (the Rothschild report) encouraged greater government control over the research it funded and proposed the need for applied research which the report distinguished from 'pure' research (whose end product was knowledge without any particular application to policy or practice).[10] Possibly the emerging research 'contract culture' may have been one reason for change within the DHSS to a more proactive stance. However, the department was also beginning to build up internal knowledge and experience on the subject and may have been less reliant than formerly on outside expertise.[11] Within the department, a number of 'research liaison' groups (RLGs) were set up in the early 1970s composed of policy makers, scientific advisers and research managers whose task it was to develop, implement and monitor research programmes in specific areas of policy interest. The Homelessness and Addictions RLG was formed in 1974 to consider research on a number of problems involving health and personal social services. It became one of the most active and longest surviving of the RLGs. Prior to this time, research had filtered into the department largely via links between the medical stream of civil servants and their colleagues in the field. This changed in the 1970s.

Examination of Department of Health activity in the late 1970s and 1980s reveals clearly that civil servants sought to commission research which would provide them with the information they needed to further current policies and that they negotiated service-related research development directly with researchers known to them (Robinson, interview; Wawman, interview). According to an account given by one department official, when he joined the DHSS in 1980, there was plenty of money and not enough good researchers to fund. 'The research strategy was that if someone came up with a good idea you funded it.' When, soon after, the money started getting short, and they 'were desperately trying to see how to influence government policy in this new situation', it was decided to draw up a research strategy prioritising areas of work the department wished to support (Wawman, interview). Research on local initiatives in prevention was one area where known researchers were deliberately sought out; studies of the economic costs of alcohol misuse was another. David Robinson remembered a conversation in the late 1970s over lunch with Chris Ralph where the latter had announced the intention of shifting from national studies to local prevention studies, and of moving research money out of London to places such as Exeter (where Jim Orford had moved), to Hull (David Robinson's unit) and York (where Alan Maynard, an economist, was becoming active in issues of the cost of alcohol misuse). That these actions were also in line with the ideological 'fame shift' from a treatment to a prevention perspective on alcohol misuse was underlined by Robinson's personal experience that it had taken almost a decade to secure funding for prevention studies (Robinson, interview). Thus, while earlier research liaison had been predominantly with psychiatrists and doctors and their research teams, relationships were now sought with professionals from disciplinary backgrounds in economics, policy science, and psychology, resulting in a widening of the consultative base of alcohol policy making and, to some extent, of the types of professionals within the core of the policy community. This was happening slowly over the course of the 1970s even before the Advisory Committee on Alcoholism had completed its term although the decline in available funds in the post-Kessel period accelerated the process.

DHSS research priorities were set out in departmental documents in the early 1980s. The 1984 document *The Strategy of the Homelessness and Addictions Research Liaison Group for Research on Alcohol Misuse* lists eight different research projects and five evaluation studies of experimental projects (see Boxes 3 and 4 overleaf).

Earlier chapters have illustrated how, in the 1960s, the policy-research community centred largely on a few prominent doctors and medical institutions. As it developed from the early 1970s, the medico-policy community broadened to encompass a wider range of

---

Box 3 RESEARCH PROJECTS

- Alcoholic liver disease and simple interventions (1978–84)
- Economics of alcohol abuse (1983–86)
- Development of a local alcohol prevention strategy (1982–85)
- Young adult children of problem drinkers (1980–84)
- Accept (a treatment service) evaluation (completed in 1984)
- Screening and early detection tests for alcoholism in hospital and general practice (completed in 1984)
- Cognitive status as a predictor of outcome for alcoholism (1984–87)
- Randomised control trial of day centre treatment of alcoholism (1982–84)

Box 4 EVALUATION OF EXPERIMENTAL ALCOHOL PROJECTS

- Community Alcohol Teams (Liverpool, Salford, Exeter, Medway, Norwich, Prestwich)
- Diploma in alcohol counselling and consultation
- Evaluation of the National Council on Alcoholism scheme (four types of voluntary counsellor training schemes)
- Plymouth night shelter for homeless drinkers
- Problem drinkers and the statutory services in Humberside (to improve responses in A&E departments by probation and social services)

---

institutional and interest group 'players' which included economists, social scientists, psychologists and epidemiologists. Although the key relationships within the policy community remained those between doctors externally and internally in government, the focus on prevention and early intervention strategies gave rise to a need for studies which could not be carried out on clinical populations. But how effective was research in helping to achieve the goal of an integrated service structure?

Although research successfully influenced the policy environment and, in turn, was influenced by policy needs, its impact on policy decisions is less clear. The fate of the 'Think Tank' report, discussed in Chapter 6, amply conveys the lesser importance of research findings relative to other factors in policy making. Despite the close relationship between civil servants and a small community of medical and other experts, within which research may be accorded a high degree of importance, one significant factor is the larger more heterogeneous set of players involved in the alcohol policy arena, the Treasury and the drink industry among them. This study has concentrated on the policy community surrounding the health departments and concerned with issues of alcohol consumption and health; but policy activity was influenced by other, overlapping 'policy communities' and interest networks revolving around the Home Office, the Department of Trade and Industry and other government departments (Tether and Harrison 1988). Ministerial action, touched on in this and previous chapters, was also instrumental particularly as the focus of concern switched from treatment issues towards prevention of alcohol-related harm at population level. These factors acted as constraints on policy action within the health departments and on the place of research-based policy formation and implementation. Another constraint on the influence of research was the difficulty of implementing research findings in the face of professional reluctance to comply with pressure or persuasion from government or professional sources – such as the case of GPs discussed earlier. Thus at one level, the use of research can be seen as a device to legitimate particular interests, which are determined by influences quite other than 'science' or the 'facts'. At another level, there is the argument that research bears fruit through a slow process of accumulated evidence, especially where the evidence is presented in an 'authoritative and integrative scientific review' which accommodates policy needs (Edwards 1993). As Weiss (1991, p. 308) argues, there are many uses of research but 'the place of information generally, and of research information particularly, is best seen as helping policy makers decide which policies are best suited to the realisation of their ideologies and interests'.

Whether on the strength of their scientific value, or on their appeal to the policy community, or their success in gaining consensus within competing interest networks, by the end of the 1980s, research and reviews in support of brief interventions, community initiatives and strategy to encourage 'sensible drinking' had become the framework for action at national and local level.

The Alcohol Treatment Arena at the End of the 1980s

In some ways the alcohol field at the end of the 1980s had achieved a new consensus. The relationship between alcohol consumption and harm was widely accepted as was the 'unit' system of measuring individual levels of consumption and the unit guidelines for assessing problematic drinking. Prevention and early intervention had overtaken treatment as the dominant policy concern. Within treatment, the drive to provide community-based treatment services, the emphasis on primary care and on training generic health and social workers to respond to drinking problems was generally regarded, within the alcohol policy community, as the appropriate way forward for service delivery. These trends were underpinned by a rapidly growing body of national and international research and supported by the World Health Organization (Bruun *et al.* 1975; Edwards *et al.* 1994). The increasing involvement of different professions and disciplines within the alcohol arena had resulted in a wide range of treatment theories and approaches and in the expansion of research efforts to find 'effective' treatments for different target groups. Whereas the alcohol treatment arena of the 1960s and early 1970s had revolved around a small number of centres and a few prominent individuals, by the late 1980s, new centres of excellence and new networks of influence had evolved in both the statutory and voluntary services.[12] Viewed by some as a sign of maturity, others saw the field as becoming increasingly fragmented and increasingly lacking a sense of identity (interview material).

By the end of the 1980s many of the tensions in the field appeared to have eased at policy level also. Relationships with the burgeoning non-statutory sector were filtered through Alcohol Concern for treatment services and through the Health Education Authority for prevention and awareness programmes. There were continuing tensions between different departments with interests in alcohol. Within the DHSS there was support for measures to control alcohol consumption but at wider departmental levels and at ministerial level the emphasis remained on strategies to reduce levels of harmful drinking and on preventing alcohol-related harms. However, inter-departmental tensions were lessened through the formation of an inter-departmental Ministerial Committee. This arose from pressures on government in the mid-1980s to address the perceived increase in alcohol-related health and social problems, epitomised by concerns over alcohol misuse among young people (BMA 1986; Home Office Standing Conference on Crime Prevention 1987). Coming at a time when the government was again considering proposals to relax the licensing laws (Baggott 1990), the need to satisfy critics – including a group of concerned MPs – was one factor in the formation of an inter-ministerial group on alcohol abuse. Set up in September 1987, the Wakeham Committee – named after its chairman, John Wakeham, leader of the House of Commons – consisted of representatives from twelve government departments and was intended 'to review and develop the Government's strategy in this area' (Ministerial Group on Alcohol *First Annual Report* 1987–88). The intention was to co-operate with the alcohol industry (anonymous, interview), and to this end the Portman Group, representing the eight largest UK drinks companies, was established in 1989.[13] According to one account, the ministerial committee was enormously important, in raising the profile of alcohol on the policy agenda, in necessitating collaboration from departments which had hitherto been 'bit players in the drama', and, to some extent, in de-fusing problems of conflicting departmental interests (anonymous, interview). The committee's achievements were summarised in the Lord President's report published in 1991, and probably the most significant outcome was the setting of targets for the reduction of alcohol-related harm in *The Health of the Nation* (DoH 1992; anonymous, interview). But the focus was on prevention rather than on treatment and the work of the committee made little if any impact on thinking around alcohol services. A survey of treatment issues was undertaken, the main outcome being support for attempts to secure greater co-ordination of services (Means *et al.* 1990), an aim which the department had been pursuing for some time already.

Certainly as the 1990s approached, alcohol treatment issues were taking a back seat on the policy agenda to issues of prevention and early intervention. The main concerns at policy level were with finding an acceptable strategy to achieve a reduction in alcohol misuse. As discussed in Chapter 6, this reflected general trends within the NHS. Even so, by 1990, new research and new debates were once again rippling the surface of consensus within the alcohol policy community; questions were being asked about the appropriateness of setting national targets for the reduction of alcohol-related harm and about the most appropriate prevention and treatment strategies. These signs of constant shift and modification in the response to alcohol consumption and intervention became more pronounced in the 1990s as alcohol-related harm became a public health and safety issue and as pressure for a national alcohol strategy strengthened.

10 Managing the Alcohol Problem: 1950 to the 1990s

Two distinct periods have emerged in the history of post-war alcohol treatment policy, with the early 1970s as the watershed. By 1970, the problem of alcohol had been redefined as 'medical', the need for appropriate treatment services had been demonstrated – supported in part by clinical research – and a policy network had emerged, emanating initially from a powerful professional and institutional base within psychiatry. Strong bonds were forged between medical civil servants in the Ministry of Health and a small group of experts, largely psychiatrists, and their clinical and research teams. This formed the core of a 'policy community' which survived into the 1990s despite expansion and growing diversity of the policy networks around alcohol issues after 1970. In this 'pioneering' phase between 1950 and 1970, initiatives for change came from the 'bottom up'; the policy community rallied around the disease concept of alcoholism; policy implementers (practitioners largely within psychiatric services) became proactive in initiating research and in providing colleagues within the professional stream of the civil service with research evidence and expert knowledge to back policy decisions. By and large, there was a general consensus, which included both statutory and voluntary service workers and the alcohol industry, that adequate treatment for alcoholism was a responsibility of the health care system. These factors were important in gaining 'respectability' and legitimacy for the new concern and in winning a foothold for issues of alcoholism treatment on the policy agenda of the Ministry of Health.

The policy network around issues of alcoholism treatment was, however, only one of a number of overlapping networks concerned with different aspects of the response to alcohol consumption and alcoholism. Despite overlap, there was no consensus between networks or between government departments on the nature of the alcohol problem or on appropriate action to address alcohol-related problems. For instance, temperance perspectives, which continued to emphasise alcohol consumption and related problems such as juvenile drunkenness and drink driving, did not fit within the new disease paradigm of the 1950s and 1960s. There was continuing temperance activity at public and parliamentary level during this period, notably in opposing moves to liberalise the licensing laws and in adding to pressures for action on drink driving.[1] But these issues 'belonged' to the Home Office and the Ministry of Transport and there was no co-ordinated policy view or conceptual framework for linking alcohol consumption, alcoholism and issues such as road safety. Although the problem of the habitual drunken offender raised questions concerning the boundaries of departmental responsibility for alcohol, during this period policy action on alcoholism treatment was separated from wider issues of alcohol control policy and was steered by a medical view of the alcohol problem which posed a medical solution – treatment for the minority who needed help.

In a sense, the years between 1950 and 1970 were the heyday of alcohol treatment policy. By 1970, the alcohol field was entering a new phase in which alcohol *treatment* no longer featured on the policy agenda. Over the first few years of the 1970s, the paradigmatic shift in perceptions of the problem towards a consumptionist perspective, the broadening of the base of professionals, target groups and intervention activities within the alcohol arena meant that, in policy terms, 'treatment' was no longer an appropriate descriptor of policy concern or professional activity. Against a backdrop of wider change in the NHS towards prevention, public health, and the management of health 'risk' in the population, the 1970s saw the start of a transformation from a largely clinical treatment response to alcoholism to a social, community-based response to problem drinking. Policy now had to consider a range of 'interventions' which encompassed control strategy (the control of availability of alcohol through, for instance, price or licensing regulations), demand reduction approaches (using, for example, public awareness campaigns, health education approaches), early intervention in problem drinking (which drew in primary health and social care services) and the provision of specialist care for individuals with severe drinking problems (the more traditional treatment and rehabilitation services). Although the health department did not claim responsibility for all these aspects of alcohol policy, policy discourse on treatment was now located within a more comprehensive framework which included consideration of the prevention of harmful drinking. Thus by the 1990s, policy was concerned with the management of 'risk' and the reduction of harm from alcohol consumption rather than with the treatment of alcoholism. Indicative of changing ideological frames within the DoH was the transfer of alcohol issues from the mental health division to the division dealing with prevention (which included tobacco and drug use). Within the DoH, there was now greater knowledge and experience of dealing with alcohol issues, resulting, as Harrison *et al.* (1996) have observed, in a

more interactive policy process through the use of advisory committees and systematic policy reviews.

By the end of the 1980s, within the DHSS there was
considerable sympathy towards a consumptionist perspective (which
addressed the relationship between per capita consumption and
alcohol-related harm). Inevitably, this entailed increased difficulties
in working across departmental boundaries and greater conflict with
opposing interests from the alcohol industry. The establishment of
the inter-departmental committee in 1987 (the Ministerial Group
on Alcohol Misuse), greeted as a positive move in promoting a more
collaborative relationship between government departments, nevertheless did not succeed in solving the fundamental dilemma over
the adoption of a strategic response to address alcohol-related
problems. Many of the individuals involved in the policy community
revolving around the DoH advocated the use of control measures
such as price and taxation to achieve a reduction in levels of
consumption and alcohol-related harm; but this did not gain wider
ministerial support. Policy moves to implement strategies to address
alcohol-related problems concentrated on demand reduction
approaches using education and awareness, professional training,
and control of drinking behaviour such as drink driving or street
drinking or, less frequently, adaptation of drinking venues and
environments.[2] Inter-departmental collaboration as manifest in the
work of the Wakeham Committee did not take on board issues of
national control policy (the approach with the greatest potential for
conflict), concentrating instead on less controversial issues and
approaches where consensus could be achieved. Despite this, the
committee's work emphasised the shift towards a prevention rather
than a treatment focus and treatment issues received little policy
attention. These trends had been visible as early as the mid-1970s
in the reports from the Advisory Committee on Alcoholism which
had already moved away from a medical model of alcoholism
treatment. The Advisory Committee's report on service delivery had
stressed the importance of reaching different groups of problem
drinkers, many of whom could not be recruited using a treatment
approach.

At practice level, adopting a 'problem-drinking' perspective along
with a concern to address health 'risks' meant that services and service
approaches became more diversified – 'fragmented' according to the
views of some commentators reported in earlier chapters – as
treatment agencies began to broaden their role to include, for example,
early intervention approaches, outreach work, the provision of training
for health professionals, and the development of courses for drink

drivers. Even within 'treatment' services, therefore, the broadening of the role meant that by the 1990s 'management' rather than 'treatment' had become a more accurate descriptor of agency activities.

As previous chapters have indicated, there were continuing tensions within alcohol policy networks of the late 1980s. However, a new consensus underpinned by research evidence from national and international studies, formed the basis of policy advocacy on treatment and the delivery of treatment services. It was agreed that the 'treatment' element of policy required a primary care response, emphasising early intervention and brief interventions, supported by a co-ordinated system of statutory and non-statutory services for problem drinkers. But, the move towards a primary care, community-based response to alcohol problems was endorsed by policy and professional leaders to a greater extent than by those working on the ground in the health and social care professions. The latter, as we have seen, were not easily persuaded to adopt a preventive role or to become more centrally involved in the management or treatment of alcohol problems in their patients and clients. Thus by the 1990s, while policy on treatment provision and service delivery was consistent and clearly stated, alcohol *treatment* occupied a weak position on the policy agenda and its grassroots implementation remained subject to local influences and variable institutional and professional application. Moving from a statement of policy intent to the implementation of change in service provision or service structures proved difficult despite efforts to secure co-ordination through the establishment of different 'umbrella' organisations at various times over the years.

Practitioners, service purchasers and policy makers were, however, eager to find the most cost-effective treatments and forms of service provision for the expanding numbers of people now defined as appropriate intervention targets. Over the 1980s, treatment research continued to expand resulting in a large, international body of studies, designed to find the most effective treatments, and providing the advocates of some treatment approaches (for instance, cognitive behavioural treatments, or brief interventions) with evidence of effectiveness. Unsurprisingly, in an era when problem management reached out to populations outside groups seeking help specifically for alcohol problems, psychological and behavioural treatment approaches, such as brief interventions, counselling, or cognitive-behavioural techniques which could be used by a range of therapists in many different settings, gained wide acceptance as effective therapies. By 1990, few questioned the need to develop an alcohol intervention strategy which would target both treatment seeking and non-treatment seeking groups; but research had still failed to provide the definitive answers on the most effective methods sought by policy makers and local purchasers of services (Lindstrom 1992; Thom *et al.* 1994; Society for the Study of Addiction 1999).

These shifts and developments in treatment approaches and service delivery in the alcohol field have to be seen within the political, social and economic context of the time. The history of post-war alcohol policy is intimately linked with the history of change in the organisation and funding of health and welfare services. Key influences were change in the relationship between the voluntary sector and the state, increasing professionalisation in the 'caring' occupations, shifts in the laws, sanctions and fashions which help to shape public views on alcohol use and misuse. These influences, which became more intricately linked with alcohol policy as the treatment focus gave way to a prevention and early intervention perspective from the 1970s, have been noted in preceding chapters. More particularly, the emergence of the new public health model of alcohol problems was located within general trends in public health towards employing an epidemiological and economic perspective of health and social problems, exemplified in approaches to tobacco smoking or the intake of certain foods (Rose 1992). This shift in the target groups for intervention away from those with an identified need and towards populations and communities represents a fundamental change in the theoretical position from which health policy developments have been derived. But the value system underlying the 'new public health' and the technologies which are the building blocks of public health interventions have been subject to varying interpretations.

Rose (1992), for instance, provides a sophisticated epidemiological argument in favour of a population-wide approach to health policy intervention based on a fundamentally humanitarian, functionalist and consensual model of human relationships and of the role of policy in achieving social change. He acknowledges conflicts of interest but interprets population control strategies as an essentially benign, enabling force which, at the societal level, aims to reduce inequalities in health and, at the individual level encourages people to make and implement healthy choices. On the whole, this is the dominant ideology underlying much of the current policy discourse on tackling alcohol problems. Since the 1970s there has been strong advocacy for a co-ordinated strategy to reduce alcohol-related problems using national and locally-based methods aiming to achieve cultural change in attitudes towards alcohol use and in drinking behaviours.[3] The savings in individual misery and costs to society as a whole are advanced as the benefits of such a policy.

The lack of critical attention to the latent assumptions of the public health paradigm has been challenged by Bunton (1990) who proposes quite a different viewpoint. Basing his argument on the theories of Foucault, Bunton adopts a conflict model in his analysis of the 'new public health' which he sees as 'part of a new social regulatory mechanism' within which problem-prevention occurs 'by manipulating the detail of the drinking individual's physical and social context on the one hand, and the national policy on the other'. Bunton cites shifting perspectives on alcohol problem management within broader changing mechanisms of social control over the past two centuries. He illustrates how different spheres of 'correction' (criminal and deviant behaviour, disease and mental health) have moved from institutionally based forms of care and control targeted on specific 'deviant' groups towards community-based forms of intervention and correction which encompass 'a growing clientele of potential deviants'. The process of increasing surveillance and control of populations extends interventions to primary health care settings, educational establishments, criminal justice agencies, social services, and many other organisational structures and groupings within the community. It is a dispersed form of control which permeates a large number of institutions and networks of social interaction and which, in the past two decades, has extended regulation beyond concern with the quantity of alcohol consumed to more widespread regulation of drinking practices and drinking settings. According to this interpretation of public health approaches to alcohol problem management, community-based, localised intervention (for instance, in the workplace, youth centres, or any other community services) is as much an aspect of the regulation of deviance as are centralised, national regulations (such as price or supply). Public health interventions may, therefore, be less benign than Rose's interpretation suggests; they are a form of social control linked to power structures and power relationships.

Gusfield's (1991) examination of the concept of 'social control' recognises this Janus-like quality where 'concepts and counterconcepts go together like husband and wife, locked in loving conflict'. What professes to be a way of helping people – the humanitarian vision of social control – becomes interpreted as the attempt by one part of society to enforce its standards and values over another part of society holding opposing standards, values and interests. Which interpretation is chosen, Gusfield argues, depends on whether the focus of the analysis is on the deviant as a troubled person requiring help or on the trouble the deviant activity causes for other people or for society as a whole.

Over the fifty years covered by this study, the policy agenda has reflected the interplay between these two facets of the alcohol problem. Within the Ministry of Health in the 1950s and 1960s, the disease concept of alcoholism and the 'medical' boundaries on policy action kept the focus on 'troubled persons'. Within the Home Office, concerns with issues such as drink driving or drunkenness offences placed the emphasis on 'troublesome activities'. In the early years of the post-war period, these distinctions were clearly preserved and despite overlap, policy networks around issues of alcohol and health tended to divide accordingly. The 1970s and 1980s saw the extension of 'troubled persons' to include individuals at risk of becoming 'troubled persons', and the inclusion (to a greater extent than in former times) within the intervention orbit of individuals who were 'troubled persons' by virtue of their relationship to dependent or problem drinkers. The DHSS broadened its remit beyond the narrowly medical definition of the 1950s to consider the socio-economic aspects of alcohol consumption and the need for prevention and early intervention as well as treatment responses. As the definition of 'troubled persons' became more elastic, the boundaries between a 'troubled persons' and a 'troublesome activities' response to the alcohol problem were also becoming less distinct. The case of habitual drunken offenders, discussed in Chapter 5, had drawn attention to the dynamics of problem interpretation underlying departmental boundaries and had indicated the shifting interface between the penal-medical response to alcohol problems. This emerged strongly in a different form in the 1990s when the policy focus began to turn towards the management of acute problems related to intoxication and binge drinking. Whereas in the 1950s these issues would have been seen as the domain of the Home Office, in the 1990s concern to address the harms associated with intoxication and binge drinking are shared by the Department of Health. The former conceptual division between issues of treatment on the one hand and issues of the control of consumption and of drinking behaviour on the other have been replaced by a more comprehensive explanatory framework which links consumption levels, alcohol-related harms and drinking behaviours (DoH 1995). These trends are reflected in the changing composition and size of the policy networks and policy community around alcohol. In the 1990s, workers within the criminal justice system, in social welfare organisations and health promotion agencies have become more prominent in the policy networks involved in the formation and implementation of strategies to address alcohol-related harms, including health issues. It could be argued that a third paradigm, characterised by a 'top-down' approach, has been emerging (Harrison *et al.* 1996).

Alcohol Problems Management:
Striving for Consensus in the 1990s

Clearly, the history of alcoholism treatment does not begin in the 1950s. Ideas concerning the nature of the problem of alcohol and the nature of appropriate social and policy responses have been framed and reframed over the centuries. Thus, many of the themes and issues which emerged in the second half of the twentieth century find a precedent in earlier ideological and institutional responses to alcohol use and problem use. But as others have commented, the alcohol field tends to suffer from amnesia (Heather undated; Berridge 1989). By the 1950s, the starting point for this study, those interested in alcoholism tended to look exclusively to the US and the 'modern alcoholism movement' originating in the work of the Yale Laboratory of Applied Physiology in the early 1940s. Perhaps such forgetfulness of the past serves a function. It is, possibly, easier to arouse interest and enthusiasm for a 'new' idea or discovery, and research findings which provide 'new' evidence for a shift in policy or practice are more likely to grasp the imagination and initiate action. The marketing and selling of concepts and recommendations for action has been as important in alcohol policy and practice (and in health care more generally) as in other areas of economic or political activity. The history of post-war alcohol policy throws up more than one instance where gaining consensus and acceptance for shifting perceptions of the problem or for 'new' policy initiatives has united diverse interests within the policy community, albeit temporarily. This was the case with the adoption of the disease concept of alcoholism in the 1950s which was used to help change public and professional perceptions of the alcoholic and to stimulate policy action. It was also a fundamental consideration in the consensus on unit measures of alcohol consumption emerging from the Royal Colleges in the mid-1980s; there, agreement among 'the experts' was a vital element in successfully opposing the advertising strength of the alcohol industry. It was also part of the *raison d'être* of the New Directions in Alcoholism Group which aimed to promote psychological perspectives of 'problem drinking' as an alternative to disease theory. It is currently a factor in policy and media attention directed towards young people's drinking. These few examples, and others discussed in preceding chapters, illustrate the process of reframing as not only a conceptual and ideological process but also as an economic and political process in

which individuals, groups and institutions are 'stakeholders'. Innovation and the diffusion of innovation plays an important part in gaining
credence for changes in policy and practice and in marking the entry
and continuing status of new 'stakeholders' within the field of activity.
It is unsurprising, therefore, that the emerging policy community in
the 1950s should emphasise the differences rather than the continui-
ties between past and present and that policy activists then, and
subsequently, should argue their case using the language of 'scientific
progress'.

This is not to say that arguments for policy action and policy
change are always spurious or spring from purely selfish motives.
Many of the individuals involved in alcoholism treatment at both
practice and policy levels were genuinely concerned to find the best,
affordable methods of addressing the individual and social harms
associated with problem alcohol use. Civil servants (administrative
and medical) were actively involved in examining current theories and
developments in treatment methods, in evaluating the evidence at
their disposal, stimulating research and discussion and bringing issues
to the notice of ministers. Research-based evidence has undoubtedly
played an increasingly important part in informing policy action even
if it was not always the primary factor in the decision-making process.

But political contexts constrain policy action even when consensus
is strong; and individuals within the 'policy community' are subject to
differing institutional interests and pressures. The role of conflicting
departmental interests in influencing policy statements from the
health departments has already been noted in previous chapters as has
the tension between different professional groups working in alcohol
problems treatment, and the 'competition' between those perceived to
be part of an 'insider' policy network by virtue of their connections
with particular institutions, and individuals who remained on the
outside. Such tensions act both as constraints on action and as
catalysts (along with other influences) to continuing re-examination of
policy and practice.

Underlying tension was a key element in shifting the theoretical
basis of consensus and, consequently, the direction of policy on
alcohol from curative to preventive approaches and from specialist to
general service provision. This has been illustrated in Chapter 6 which
showed how the consensus emerging in the 1970s within the policy
network linked to the DHSS began to favour a consumptionist view of
alcohol problems which was challenged from the start by other policy
networks and other government departments. At the same time, the
pressures to move policy in a particular direction – towards a
population and community-based approach to the management of

alcohol-related harm – left little room for dissenting voices. Debate centred around the efficacy of different strategies to lower harmful levels of alcohol consumption and to achieve the targets set, eventually, by the government in 1992.[4] But by the 1990s new evidence on the relationship between alcohol consumption and alcohol-related harm was entering the policy arena (Stockwell *et al*. 1996) and shifting the policy agenda away from consideration of strategies to achieve national targets towards consideration of effective means of managing alcohol-related risks and harms related to intoxication. Looking back to the rejected Home Office report of 1980, we find the suggestion that policy could adopt a 'situational' approach to the control of alcohol-related problems:

> It is conceivable that alcohol policy could concentrate on encouraging safer drinking habits, devising safer drinking environments, rather than simply discouraging drinking. (Tuck 1980, p. 3)

The statement contains the notion of 'harm reduction' which was already available both as a policy option to control harmful drinking practices (Robinson *et al*. 1989) and as part of a treatment repertoire (Heather n.d.). But prior to the 1990s there was no acceptable conceptual framework for the development of a comprehensive harm reduction strategy. Home Office and DHSS responsibilities still emphasised different aspects of the alcohol problem, and the policy community around alcohol and health issues threw its weight behind the promotion of 'sensible drinking' as the major strategy for tackling alcohol-related harms.

By the 1990s, when advocacy for a 'harm reduction' approach was emerging, its proponents drew on theoretical insights from drugs and HIV policy as evidence of effectiveness and of public and political acceptability (Single 1997; Stimson and Thom 1997). The new response to alcohol-related problem behaviour appears to centre around action models borrowed from the drugs and criminal justice spheres where 'community safety' approaches have gained considerable credibility as an effective method of addressing 'troublesome behaviours'. The effects of shifts in alcohol policy towards a 'community safety' model of harm reduction have been evident in the development of partnerships between criminal justice agencies and alcohol services, in the use of camera surveillance techniques in city centres to discourage alcohol-related problems (among other things), in 'zero tolerance' policing which includes eradication of street drinking, in concern to address the problems of alcohol-related attendances in hospital Accident and Emergency Departments, and in the emphasis in recent government statements on reducing the harm related to episodes of heavy drinking and intoxication (O'Brien and Light 1993; DoH 1995; Webster and Chappell 1995; Plant *et al.* 1997). The 'community safety' perspective of the 1990s echoes temperance concerns of the 1950s but has become a professionalised rather than a lay response to alcohol problems management.

As in former policy shifts, multiple influences underpin the direction of policy action. The policy community remains an important player at the interface between policy, practice and research. The changing composition of the alcohol field has brought new players to the fore in the 1990s and reshuffled the position of older groups. The non-statutory services, for instance, are now the main providers of services; new professional groups such as criminal justice workers or health promotion experts are entering the alcohol arena bringing with them their theoretical understandings and practical experiences. The policy community around alcohol has grown and is, perhaps, more structured than previously with less direct contact between civil servants and wider groups of service providers. The continuing production of new research 'evidence' has played an important role in initiating a reassessment of policy objectives. For instance, research indicating that alcohol use can bring health benefits, in particular that it may have a protective effect for coronary heart disease, influenced reassessment of drinking guidelines for policy and health education statements (DoH 1995). A review of the evidence on the relationship between per capita consumption and alcohol-related harm stimulated a reassessment of the effectiveness of lowering average consumption of alcohol as a means of reducing all forms of related harm. The results of this research indicated the importance of episodes of heavy drinking (binge and intoxication drinking) as a public health and safety issue (Stockwell *et al.* 1996).

The search for consensus to activate and implement policy and policy change has been a feature of the alcohol arena since the 1950s. But competing interpretations of the alcohol problem have always co-existed within the dominant paradigm of the time and draw attention to latent tensions within the fragile consensual framework around issues of alcohol problems management. What we have seen over past years is not one model replacing another but competing perspectives jostling for dominance within particular socio-historical contexts. We appear to be witnessing the emergence of a new dominant paradigm in alcohol policy and practice with an emphasis on the reduction of risk and harm. Within this paradigm, the focus of action is on policy and programmes which 'attempt to reduce the harm associated with drinking without the drinker necessarily giving up his or her use of alcohol at the present time' (Plant *et al.* 1997, p. 6). As others have argued, harm reduction strategies are not incompatible with policies to control per capita consumption and there continues to be a strong argument in favour of control measures at both national and local level (Alcohol Concern 1999). In striving for consensus in an arena which is politically sensitive, and which encompasses a very wide range of interest groups subject to differing institutional pressures, harm reduction approaches may furnish a common meeting place from which to extend help to 'troubled persons' and to tackle 'troublesome behaviours' as currently defined. Whether the introduction of a national alcohol strategy (DoH 1998a) can achieve this by building on the successes and failures of the past remains to be seen.

Notes

Chapter 2

1 Public Record Office (PRO), London, MH 58.666: Correspondence (12 June 1956).

2 PRO MH 58.666 Pilkington correspondence (12 June 1958).

3 PRO MH 58.666: Circular from Congress of Mental Specialists and Neurologists of France and French Speaking Countries (19 August 1954); Temperance Resolution from the Order of the Sons of Temperance (22 June 1956); Resolution from the Order of the Sons of Temperance (5 June 1958); Independent Order of Rehabites (September 1959).

4 PRO MH.58.666: Note from Home Office, J.C.H. Holden (3 January 1957); notes from R. Ellerington and G. Godber (22 January 1957); suggested reply to Home Office (28 January 1957); reply to Home Office (21 February 1957). Exchange between Mr Hastings, Labour MP for Barking and Mr Thompson, Minister for Health (1 December 1958). This was because local authorities were responsible for health education funding.

5 PRO MH 58.666: Parr report (17 September 1954).

6 PRO MH 58.666: Correspondence (25 March 1952 to 25 June 1952). Correspondence, Esher (25 March 1952) and reply to Esher (27 March 1952).

7 PRO MH 58.666: Correspondence from Casson (6 March 1958) and reply (12 March 1958).

8 Discovery announced in the *Lancet* (1948) 2, 1004; *British Journal of Addiction* (1950) 1. Although hailed as a new discovery, the possible effects of tetramethylthiuram disulphide were known as early as 1910 and were reported by a doctor working in a chemical company in 1937. See Williams (1937).

9 PRO MH 58.666: Correspondence (24 February 1954).

10 PRO MH 58.666: Maclay (12 March 1958).

11 Joint Committee of the British Medical Association and Magistrates Association, minutes of the meeting (12 May 1959); PRO MH 58.667: Benner to Brough (8 September 1960).

12 Obituary in *British Journal of Addiction* (1972) 67, 149–52; quotation from Barry Richards' unpublished autobiography (Maryse Metcalf, private papers).

13 D.L. Davies' paper given at a conference (25 May 1975) Royal College of Physicians. Held at the Institute of Psychiatry Library, folder 'Typescripts and Correspondence'.

14 BMA/Magistrates' Committee, Document submitted for the meeting (21 May 1959), 'Memorandum on the treatment of alcoholics' by M. Glatt (BMA/Mag).

Chapter 3

1   PRO MH 58.666: Correspondence, Paull (June 1952); Esher (23 June 1952): Correspondence, Maclay (29 April 1952); Esher (23 June 1952); Maclay (22 July 1953); Dudley (8 March 1956); Correspondence, Parr (17 December 1954); Rev. Allen (17 November 1958); Correspondence, Pilkington (15 September 1958).

2   PRO MH 58.666: Graham (1952); Esher (25 March 1952); Manning-Buller (25 April and 28 May 1952); Cooke (2 May 1953); Cary (15 February 1954); a teacher (5 July 1956); Cardew (25 November 1957); Casson (6 March 1958).

3   PRO MH 58.666: Smith-Moorhouse (11 January 1959).

4   Council of the British Medical Association, Minutes 33 and 34 (7 July 1952).

5   BMA/Magistrates' Committee, Minutes (5 November 1958).

6   BMA/Magistrates' Committee, Minutes (12 March 1959).

7   BMA/Magistrates' Committee, Document submitted for the meeting (21 May 1959); 'Memorandum on the treatment of alcoholics' by M. Glatt (BMA/Mag.); Minutes (21 May 1959).

8   PRO MH 58.667: Inpatient Units for Alcoholics. Letter and document from MacKeith to Maclay (7 September 1959); Memo to Mr Brough (15 June 1960); Memo to P. Benner (9 August 1960).

9   PRO MH 58.667: Memo to P. Benner (8 August 1960); Letter to Home Office (23 August 1960); Memo P. Benner to Emery (14 November 1960).

10 PRO MH 58.667: Memo to P. Benner (8 September 1960).

11 PRO MH 58.667: Memo to Brough (9 August 1960); Memo to Mr Benner from Brough (8 September 1960); Letter to Stotesbury at Home Office from P. Benner (23 September 1960).

12 PRO MH 58.667: Note from Dodds to Emery (21 November 1960); draft on treatment from P. Benner.

13 PRO MH 58.667: Note of a meeting with the Home Office and Prison Commission (14 November 1960).

14 PRO MH 58.667: Memo to Emery (23 November 1960).

15 PRO MH 58.669: Returns from questionnaires to Hospital Boards of Governors, Regional Hospital Boards and Private Establishments (1961).

16 Wellcome: SA/CCA/17 (13 June 1965).

17 Davies would not admit vagrant drinkers to the Maudsley ward (Edwards, interview); Conversation with Thomas Bewley, interview in *Addiction* (1995) 90, 883–92: Bewley notes how he was one of the few psychiatrists treating alcoholism in the 1950s and that he accepted 'skid row' types.

18 Dr Anthony Clare warned of the dangers in the trend towards 'brief interventions' which could not cater for patients needing more intensive care. Paper at the Ninth International Conference on Alcohol, Liverpool 14–17 September 1993.

19 Stallings (1973) illustrates how the homogeneity and consensus in any social movement may be more apparent than real, the 'public image' covering differences between individuals and groups. In particular, Stallings notes ideological differences between leaders and followers and increasing heterogeneity of beliefs and perceptions as one moves from the centre to the periphery of a network or, in this case, a 'policy community'.

Chapter 4

1 Home Office, Working Party on Habitual Drunken Offenders documentation: WPHDO (67) 14, T.H. Bewley, 'Treatment of compulsorily detained alcoholics' in *The Prison Medical Journal*; WPHDO (67) 17, Dr Tropp (Edwards, private papers); also mentioned by Bewley in 'Conversation with Thomas Bewley' interview in *Addiction* (1995) 90, 883–92.

2 Unpublished interview with Norman Ingram-Smith conducted by Professor Ilana Crome (private papers).

3 'Wet' accommodation means that individuals were accepted even if they had been drinking. Most hostels insisted that residents should arrive sober and remain abstinent during their stay.

4 Complaints about vagrant drinkers and dissatisfaction with the efforts of voluntary associations to deal with the problem were voiced by the residents of Tower Hamlets and Southwark and the London Boroughs Association in statements made to the Home Office Working Party on the Drunken Offender, 20 July 1967, WHPDO (67) 19–21, WHPDO (67) 27.

5 Herbert D. Chalke, Medical Officer of Health for Camberwell was an exception. He was involved in the response to alcoholism in Camberwell and wrote on the subject.

6 The term 'counselling' was not widely used until the late 1970s, when different models and approaches to 'counselling' (many drawn from psychotherapeutic sources) became popular and were employed by the increasing number of social workers and professional 'counsellors' entering the alcohol field. In the earlier period, counselling was generally spoken of as 'advice' and information. See Cook (1989).

7 SA/CCA/18 Constitution; Minutes of meeting 4 December 1961; and 16 February 1963.

8 As documented in a later draft fund-raising document: E. Kyle 1971, SA/CCA/22; and in Chalke (1970).

9 For example, SA/CCA/18 Constitution, Mr Kenneth Robinson MP, 5 July 1963; CCA Minutes of meetings indicate frequent attendance by Dr Richard Phillipson (MoH).

10 SA/CCA/18 Constitution, April 1966.

11 SA/CCA/1 Minutes 12 October 1967. The CCA published a bulletin of its activities – later the *CCA Journal on Alcoholism*. In education, a Working Party was set up to look at incorporating alcohol into secondary schools' health education curriculum and a handbook for teachers was planned: see SA/CCA/1 Executive Committee Minutes March 1966 to December 1966. These efforts do not seem to have been successful despite requests from educational bodies for information and guidance: see SA/CCA/1 Report made to the CCA by Father John Jukes, 1968 and SA/ CCA/1 Minutes, 15 November 1966, Elizabeth Keys. The Council ran numerous information and training events which targeted members of the general public as well as the medical and social welfare professions: see SA/ CCA/22 draft fund-raising document, Kyle 1971.

12 Edwards suggestion is minuted: SA/CCA/1 Minutes 23 February 1967; Davies recalled the impetus as coming from Peter Waters who had attended the Rutgers' summer school in the US and on his return had secured funding for a similar venture from the Rowntree Social Services Trust. According to Davies' account, this was how he had become associated; see 'Interview with D.L. Davies' in Edwards (1991).

13 SA/CCA/1 Minutes 2 October 1969 and SA/CCA/88 *CCA Journal on Alcoholism*, (1969) 1, no. 4, report.

14 SA/CCA/11 CCA *Annual Report* 1969–70; SA/CCA/13 Cook in CCA *Annual Report* 1975–76. Note: much earlier Cook had registered his concern that the emphasis of the CCA should be to remain 'a truly local community-based organisation'. As part of this aim, they had created a Community Council made up of lay members of the public as distinct from the executive committee, composed mainly of medical and social workers; SA/CCA/11 CCA *Annual Report* 1969–70; SA/CCA/96 22 May 1978.

15 Correspondence Morrell to Editor of *British Journal of Addiction* 29 November 1954 (Morrell papers).

16 Correspondence from Mrs Mann to Mr Walton 9 August 1951 (Morrell papers).

17 Correspondence from Forbes Cheston to Morrell 13 January 1953 (Morrell papers).

18 Publication from the Advisory Council on Alcoholism, 'Alcoholism: A Social Problem' (Morrell papers).

19 Correspondence to Munro from JL or JH (signature unclear) 14 January 1953 (Morrell papers).

20 Correspondence from Pullar-Strecker to Morrell 1955 (Morrell papers).

21 Various correspondence; for example, 13 January 1953, Cheston wrote to Morrell to ask him to try for Rowntree funding to sponsor a visit to the UK by Mrs Marty Mann. In May 1956 Morrell refused a request from

Robertson (Dumfries) for funds to start a British Council on Alcoholism (Morrell papers).

22 Correspondence from Morrell to Philip Rowntree 2 December 1955 (Morrell papers).

23 Agenda for the Steering Group meeting on 7 March 1961 and letter from Dr Smith-Moorhouse dated 5 February 1961 (Morrell papers).

24 Minutes of meetings in 1959 contain references to a forthcoming article by Dr Casson in the national press (his correspondence with the MoH is commented on in Chapter 2). The article was expected to press for better information on alcoholism and better facilities. The Steering Group aimed to promote this kind of awareness material. They also distributed to GPs reprints of papers on the role of GPs in responding to alcoholism – published by Max Glatt and Basil Merriman who were in touch with the Steering Group. Minutes, 17 March 1960; Editorial *British Journal of Addiction* (1966).

25 Correspondence from Rev. Harrison to Morrell 28 November 1956 (Morrell papers).

26 Correspondence from Morrell to Pullar-Strecker 15 March 1956; and from Morrell to Goodwin 9 March 1956 (Morrell papers).

27 SA/CCA/88 *CCA Journal on Alcoholism* (1970) Special Regional Issue.

28 SA/CCA/20. Documents that affiliation was agreed in August 1970.

29 SA/CCA/13, CCA *Annual Report* 1974–75.

30 Information from Alcohol Concern, London (personal communication).

31 Obituary, National Council on Alcoholism *Fifth Annual Report* 1968.

Chapter 5

1 Evidence presented to Home Office Working Party on Habitual Drunkenness Offenders: WPHDO (67) 24, 18 August 1967; WPHDO (67), Sorenson; WPHDO (67), Swinney; WPHDO (67) 54 Brighton.

2 National Assistance Board Survey carried out October 1965. See evidence to the Home Office Working Party. The incidence of alcoholism amongst users of reception centres; memorandum from the Supplementary Benefits Commission A.H., 15 June 1967, WPHDO (67) 3.

3 Out of Court (1988 p. 16) describes a 'drinking school' as 'a social unit of mainly alcohol dependent men (sometimes mixed sexes) who share the three central needs of the "skid row" drinker: alcohol, money and shelter'.

4 General statement of case to be presented to Lord Stonham, July 1967; London Borough of Southwark, general statement of case and supplementary statement, evidence to Home Office Working Party WPHDO (67) 19–21; report of deputation to Lord Stonham WPHDO (67) 27. Archard (1975) documents media and public attitudes towards this group of drinkers for the period around 1970.

5 General statement of case to be presented to Lord Stonham, July 1967, pp. 1–4.

6 For example, discussed in the BMA/Magistrates' Committee in the Home Office Working Party on Habitual Drunken Offenders and in the Advisory Committee on Alcoholism (to be discussed in Chapter 6).

7 According to the accounts of individuals involved at the time, the approach was influenced by the work of Maxwell Jones (US), for example Jones 1952; 1968.

8 Advisory Council on the Treatment of Offenders (1963) cited in: Home Office (1966).

9 Home Office 1966, evidence to the Working Party provided among others by Anton Wallich-Clifford, Norman Ingram-Smith, Professor Griffith Edwards, Dr B. Merriman; Appendix B on the use of hostels for alcoholics (attributed to Griffith Edwards).

10 SA/CCA/1 Minutes (10th December 1964). Also present at the meeting: Dr Phillipson (MoH); Barry Richards.

11 Correspondence from Lady Reading to Griffith Edwards (28 May 1965).

12 Correspondence from Griffith Edwards to Lady Reading (23 June 1965, 24 June 1965, 1 July 1965).

13 Correspondence between Griffith Edwards and Lady Reading (5, 7, 10, 11 August 1965).

14 Correspondence between Lady Reading and Griffith Edwards indicates the importance of influential contacts in securing funding, finding a house and rallying support for the hostel; for example, contact was made with Mrs Denington, chairman of the Greater London Council Housing Committee, of whom it was noted 'poor woman, we are hot on her tail' (10 November 1965); members of the Carnegie Trust steering committee were canvassed at a lunch (1 November 1965); dinner at Lady Reading's home to discuss funding included, Lord Stonham, and Professor Titmuss from the London School of Economics (22 May 1967).

15 *The Barry Richards Interview*, news sheet issued for the twenty-five years of Turning Point (Maryse Metcalf, private papers).

16 SA/CCA/1 Minutes (15 March 1966) state that ideas for Rathcoole came originally from a report made to the CCA Working Party on 'skid row' which produced a paper *The Drunkenness Offender: A Therapeutic Alternative to Repeated Imprisonment*. Rathcoole House, which opened in 1966 with Timothy Cook as warden, became the model for this type of provision and had a considerable influence on the Home Office Working Party on Habitual Drunken Offenders. Early publications describing the house included Cook *et al.* (1968); Cook and Pollak (1970). Rathcoole House became Alcoholics Recovery Project (ARP) in 1969.

17 For a brief account of the Seebohm Committee and the 'professionalisation' of the personal social services see Brown (1975, pp. 115–31). Social

work made little impact as a profession on the alcohol field during the 1960s and 1970s although some of the techniques introduced in the 1970s, such as counselling, were brought in by social workers (Larry Harrison, personal communication).

18 Quotations are taken from interviews with: Ms Elspeth Kyle, Dr Benno Pollak, Mr David Kitchen and Mr Timothy Cook. Similar views about the importance of Edwards' leadership at this time were also made by other people.

19 SA/CCA/1 Minutes (1 June 1967); International Symposium on the Habitual Drunken Offender held at the Institute of Psychiatry in 1968, proceedings; Cook et al. (1969); CCA AGM (29 April 1969) on the topic of 'The Vagrant Alcoholic' aroused high feelings among local residents present at the meeting who wanted something done; CCA/88, *CCA Journal on Alcoholism* vol. 2, no. 1 (October 1969).

20 Correspondence from George Hepburn, Director of Greater London Alcohol Advisory Service to a civil servant 10 June 1986, commenting on themes to emerge from a review prepared for a DHSS-sponsored conference on detoxification services, 13 June 1986 in London. The 'political' nature of the debate on detoxification services was also referred to by B. Hore in a paper prepared for the same conference (papers and correspondence made available by civil servant, personal communication during research prior to this project).

21 Dr Brian Hore pointed out that the criteria used to judge the success of detoxification units should not have been based on recovery rates (always low with this group of drinkers). 'The spirit of the initiative was to offer these individuals who are seriously affected by alcohol, entry into the treatment system and away from the criminal system' (personal communication).

22 Various interviews. Also, younger doctors entering the addictions field may have been more attracted to working with illicit drugs – thereby losing potential leaders to the alcohol arena.

Chapter 6

1 For a critical description of the syndrome and reactions to it from workers in the alcohol arena, see Heather and Robertson (1985); Shaw *et al.* (1978).

2 The most common indicators used to assess alcohol-related harm in the population were alcohol-related liver cirrhosis; deaths; admission to hospital with a diagnosis of alcoholism or alcohol-related illnesses; drink driving and other offences relating to alcohol use.

3 A position paper, *Proposal for a Scientific Conference on the National Implications of Alcohol Use*, prepared by Griffith Edwards on the basis of discussions held at the DHSS on 14 September 1972, indicates moves towards an epidemiological analysis of the demographic correlates of

'alcoholism' and consideration of prevention strategies (Edwards, private papers).

4 D. Ennals, speech at the opening of the Health Education Council's North East Campaign on Alcohol Education, DHSS, 7 November 1977.

5 Accounts were given by interviewees of Sir Keith's interest. Derek Rutherford pointed out that Harry Vincent, chairman of the National Council on Alcoholism, was a relative of Sir Keith Joseph. Harry Vincent influenced the appointment of Sir Bernard Braine as chairman of the NCA and, in 1973, Sir Bernard appointed Derek Rutherford as director.

6 Even in the early 1990s, when I was conducting interviews, I was advised by several interviewees not to bother about the Tuck report because it was unimportant or completely misguided. As we shall see in the last chapter, some of the perceptions of the problem contained in the report were revisited in the mid-1990s.

7 Correspondence Owen–Edwards 21 February 1975 (Edwards, private papers).

8 DHSS Advisory Committee on Alcoholism Minutes 23 April 1977 (Edwards, private papers).

9 Tension among committee members was reported by interviewees both from first hand knowledge and from hearsay, for example Professor Griffith Edwards, interview; Mr Derek Rutherford, interview; Dr Anthony Thorley, interview. It is also indicated in the minutes of the first meeting of the committee on 23 April 1975 in discussion of the terms of reference (Edwards, private papers).

10 DHSS Advisory Committee on Alcoholism Minutes 23 April 1975 (Edwards, private papers); a note by the committee acknowledges the work undertaken by the members of staff of the department and adds: 'Whilst they did not indicate to us the road we should take, they nevertheless steered us away from entering blind alleys and following wrong tracks' (Advisory Committee on Alcoholism 1978b, p. iii). As examples in previous chapters have shown, the department was concerned to maintain its boundaries of responsibility.

11 DHSS Advisory Committee on Alcoholism Minutes 23 April 1975 (Edwards, private papers).

12 The significance of this was pointed out by Professor Neil Kessel (interview). See Advisory Committee on Alcoholism (1978b, para. 4.24).

13 Camberwell Council on Alcohol Annual Report 1977–78, p. 2. Several interviewees spoke about the abrupt ending to the committee; some thought that the committee had probably ended its useful lifespan; others felt that the alcohol field would have benefited from its continuation. No satisfactory answer was given to the committee members I spoke to for the apparently dismissive way in which the committee ended.

14 It is widely quoted in the literature and many of the interviewees referred

to its importance; from the perspective of the DHSS, Dr Ron Wawman commented that the core of policy activity during his time in the department was based on the three Kessel reports.

15 Letter from Griffith Edwards to Neil Kessel 29 June 1977 (Edwards, private papers); A. Thorley (1979, p. 131).

16 Interview material from several respondents indicated that considerable divergence of views had developed regarding the needs for specialist inpatient facilities, and that the Kessel report was seen as endorsement for a move away from hospital based treatment under psychiatric supervision towards community-based provision with less emphasis on the need for medical expertise.

17 DHSS Advisory Committee on Alcoholism Minutes 8 July 1976; Camberwell Council on Alcohol *Annual Report* 1977/78, p. 2.

18 DHSS Homelessness and Addictions Research Liaison Group (1984) Strategy for Research on Alcohol.

19 For example, Breeze (1985, p. 2): 'The 4 pint limit itself was a judgement which could not be justified by hard evidence of dramatic symptoms when marginally exceeded.'

Chapter 7

1 According to the Chief Medical Officer's Report for 1959, there were 100 clinical psychologists and 293 social workers employed in mental health services as a whole. Numbers employed in alcohol services are not available but oral accounts suggest low numbers rising slowly from the 1970s. This would appear to be supported by Webster's (1996, p. 447) figure of 600 clinical psychologists in mental health services by the end of the 1970s.

2 Discussion on the roots of clinical psychology is based on accounts in Routh (1994); Walker (1991). Although much of the discussion is relevant to the development of clinical psychology generally, both accounts are specific to issues of professionalisation in the US. I did not find an historical account of clinical psychology as a profession in the UK.

3 Francis Edward Camps was a Council member of the Society for the Study of Addiction since 1960 and President of the Society from 1966 until his death in 1972. See obituaries in *British Journal of Addiction* (1972) 67, 149–52; Barry Richards' autobiography (Mrs Maryse Metcalf, private papers).

4 According to one estimate there were 1350 AA groups in England and Wales by 1990; see Collins, Ottley and Wilsin (1990 p. 21). For a description and history of the Minnesota Model of treatment see Cook (1988a). According to Cook, the first Minnesota Model treatment centre opened in Britain was Broadway Lodge at Weston-super-Mare in 1974. Since then other centres, run as private or voluntary facilities, have

opened, largely in the south and south-west of England. For an evaluation of the approach see Cook (1988b).

Chapter 8

1 *White Ribbon* (the official organ of the national British Women's Temperance Association) January 1905, p. 34.

2 Banks (1981) notes that when Frances Willard, the feminist president of the Women's Christian Temperance Union (WCTU) visited the British Women's Temperance Association (NWTA) in 1892, she expressed her surprise that the latter had not given support to issues of women's suffrage and women's emancipation. Efforts to involve the NWTA in suffrage campaigns were largely unsuccessful. Kitze (1986) suggests, however, that the BWTU did widen its scope to include feminist issues and that involvement in the BWTU allowed women to develop the skills and self-confidence needed to become active in other spheres of public life.

3 More recent surveys and reviews suggest that changes are taking place especially in the drinking habits of young women who are drinking more than formerly but the evidence is still patchy.

4 Camberwell Council on Alcoholism *Annual Report* 1973–74, Wellcome Institute SA/CCA/96.

5 Camberwell Council on Alcoholism Seminar Minutes (1973) 9–16 November, 23 November, 7 December, Wellcome Institute SA/CCA/95; Camberwell Council on Alcoholism (1974) *Women Alcoholics* papers by S. Otto and G. Litman, Wellcome Institute, SA/CCA/95.

6 Camberwell Council on Alcoholism *Annual Report* 1974–75, Wellcome Institute SA/CCA/96.

7 Camberwell Council on Alcoholism *Annual Report* 1977–78, Wellcome Institute SA/CCA/96; Camberwell Council on Alcoholism (June 1977) Circular Letter from C. Wilson, Wellcome Institute SA/CCA/96.

8 Camberwell Council on Alcoholism *Annual Report* 1977–78.

9 C. Wilson (1976) Women and Alcohol paper presented to USAFE course on alcoholism, 8 June, Wellcome SA/CCA/96.

10 For example, 1972 The Alcohol Education Centre; 1976 GLAAS (Greater London Alcohol Advisory Service); 1984 Alcohol Concern.

11 Wilson (1980) reported 11 per cent of women to be abstainers in 1978; Breeze (1985) from fieldwork carried out in 1982, reported 8 per cent of women to be total abstainers and the same figure can be found in the survey by Goddard and Ikin (1988). These last two authors commented that, since 1978, the proportion of women who reported having an alcoholic drink had risen from 58 per cent to 61 per cent but that the increase in consumption was largely attributable to an increase in the category of light drinkers.

12 For example, in 1978, three of the residential houses run by 'Aquarius' in

Birmingham had difficulty recruiting females to fill available spaces. Staff
who had attended workshops on women and alcohol were reported as
'very keen on the issue of the woman alcoholic' and worried that they
might lose beds reserved for women. They approached CCA for advice on
recruiting women (SA/CCA/96, letter from S. Otto, 1978). Alcoholics
Recovery Project, London, kept beds open for women despite conflict over
empty beds (Graham, interview).

13 Department of Health and Social Security (20 December 1983) 'Drinking
During Pregnancy' Press Release (83/288). Reports answer to parliamentary questions by Mr John Patten, Parliamentary Secretary for Health.

14 For a brief discussion of the American response following the publication
of the research by Jones and Smith (1973) see Little and Ervin (1994).

15 For a brief history and discussion of the British situation (including
comments that the official response in the US was far greater than in the
UK) see Plant (1985 pp. 8–19). Indications of media and service responses
in the UK are also in C. Wilson 'The Foetal Alcohol Syndrome', Addiction
Research Unit paper presented in June 1977 (Betsy Thom, personal
papers). Dr Ron Wawman (interview) commented that the DoH had never
funded research on FAS. He remembered the concern to review the
evidence carefully before writing the statement which was delivered in the
House by John Patten.

16 Home Office (1988) News Release, 24 October; and document CM13
mar.1 (personal communication, 6 September 1991).

17 SCODA (Standing Conference on Drug Abuse) was interested in women's
drug use; collaborative conferences and action on women's issues were
sometimes undertaken with Alcohol Concern and other institutions
(background paper in B. Thom, personal papers).

Chapter 9

1 PRO: MH 58.666: 17 September 1954, Parr.

2 *British Medical Journal* (1954) 1, p. 270: a report of a meeting of the
Section of General Practice of the Royal Society of Medicine on 20 January
1954 devoted to a discussion of the management of the alcoholic in
general practice. The report included views from Dent, Hobson, and
Lincoln Williams, all well-known practitioners in alcoholism treatment.

3 Dr H.K. Soltan, written evidence to BMA/Magistrates' Meeting, 21 May
1959 (British Medical Association archives).

4 For a description of Balint's approach see *British Medical Journal* (1958) 2,
585–90. Webster (1996 pp. 14–15) discusses the emergence in the early
1950s of a number of organisational groupings (for example, the College
of General Practitioners) acting as a forum for idealistic, younger
practitioners; it was practitioners allied to such groups who tended to
favour health centre practice and the ideas of Balint.

5 Dr Ron Wawman, discussion document on Alcohol Policy 1982/83 (seminar 2 May 1979, report in 1980). Conference paper: 'Policy Background to Trends' to be held at the Meeting of Consultant Psychiatrists 30 November 1982 – *The Psychiatrists on Alcohol Treatment Services – Taking Stock.*

6 Dr Alan Cartwright stressed the importance of the status of CAT workers (interview); for another example and discussion of inter-professional collaboration see Jefferys and Sachs (1983).

7 Dr Peter Anderson, telephone communication (on facilitator schemes and his work in Oxford); J. Dawson and G. Smerdon (1987) *Options*, Cornwall Council on Alcohol (report); Cornwall Council on Alcohol (1992), *The John Dawson Project Interim Report*; Maggie Findlay, Cornwall Council on Alcohol, telephone communication.

8 Also commented on by Sir George Godber as important in signifying support from the leaders of the profession (interview material).

9 The specific aim of individual councils is not clear and seems to vary from source to source. This probably reflects what was happening in reality. The Camberwell Council on Alcoholism, for instance, did not believe its function to be the provision of a treatment service. Other councils were providing 'counselling' quite early on although it is not clear whether they would have thought of counselling as a 'treatment' or a prevention approach; see Camberwell Council on Alcoholism, *Journal on Alcoholism* September 1973, Vol. 3 (2) 'Alcoholism Facilities England and Wales: A directory of facilities for advice, referral and treatment'. Also the NCA and FARE came to include a heterogeneous membership which included information/advice giving bodies and service providers of different sorts, with considerable overlap (personal communication).

10 Lord Rothschild (1971): the report aroused considerable controversy; see discussion in Bulmer (1987, p. 10–11).

11 The contribution of Chris Ralph (career civil servant) has been discussed in Chapter 6; he was involved in alcohol policy for most of the 1970s; Alan Sippert (medical officer in the department) was also knowledgeable and involved in alcohol issues. As noted earlier, several ministers during this period also took an interest in alcohol policy.

12 Centres providing some combination of treatment, prevention, research, training components emerged in Leeds, Manchester, Newcastle, Canterbury, Hull/York, Exeter, Birmingham, Liverpool and represented statutory and non-statutory services.

13 The aims of the Portman Group are stated in each issue of the *Quarterly Review of Alcohol Research* Portman, London. The aims are to promote sensible drinking, to reduce alcohol-related harm, and to develop a better understanding of alcohol misuse.

Chapter 10

1 For a discussion of government activity on licensing and drink driving issues at this time, including events leading up to the Road Safety Act of 1967, see Baggott (1990, pp. 113–42).

2 For descriptions of these approaches in the 1980s, see Robinson, Tether and Teller (1989), and for more recent examples, Plant *et al.* (1997).

3 Developing a national strategy was the theme of a conference held by the Society for the Study of Addiction, entitled, 'Tackling Alcohol Together', Leeds (1996); the main focus was on strategies to reduce consumption.

4 Department of Health (1992). The aim was to achieve a reduction from 28 per cent of men and 11 per cent of women drinking above recommended levels in 1992 to 18 per cent of men and 7 per cent of women by the year 2005.

References

Archives and Private Papers

Public Record Office, Kew, London. Files MH 58.666; MH 58.667; MH 58.669.
The files largely consist of correspondence between MoH officials and individuals outside the Ministry of Health – doctors, members of the public, with MPs, with the Home Office and other government departments, and internal memos; referenced as MH (number) in the chapter notes.

British Medical Association Archives, BMA, London.
Minutes of the BMA/Magistrates' Committee (full collection); referenced as BMA/Mag.

Wellcome Institute for the History of Medicine, Contemporary Archives Centre, London.
Collection of documents from the Camberwell Council on Alcoholism; includes minutes of meetings (incomplete), reports, issues of the Camberwell journal, correspondence; covers the period 1960 to 1980. These documents are referenced as SA/CCA.

Professor Griffith Edwards, private papers.
Includes correspondence, minutes of meetings and documentation for the Home Office working party on the Habitual Drunken Offender; minutes and documents for the Advisory Committee on Alcoholism 1975–78; general papers covering the period 1960 to 1980; referenced as Edwards, private papers.

W.B. Morrell: private papers held by Mr Derek Rutherford.
Covering the initiation and development of councils on alcoholism (1950s and 1960s); other activities of the Rowntree Trust, other miscellaneous documents; referenced as Morrell, private papers.

Barry Richards' autobiography (unpublished), held by Mrs Maryse Metcalf.

Published Sources

Abel, A. and Lewin, W. (1959) 'Report on hospital building', supplement to the *British Medical Journal*, April, 109–14.

Acheson, D. (1998) *Inequalities in Health*. The Stationery Office, London.

Advisory Committee on Alcoholism (1978a) *Report on Prevention*. DHSS and the Welsh Office, London.

Advisory Committee on Alcoholism (1978b) *The Pattern and Range of Services for Problem Drinkers*. DHSS and the Welsh Office, London.

Advisory Committee on Alcoholism (1979) *Report on Education and Training*. DHSS and the Welsh Office, London.

Ahlstrom, S. (1983) *Women and Alcohol Control Policy: A Review of Findings and Some Suggestions for Research*. Policy paper presented at the Alcohol Epidemiology Section Meeting, International Council on Alcohol and Addictions, Padua, Italy. Social Research Institute of Alcohol Studies, Helsinki. Report No. 168.

Alcohol Concern (1999) Proposals for a national alcohol strategy for England. Alcohol Concern, London.

Alcohol Education Centre (1977) *The Ledermann Curve: Report of a Symposium held in London on 6–7 January*. AEC, London.

Allen, D. (1981) 'An analysis of the factors affecting the development of the 1962 Hospital Plan for England and Wales', *Social Policy and Administration* 15(1), 3–18.

All Party Group on Alcohol Misuse (1995) *Alcohol and Crime: Breaking the Link*. Alcohol Concern, London.

Anderson, D. (ed.) (1989) *Drinking to your Health: The Allegations and the Evidence*. The Social Affairs Unit, London.

Anderson, P. (1987) 'Early intervention in general practice', in Stockwell, T. and Clement, S. (eds) *Helping the Problem Drinker: New Initiatives in Community Care*. Croom Helm, London.

Archard, P. (1975) *The Bottle Won't Leave You. A Study of Homeless Alcoholics and their Guardians*. Alcoholics Recovery Project, London.

Armor, D.J., Polich, J.M. and Stambul, H.B. (1976) *Alcoholism and Treatment*. Rand Corporation, Santa Monica.

Baggott, R. (1986) 'Alcohol politics and social policy', *Journal of Social Policy* 15(4), 467–88.

Baggott, R. (1990) *Alcohol Politics and Social Policy*. Avebury, Aldershot.

Baggott, R. (1994) *Health and Health Care in Britain*. Macmillan, London.

Baggott, R. (nd) *The Politics of Alcohol: Two Periods Compared*. Institute of Alcohol Studies, London.

Baldwin, S. (1987) 'Old wine in old bottles: Why community alcohol teams will not work', in Stockwell, T. and Clement, S. (eds) *Helping the Problem Drinker: New Initiatives in Community Care*. Croom Helm, London.

Balint, M. (1964) *The Doctor, his Patient and the Illness*. Pitman, London.

Banks, O. (1981) *Faces of Feminism. A Study of Feminism as a Social Movement*. Martin Robertson, Oxford.

Beaglehole, R. and Bonita, R. (1997) *Public Health at the Crossroads: Achievements and Prospects*. Cambridge University Press, Cambridge.

Berridge, V. (1989) 'History and addiction control: the case of alcohol' in Robinson, D., Maynard, A. and Chester, R. (eds) *Controlling Legal Addictions*. The Eugenics Society and Macmillan, London.

Berridge, V. (1990) 'The Society for the Study of Addiction 1884–1988', *British Journal of Addiction 85* special issue.

Berridge, V. (1996) *AIDS in the UK: the Making of Policy 1981–1994*. Oxford University Press, Oxford.

Berridge, V. and Thom, B. (1996) 'Research and policy: What determines the relationship', *Policy Studies* 17 (1), 23–34.

Berridge, V., Webster, C. and Walt, G. (1993) 'Mobilisation for total welfare 1948–74', in Webster, C. (ed.) *Caring for Health: History and Diversity*. Oxford University Press, Oxford.

Bien, T.H., Miller, W.R. and Tonigan, J.S. (1993) 'Brief interventions for alcohol problems: a review', *Addiction* 88, 315–36.

Bligh, J.G., Gough-Thomas, H. and Madden, J.S. (1982) 'The detection of an early case of alcohol abuse in general practice', *British Journal of Alcohol and Alcoholism* 17, 86–8.

Booth, General (1890) *In Darkest England and the Way Out*. International Headquarters of the Salvation Army, London.

Breeze, E. (1985) *Women and Drinking*. HMSO, London.

Brewers and Licensed Retailers Association (1997) *Statistical Handbook: A Compilation of Drinks Industry Statistics*. Brewing Publications Limited, London.

British Medical Association (1970) *Primary Medical Care*. Planning Unit Report No. 4. BMA House, London.

British Medical Association (1986) Report of the Board of Science and Education, *Young People and Alcohol*. BMA, London.

Brown, R.G.S. (1975) *The Management of Welfare*. Fontana, Glasgow.

Bruun, K. (1982) 'Alcohol policies in the United Kingdom', *British Journal of Addiction* 77, 435–44.

Bruun, K., Lumio, M., Mekela, K., Pan, L., Popham, R., Room, R., Schmidt, W., Skog, O., Sulkunnen, P. and Osterberg, E. (1975) *Alcohol Control Policies in Public Health Perspective*. Finnish Foundation for Alcohol Studies; WHO Regional Office for Europe; Addiction Research Foundation of Ontario, Helsinki.

Bulmer, M. (ed.) (1987) *Social Science Research and Government*. Cambridge University Press, Cambridge.

Bunton, R. (1990) 'Regulating our Favourite Drug', in Abbott, P. and Payne, G. (eds) *New Directions in the Sociology of Health*. Falmer Press, London.

Busfield, J. (1986) *Managing Madness: Changing Ideas and Practice*. Unwin Hyman, London.

Bynum, W.F. (1984) 'Alcoholism and degeneration in 19th century European medicine and psychiatry', *British Journal of Addiction*, 79, 59–70.

Caddy, G.R. and Lovibond, S.H. (1976) 'Self-regulation and discriminated aversive conditioning in the modification of alcoholics' drinking behaviour', *Behaviour Therapy* 7, 223–300.

Caldwell, D. (1975) 'The Medical Council on Alcoholism', in Caruana, S. (ed.) *Notes on Alcohol and Alcoholism*. Edsall, London.

Camberwell Council on Alcoholism (1980) *Women and Alcohol*. Tavistock, London.

Cartwright, A., Shaw, S.J. and Spratley, T.A. (1975) *Designing a Comprehensive Community Response to Problems of Alcohol Abuse*. Report to the Department of Health and Social Security by the Maudsley Alcohol Pilot Project (MAPP), The Bethlem Royal and Maudsley Hospitals, London.

Central Policy Review Staff (1982) *Alcohol Policies in the UK*. Sociologiska Institutionen, Stockholm.

Chalke, H.E. (1970) 'The role of voluntary organizations in combatting alcoholism', in Phillipson, R.V. (ed.) *Modern Trends in Drug Dependence and Alcoholism*. Butterworth, London.

Clemmons, P. (1985) 'Reflections of social thought in research on women and alcoholism', *Journal of Drug Issues* 15, 73–80.

Collins, M.N., Burns, T., van den Berk, P.A.H. and Tubman, G.F. (1990) 'A structured programme for out-patient alcohol detoxification', *British Journal of Psychiatry* 156, 871–4.

Collins, S. (ed.) (1990) *Alcohol, Social Work and Helping*. Routledge, London.

Collins, S., Ottley, G. and Wilsin, M. (1990) 'Historical perspectives and the development of community services', in Collins, S. (ed.) *Alcohol Social Work and Helping*. Routledge, London.

Committee of Enquiry into the cost of the National Health Service. Report (London, 1956). Cmnd. 663 (Guillebaud).

Committee on Labor and Public Welfare (1976) United States Senate, 94th Congress Second Session, *Examination of the Special Problems and Unmet Needs of Women Who Abuse Alcohol*. United States Government Printing Office, Washington.

Cook, C.C.H. (1988a) 'The Minnesota Model in the management of drug and alcohol dependency: miracle, method or myth? Part I. The philosophy and the programme', *British Journal of Addiction* 83, 625–34.

Cook, C.C.H. (1988b) 'The Minnesota Model in the management of drug and alcohol dependency: miracle, method or myth? Part II. Evidence and conclusions', *British Journal of Addiction* 83, 735–48.

Cook, T. (1989) *Confronting Change.* Keynote address to a seminar of alcohol workers in London on 19 July, published in GLAAS Briefing, London.

Cook, T., Gath, D. and Hensman, C. (eds) (1969) *The Drunkenness Offence.* Proceedings of an International Symposium, Pergamon Press, London.

Cook, T., Morgan, H.G. and Pollak, B. (1968) 'The Rathcoole experiment: First year at a hostel for vagrant alcoholics', *British Medical Journal* 1, 240–2.

Cook, T. and Pollak, B. (1970) *In Place of Skid Row: The First Three Years of the Rathcoole Experiment, May 1966 – May 1969.* NACRO paper, no. 4, National Association for Care and Rehabilitation of Offenders, London.

Coxall, W.N. (1985) *Parties and Pressure Groups* (second edition). Longman, London.

Culyer, A. (1994) *Supporting Research and Development in the NHS.* A report to the Minister for Health by a Research and Development Task Force. HMSO, London.

Davies, D.L. (1962) 'Normal drinking in recovered alcoholics', *Quarterly Journal of Studies on Alcohol* 23, 94–104.

Davies, D.L., Shepherd, M. and Myers, E. (1956) 'The two years prognosis of 50 alcohol addicts after treatment in hospital', *Quarterly Journal of Studies on Alcohol* 17, 485.

Davin, A. (1978) 'Imperialism and motherhood', *History Workshop*, vols 5/6, 19–65.

DAWN (1980) *Report from the First Symposium.* DAWN, London.

DAWN (1981) *Report of the First Annual Conference,* 13 November. DAWN, London.

DAWN (1984) *Survey of Facilities for Women Using Drugs (Including Alcohol).* DAWN, London.

Department of Health (1989) *Caring for People: Community Care in the Next Decade and Beyond.* Cm 849, HMSO, London.

Department of Health (1992) *The Health of the Nation: A Strategy for Health in England.* HMSO, London.

Department of Health (1993) *Alcohol and Drug Services and Community Care.* LAC (93) 2, Department of Health, London.

Department of Health (1995) *Sensible Drinking: The Report of an Inter-Departmental Working Group.* Department of Health, London.

Department of Health (1998a) *Our Healthier Nation: A Contract for Health. A Consultation Paper.* The Stationery Office, London.

Department of Health (1998b) *The New NHS: Modern, Dependable.* White Paper. The Stationery Office, London.

Department of Health and Royal College of General Practitioners (1992) *Women and Alcohol.* HMSO, London.

Department of Health and Social Security (1973) *Community Services for Alcoholics.* Circular 21/73, HMSO, London.

Department of Health and Social Security (1975) *Better Services for the Mentally Ill.* HMSO, London.

Department of Health and Social Security (1976a) *Prevention and Health: Everybody's Business.* HMSO, London.

Department of Health and Social Security (1976b) *Priorities for Health and Personal Social Services in England.* HMSO, London.

Department of Health and Social Security (1981a) *Care in Action.* HMSO, London.

Department of Health and Social Security (1981b) *Drinking Sensibly.* HMSO, London.

Department of Health and Social Security (1986) *Neighbourhood Nursing: A Focus for Care.* Report of the Community Nursing Review, (Cumberledge Report). HMSO, London.

Department of Health and Social Security (1987) *Promoting Better Health in 1987.* White Paper, Cmnd 249. HMSO, London.

Department of Health and Social Security (1988) *Community Care: Agenda for Action,* (Griffiths Report). HMSO, London.

Department of Health and Social Security Homelessness and Addiction Research Liaison Group (1994) *Strategy for Research on Alcohol Misuse.* DHSS RLG, London.

Department of Health and Social Security/National Council for Voluntary Organizations Joint Committee of Enquiry (1982) *National Voluntary Organizations and Alcohol Misuse.* DHSS, London.

Duffy, J.C. (1980) 'The association between per capita consumption of alcohol and the proportion of excessive consumers', *British Journal of Addiction* 75, 147–51.

Duffy, J.C. (1982) 'Fallacy of the distribution of alcohol consumption', *Psychological Reports* 50, 125–6.

Duffy, J.C. (1993) 'Alcohol consumption and control policy', *Journal of the Royal Statistical Society, Series A, (Statistics in Society)* 156, Part 2, 225–30.

Eckstein, H. (1958) *The English Health Service: Its Origins, Structure and Achievements.* Harvard University Press, Cambridge, MA.

Edwards, G. (1960) 'Encounter with an alcoholic', *Medical World* 94, 512.

Edwards, G. (1961) 'Early diagnosis of alcoholism', *Medical World* 95, 372.

Edwards, G. (1962a) 'Alcoholism as a public health problem in the USA', *Lancet* 1, 960–2.

Edwards, G. (1962b) 'Prevention of alcoholism', *Medical World* 96, 182.

Edwards, G. (1970) 'The status of alcoholism as a disease', in Phillipson, R.V. (ed.) *Modern Trends in Alcoholism.* Butterworth, London.

Edwards, G. (1985) 'Paradigm shift or change in ownership? The conceptual significance of D.L. Davies's classic paper', *Drug and Alcohol Dependence* 15, 19–35.

Edwards, G. (1989) 'The Addiction Research Unit of the Institute of Psychiatry, University of London – 1. The work of the unit's drug and alcohol section, and general issues', British Journal of Addiction 84, 715–25.

Edwards, G. (ed.) (1991) Addictions, Personal Influences and Scientific Movements. Transaction Publications, New Brunswick.

Edwards, G. (1992) 'Problems and dependence: the history of two dimensions', in Lader, M., Edwards, G. and Drummond, D.C. (eds) The Nature of Alcohol and Drug Related Problems. Society for the Study of Addiction Monograph 2, Oxford University Press, Oxford.

Edwards, G. (1993) 'Substance misuse and the uses of science', in Edwards, G. et al. (eds) Drugs, Alcohol and Tobacco: Making the Science and Policy Connections. Oxford Medical Publications, Oxford.

Edwards, G. (1994) 'D.L. Davies and normal drinking in recovered alcohol addicts: the genesis of a paper', Drug and Alcohol Dependence 35, 249–59.

Edwards, G. et al. (1994) Alcohol Policy and the Public Good. Oxford University Press, Oxford.

Edwards, G. and Gross, M.M. (1976) 'Alcohol dependence: Provisional description of a clinical syndrome', British Medical Journal 1, 1058.

Edwards, G., Gross, M.M., Keller, M., Moser, J. and Room, R. (1977) Alcohol Related Disabilities. WHO Offset Publication no. 32, WHO, Geneva.

Edwards, G. and Guthrie, S. (1966) 'A comparison of in-patient and out-patient treatment of alcohol dependence', Lancet 1, 467–8.

Edwards, G. and Guthrie, S. (1967) 'A controlled trial of in-patient and out-patient treatment of alcohol dependence', Lancet 1, 555–9.

Edwards, G., Hawker, A., and Hensman, C. (1966) 'Setting up a therapeutic community', Lancet 2, 1407–8.

Edwards, G., Hawker, A., Hensman, C., Peto, J. and Williamson, V. (1973) 'Alcoholics known or unknown to agencies: Epidemiological studies in a London suburb', British Journal of Psychiatry 123, 169–83.

Edwards, G., Hawker, A., Williamson, V. and Hensman, C. (1966) 'London's skid row' Lancet 1, 249–52.

Edwards G., Hensman C., Hawker A., and Hodson V. (1965) 'Who goes to AA?' Paper given at the 11th European Institute on the Prevention and Treatment of Alcoholism 14–15 June, Oslo.

Edwards, G., Williamson, V., Hawker, A., Hensman, C. and Postoyan, S. (1968) 'Census of a reception centre', British Journal of Psychiatry 114, 1030–9.

Ettorre, B. (1984) 'A study of alcoholism treatment units – 1. Treatment activities and the institutional response', Alcohol and Alcoholism 19 (3), 243–55.

Ettorre, B. (1985a) 'A study of alcoholism treatment units: some findings on links with community agencies', British Journal of Addiction 80, 181–9.

Ettorre, B. (1985b) 'A study of alcoholism treatment units: some findings on units and staff', *Alcohol and Alcoholism* 20 (4), 371–8.

Ettorre, B. (1985c) 'A study of alcoholism treatment units: Some findings on patients', *Alcohol and Alcoholism* 20 (4), 361–9.

Ettorre, B. (1992) *Women and Substance Use*. Macmillan, London.

Ettorre, E. (1997) *Women and Alcohol. A Private Pleasure or a Public Problem?* Women's Press, London.

Evans, M. (1967) 'The Cardiff plan and the Welsh Unit', *British Journal of Addiction* 62, 29–34.

Faculty of Public Health Medicine, Royal College of Physicians (1991) *Alcohol and the Public Health*. Macmillan, Basingstoke.

Falner, R.D., DuBois, D. and Adan, A. (1991) 'Community-based intervention and prevention. Conceptual underpinnings and progress toward a science of community intervention and evaluation', in Walker C.E. (ed.) *Clinical Psychology: Historical and Research Foundations*. Plenum Press, New York.

Fillmore, K.M. (1984) 'Issues in the changing drinking patterns among women in the last century', discussion paper presented at the NIAAA Women and Alcohol Conference, Seattle, Washington, May 1984.

Finlayson, G. (1990) 'A moving frontier: voluntarism and the state in British social welfare, 1941–1949', *Twentieth Century British History* 1, 183–206.

Finlayson, G. (1994) *Citizen, State, and Social Welfare in Britain 1830–1990*. Clarendon Press, Oxford.

Finn, P. (1985) 'Decriminalisation of public drunkenness: Response of the health care system', *Journal of Studies on Alcohol* 46, 7–23.

Florin, D. (1996) 'Research and Policy: The prevention of heart disease in general practice', paper given at the workshop on 'Science Speaks to Policy', London School of Hygiene and Tropical Medicine, 12–13 July, London.

Folkson, A. (1965) 'The treatment of the alcoholic', *Journal of the College of General Practitioners* 10, 151–5.

Forsyth, G. and Logan, R.F.L. (1960) *Demand for Medical Care*. Oxford.

Fox, D.M. (1990) 'Health policy and the politics of research in the United States', *Journal of Health Policy, Politics and Law* 15 (3), 481–99.

Gardiner, T. (1971) 'Alcoholism treatment in general practice', *Journal of the Royal College of General Practitioners* 21, 379–81.

Giesbrecht, N. and Pernanen, K. (1987) 'Sociological perspectives on the alcoholism treatment literature since 1940', in Galanter, M. (ed.) *Recent Developments in Alcoholism*. Plenum Press, New York.

Glanz, A. (1994) 'The fall and rise of the general practitioner', in Strang, J. and Gossop, M. (eds) *Heroin Addiction and Drug Policy: The British System*. Oxford Medical Publications, Oxford.

Glatt, M. (1955a) 'Treatment centre for alcoholics in a mental hospital', *Lancet* 1, 1316–20.

Glatt, M. (1955b) 'A treatment centre for alcoholics in a public mental hospital: Its establishment and its working', *British Journal of Addiction* 52, 55–133.

Glatt, M (1959) 'An alcoholic unit in a mental hospital', *Lancet* 1, 397–8.

Glatt, M. (1960) 'The key role of the family doctor in the rehabilitation of the alcoholic', *Journal of the College of General Practitioners* 111, 292–300.

Glatt, M. (1961a) Correspondence, *Lancet* 1, 1112–13.

Glatt, M. (1961b) Correspondence, *British Medical Journal* 1, 1246.

Glatt, M. (1961c) 'The alcoholism memorandum of the BMA and the Magistrates' Association', *British Journal of Addiction* 57, 131–3.

Glatt, M. (1961d) 'Drinking habits of English (middle class) alcoholics', *Acta Psychiatrica Scandinavia* 37–88.

Glatt, M. (1979a) 'The future of regional alcoholic units', *Lancet*, April, 814–16.

Glatt, M. (1979b) Commentary, *British Journal of Addiction* 74, 133–8.

Glatt, M. (1982) *Alcoholism*. Hodder and Stoughton, Sevenoaks.

Godber, G. (1961) 'Trends in specialisation and their effect on the practice of medicine', *British Medical Journal* 2, 843–7.

Goddard, E. (1991) *Drinking in England and Wales in the Late 1980s*. HMSO, London.

Goddard, E. and Iken, C. (1988) *Drinking in England and Wales in 1987*. HMSO, London.

Goodwin, D.W. (1991) 'Inpatient treatment of alcoholism – new life for the Minneapolis plan', *New England Journal of Medicine*, 804–6.

Grant, A.P. and Boyd, M.W.J. (1962) 'Chronic alcoholism: a survey of the incidence of chronic alcoholism in N. Ireland', *British Journal of Addiction* 58, 39.

Grant, M. (1979) Commentary, *British Journal of Addiction* 74, 119.

Gusfield, J.R. (1982) 'Deviance in the Welfare State: the alcoholism profession and the entitlements of stigma', *Research in Social Problems and Public Policy* 2, 1–20.

Gusfield, J. (1991) 'Benevolent repression: popular culture, social structure, and the control of drinking', in Barrows, S. and Room, R. (eds) *Drinking Behaviour and Belief in Modern History*. University of California Press, Oxford.

Gutzke, D. (1984) '"The cry of the children": the Edwardian medical campaign against maternal drinking', *British Journal of Addiction* 79, 71–84.

Haig, R. and Hibbert, G. (1990) 'When and where to detoxify single homeless drinkers', *British Medical Journal* 301, 848–9.

Harrison, B. (1971) *Drink and the Victorians: The Temperance Question in England*. Faber, London.

Harrison, L., Guy, P. and Sivyer, W. (1996) 'Community care policy and the future of alcohol services', in Harrison L. (ed.) *Alcohol Problems in the Community*. Routledge, London.

Heath, D.B. (1988) 'Alcohol control policies and drinking patterns: An international game of politics against science', *Journal of Substance Abuse* 1, 109–15.

Heather, N. (1987) 'DRAMS for problem drinkers: The potential of a brief intervention by general practitioners and some evidence of its effectiveness', in Stockwell, T. and Clements, S. (eds) *Helping the Problem Drinker: New Initiatives in Community Care*. Croom Helm, London.

Heather, N. (1993) 'Disulfiram treatment for alcohol problems: is it effective and, if so, why?', in Brewer, C. (ed.) *Treatment Options in Addiction Medical Management of Alcohol and Opiate Abuse*. Gaskell, London.

Heather, N. (nd) 'Application of harm reduction principles to the treatment of alcohol problems', in Heather, N., Wodak, A., Nadelmann, E. and O'Hare, P. (eds) *Psychoactive Drugs and Harm Reduction*. Whurr Publishers, London.

Heather, N. and Robertson, I. (1985) *Problem Drinking: The New Approach*. Penguin Books, Harmondsworth.

Helping Hand Organization (1976) *Report on the Female Alcoholic*. Helping Hand Organization, London.

Hensman, C., Chandler, J., Edwards, G., Hawker, A. and Williamson, V. (1968) 'Identifying abnormal drinkers: prevalence estimates by general practitioners and clergymen', *Medical Officer* 120, 215–20.

Higgins, J. (1980) 'The unfulfilled promise of policy research', *Social Policy and Administration* 14 (3), 195–208.

Hilton, M.E. (1989) 'How many alcoholics are there in the United States?', *British Journal of Addiction* 84, 459–60.

Hodgson, R.J. (1979) Commentary, *British Journal of Addiction* 74, 227–34.

Home Office (1966) *Residential Provision for Homeless Discharged Offenders: Report of the Working Party on the Place of Voluntary Service in After-Care*. HMSO, London.

Home Office (1971) *Habitual Drunken Offenders: Report of the Working Party*. HMSO, London.

Home Office (1972) *Report of the Departmental Committee on Liquor Licensing in England and Wales* (the Erroll Report). Cmnd. 5154, HMSO, London.

Home Office Standing Conference on Crime Prevention (1987) *Report of the Working Party on Young People and Alcohol*. Home Office, London.

Honigsbaum, F. (1979) *Division in British Medicine*. Kogan Page, London.

Hore, B.D. (1974) 'The community approach – fact or fantasy', *CCA Journal on Alcoholism* 3 (3), 7–11.

Hore, B. and Smith, E. (1975) 'Who goes to alcoholic units?', *British Journal of Addiction* 70, 263–70.

Hunt, G., Mellor, J. and Turner, J. (1987) 'Wretched, hatless and miserably clad: women and the inebriate reformatories from 1900–1913', paper presented at ICAA Alcohol Epidemiology Section, Aix en Provence.

James, W.P. *et al.* (1972) *Alcohol and Drug Dependence – Treatment and Rehabilitation: A Report Correlating Therapeutic Principles with Planning and Design of Facilities for the Treatment of Alcohol and Drug Dependence*. King Edward's Hospital Fund for London, London.

Jefferys, M. and Sachs, H. (1983) *Rethinking General Practice: Dilemmas in Primary Medical Care*. Tavistock, London.

Jones, K.L. and Smith, D.W. (1973) 'Recognition of the foetal alcohol syndrome in early infancy', *Lancet* 2, 999–1001.

Jones, M. (1952) *Social Psychiatry: A Study of Therapeutic Communities*. Tavistock, London.

Jones, M. (1968) *Beyond the Therapeutic Community: Social Learning and Social Psychiatry*. Yale University Press, London.

Joseph Rowntree Social Service Trust, Steering Group on Alcoholism (1960–63) *Chronic Alcoholics. A Report on the Incidence Apparent to Health Visitors and Probation Officers in Harrow, Peterborough, York, Salford and Gateshead, together with a Discussion of the Probable Magnitude of the Incidence in England and Wales*. Report prepared by G. Prys Williams, MBE, BCom, FIS.

Keller, M. (1981) 'Perspective on medicine and alcoholism', paper delivered at the National Council on Alcoholism – American Medical Society on Alcoholism Medical–Scientific luncheon, 13 April, New Orleans, Louisiana.

Kelynack, T.N. (1902) 'Alcohol and the alcoholic environment in its relation to women and children', *Medical Temperance Review* 5, 195–205.

Kendell, R.E. and Staton, M.C. (1966) 'The fate of untreated alcoholics', *Quarterly Journal of Studies on Alcohol* 27, 30–41.

Kenyon, W.H. (1970) 'Mersyside Council on Alcoholism. The development and function of a Regional Council', *CCA Journal on Alcoholism* 2 (3), 8–12.

Kessel, N., Hore, B., Makenjuola, J.D.A., Redmond, A.D., Rossall, C.J., Rees, D.W., Chand, T.G., Gordon, M. and Wallace, P.C. (1984) 'The Manchester detoxification service – description and evaluation', *Lancet* 1, 839–42.

Kingsley, S. and Mair, G. (1983) *Diverting Drunks from the Criminal Justice System*. Research and Planning Unit, Paper 21, Home Office, London.

Kitze, J.L. (1986) 'Enter every open door. The British Women's Temperance Association 1876–1900', dissertation for the Diploma in Historical Studies, University of Cambridge.

Klein, R. (1983) *The Politics of the National Health Service*. Longman, London.

Kurtz, E. (1979) *Not God: A History of Alcoholics Anonymous.* Center City, Hazelden.

Lalonde, M.A. (1974) *New Perspectives on the Health of Canadians.* Canadian Department of National Health and Welfare, Ottawa.

Leach, B. and Norris, J.L. (1977) 'Factors in the development of Alcoholics Anonymous (AA)', in Kissin, B.L. and Begleiter, H. (eds) *The Biology of Alcoholism*, vol. 5. Plenum Press, New York.

Ledermann, S. (1956) *Alcool, Alcoolisme, Alcoolisation.* Presses Universitaires de France, Paris.

Leech, K. (1990) *Care and Conflict: Leaves from a Pastoral Notebook.* Darton, Longman and Todd, London.

Levine, H. (1978) 'The discovery of addiction: Changing conceptions of habitual drunkenness in America', *Journal of Studies on Alcohol* 39, 143–74.

Levine, H. (1984) 'What is an alcohol-related problem?', *Journal of Drug Issues* 45–60.

Lewis, J. (1980) *The Politics of Motherhood: Child and Maternal Welfare in England, 1900–1939.* Croom Helm, London.

Lewis, J. (1987) *What Price Community Medicine?* Wheatsheaf, Brighton.

Lewis, J. (1991) 'The origins and development of public health in the UK', in Holland, W., Detels, R. and Knox, G. (eds) *The Oxford Textbook of Public Health vol. 1, Influences of Public Health*, Oxford University Press, Oxford.

Lewis, J. (1994) 'Providers, "consumers", the state and the delivery of health-care services in twentieth-century Britain', in Wear, A. (ed.) *Medicine in Society.* Cambridge University Press, Cambridge.

Lightfoot, P. and Orford, J. (1987) 'Helping agent's attitudes towards alcohol-related problems: situations vacant? A test and elaboration of a model', *British Journal of Addiction* 81, 749–56.

Lindstrom, L. (1992) *Managing Alcoholism: Matching Clients to Treatments.* Oxford University Press, Oxford.

Litman, G. (1975) 'Women and alcohol: facts and myths', *New Behaviour*, 24 July, 126–9.

Litman, G. and Wilson, C. (1978) 'A review of services for women alcoholics in the UK', paper presented at the 24th International Institute on the Prevention and Treatment of Alcoholism, 25 June, Zurich.

Little, R.E. and Ervin, C.H. (1984) 'Alcohol Use and Reproduction', in Wilsnack, S.C. and Beckman, L.J. (eds) *Alcohol Problems in Women.* Guilford Press, New York.

MacAndrews, C. (1969) 'On the notion that certain persons who are given to frequent drunkenness suffer from a disease called alcoholism', in Plog, S. and Edgarton, R. (eds) *Changing Perspectives in Mental Illness.* Holt, Reinhart and Winston, New York.

McLaughlin, P. (1991) 'Inebriate reformatories in Scotland: An institutional history', in Barrows, S. and Room, R. (eds) *Drinking Behaviour and Belief in Modern History*. University of California Press, Oxford.

MacLeod, R. (1967) 'The edge of hope. Social policy and chronic alcoholism, 1870–1900', *Journal of the History of Medicine and Allied Sciences* 22 (3), 215–45.

Madden, J.S. (1988) *Enterprise Rewarded: An Historical Review of the First 25 Years of the Merseyside, Lancashire and Cheshire Council on Alcoholism Ltd*. Merseyside, Lancashire and Cheshire Council on Alcoholism Ltd.

Marland, H. (1991) 'Lay and medical conceptions of medical charity during the 19th century: the case of the Huddersfield General Dispensary and Infirmary', in Barry, J. and Jones, C. (eds) *Medicine and Charity Before the Welfare State*. Routledge, London.

Maynard, A. (1989) 'The costs of addiction and the costs of control', in Robinson, D., Maynard, A. and Chester, R. (eds) *Controlling Legal Addictions*. The Eugenics Society and Macmillan, London.

Meacher, M. (1980) 'How the Mandarins rule', *New Statesman*, 5 December, 14–15.

Means, R., Smith, R., Harrison, L., Jeffers, S. and Doogan, K. (1990) *Understanding Alcohol: An Evaluation of an Education Programme*. Health Education Authority, London.

Medical Council on Alcoholism (1970) *Annual Report*. MCA, London.

Mental Health Foundation (1996) *Too Many for the Road*. Report of MHF Expert Working Group on Persistent Street Drinkers. Mental Health Foundation, London.

Merriman, B. (1960a) Correspondence, *British Medical Journal* 1, 274.

Merriman, B. (1960b) 'Outpatient treatment of the alcoholic', *Journal of the College of General Practitioners* 111, 301–5.

Merry, J. (1966) 'The "loss of control" myth', *Lancet* 1, 1257–8.

Micale, M.S. and Porter, R. (eds) (1994) *Discovering the History of Psychiatry*. Oxford University Press, Oxford.

Miller, W.R. and Hester, R.K. (1986) 'The effectiveness of alcoholism treatment: what research reveals', in Miller, W.R. and Heather, N. (eds) *Treating Addictive Behaviours: Processes of Change*. Plenum Press, New York.

Ministerial Group on Alcohol Misuse (1987–88) *First Annual Report*. MGAM, London.

Ministry of Health (1951) *On the State of the Public Health: Report of the Chief Medical Officer*. HMSO, London.

Ministry of Health (1957) *On the State of the Public Health: Report of the Chief Medical Officer*. HMSO, London.

Ministry of Health (1959) *Annual Report of the Chief Medical Officer for the Year 1959*. Cmnd 1207, HMSO, London.

Ministry of Health (1960) *Annual Report of the Chief Medical Officer for the Year 1960.* Part 2. Cmnd 1550, HMSO, London.

Ministry of Health (1962) *The Hospital Treatment of Alcoholism.* Memorandum HM (62) 43, London.

Ministry of Health (1968) *The Treatment of Alcoholism.* Memorandum HM (68) 37, London.

Moser, C.O.N. (1989) 'Gender planning in the third world: meeting practical and strategic gender needs', *World Development* 17 (11), 1799–825.

Moser, J. (1975) 'WHO and alcoholism. Alcohol problems and national health planning in programmes of the World Health Organization', in Caruana, S. (ed.) *Notes on Alcohol and Alcoholism.* Edsall, London.

Mowbray, A. and Kessel, N. (1986) 'Alcoholism and the general practitioner', *British Journal of Psychiatry* 148, 697–700.

National Council of Social Service (1961–62) *Annual Report,* no. 43, NCSS, London.

National Council of Voluntary Organisations (1985) *Problem Drinking Experiments in Detoxification.* NCVO, London.

National Council on Alcoholism (1970) *The Alcohol Explosion.* NCA, London.

National Council on Alcoholism (1978/79) *Annual Report.* NCA, London.

Nuffield Institute for Health (1993) *Brief Interventions and Alcohol Use.* Nuffield Institute for Health, no. 7, York.

O'Brien, J. and Light, R. (1993) *Promoting Responsible Retailing: Server Training Initiatives in England and Wales.* University of the West of England, Bristol.

O'Leary, B. (1979) Commentary, *British Journal of Addiction* 74, 121–4.

Orford, J. (1987) 'The need for a community response', in Stockwell, T. and Clement, S. (eds) *Helping the Problem Drinker: New Initiatives in Community Care.* Croom Helm, London.

Orford, J. and Wawman, T. (1986) *Alcohol Detoxification Services: A Review.* Prepared for the DHSS, London.

Out of Court – Alternatives for Drunken Offenders (1988) *Drunkenness Offenders: The State of the Nation.* Action on Alcohol Abuse, London.

Owen, D. (1965) *English Philanthropy 1660–1960.* Oxford University Press, Oxford.

Page, P.B. (1988) 'The origins of alcohol studies: E.M. Jellinek and the documentation of the alcohol research literature', *British Journal of Addiction* 83, 1095–103.

Parr, D. (1957) 'Alcoholism in general practice', *British Journal of Addiction* 54, 25–39.

Parry, R.A. (1971) 'Alcoholism in general practice', *Journal of the Royal College of General Practitioners* 20, 224–9.

Patterson, H.R. (1972) 'Drinking patterns in Leicestershire', *Journal of Alcoholism* 17, 118.

Plant, Martin (1982) 'Alcohol Policies in the United Kingdom', review of a book by K. Bruun, *British Journal of Addiction* 77, 435–44.

Plant, Martin (1990) *Alcohol Related Problems in High Risk Groups.* WHO Publications, Geneva.

Plant, Martin, Single, E. and Stockwell, T. (eds) (1997) *Alcohol: Minimising the Harm: What Works?* Free Association Books, London.

Plant, Moira (1985) *Women, Drinking and Pregnancy.* Tavistock, London.

Plant, Moira (1990) *Women and Alcohol: A Review of International Literature on the Use of Alcohol by Females.* WHO Publications, Geneva.

Plant, Moira (1997) *Women and Alcohol: Contemporary and Historical Perspectives.* Free Association Books, London.

Pollak, B. (1987) 'Alcohol – a balanced view', *British Journal of Addiction* 82, 715–16.

Porter, R. (1985) 'The drinking man's disease: the "pre-history" of alcoholism in Georgian Britain', *British Journal of Addiction* 80, 383–96.

Pullar-Strecker, H. (1948) Correspondence, *Lancet*, 2, 396.

Pullar-Strecker, H. (1951) Correspondence, *British Medical Journal* 2, 1342.

Pullar-Strecker, H. (1952a) 'Facts and Figures on Alcoholism', *Lancet* 1, 55.

Pullar-Strecker, H. (1952b) 'The problem of alcoholism and its treatment as it concerns or should concern the medical profession', *British Journal of Addiction* 49, 21–32.

Radzinowicz, L. and Hood, R. (1986) *A History of English Criminal Law vol. 5. The Emergence of Penal Policy in Victorian and Edwardian England.* Stevens and Sons, London.

Rein, M. and Schon, D. (1991) 'Frame-reflective policy discourse', in Wagner, P., Weiss, C.H., Wittrock, B. and Wollman, H. (eds) (1991) *Social Sciences and Modern States: National Experiences and Theoretical Crossroads.* Cambridge University Press, Cambridge.

Richardson, J.J. and Jordan, A.G. (1979) *Governing Under Pressure.* Martin Robertson, London.

Ritson, B. (1969) 'Involvement in treatment and its relation to outcome amongst alcoholics', *British Journal of Addiction* 64, 23–9.

Robinson, D. and Ettorre, B. (1980) 'Special units for common problems: Alcoholism treatment units in England and Wales', in Edwards, G. and Grant, M. (eds) *Alcohol Treatment in Transition.* Croom Helm, London.

Robinson, D., Maynard, A. and Chester, R. (eds) (1989) *Controlling Legal Addictions.* The Eugenics Society and Macmillan, London.

Robinson, D., Tether, P. and Teller, J. (1989) *Local Action on Alcohol Problems.* Tavistock, London.

Roizen, R. (1987) 'The great controlled-drinking controversy', in Galanter, M. (ed.) *Recent Developments in Alcoholism.* Plenum, New York.

Roizen, R. (1993) 'Paradigm Sidetracked: Explaining early resistance to the alcoholism paradigm at Yale's Laboratory of Applied Physiology, 1940–44', paper given at the Alcohol and Temperance History Group's International Congress on the Social History of Alcohol, Hiron College, London, Ontario.

Roizen, R. (1994) 'Norman Jolliffe, the Rockefeller Foundation and the origins of the modern alcoholism movement', *Journal of Studies on Alcohol* 55, 391–400.

Roman, P.M. (1988) *Women and Alcohol Use: A Review of the Research Literature*. US Department of Health and Human Services, Rockville, Maryland.

Room, R. (1980) 'Treatment seeking populations and larger realities', in Edwards, G. and Grant, M. (eds) *Alcoholism Treatment in Transition*. Croom Helm, London.

Room, R. (1983) 'Sociological aspects of the disease concept of alcoholism', *Research Advances in Alcohol and Drug Problems*, vol. 7, 47–91, Plenum Press, New York.

Room, R. (1984) 'The World Health Organization and alcohol control', *British Journal of Addiction* 79, 85–92.

Room, R. (1991) 'Social science research and alcohol policy making', in Roman, P. (ed.) *Alcohol: The Development of Sociological Perspectives on Use and Abuse*. Rutgers Centre of Alcohol Studies, New Brunswick, NJ.

Rose, G. (1992) *The Strategy of Preventive Medicine*. Oxford University Press, Oxford.

Rothschild, Lord (1971) 'The organization and management of government R&D', in *A Framework for Government Research and Development* Cmnd 4184, HMSO, London.

Routh, D.K. (1994) *Clinical Psychology since 1917: Science, Practice and Organization*. Plenum Press, New York.

Royal College of General Practitioners (1986) *Alcohol: A Balanced View*. Reports from General Practice 24, Royal College of General Practitioners, London.

Royal College of Physicians (1987) *A Great and Growing Evil: The Medical Consequences of Alcohol Abuse*. Tavistock, London.

Royal College of Psychiatrists (1979) *Alcohol and Alcoholism*. Tavistock, London.

Royal College of Psychiatrists (1986) *Alcohol: Our Favourite Drug*. Tavistock, London.

Rutherford, D. (1991) 'The drinks cabinet: UK alcohol policy', *Contemporary Record* 5 (3), 450–67.

Russell, M.A.H., Wilson, C., Taylor, C. and Baker, C.D. (1979) 'Effects of general practitioners' advice against smoking', *British Medical Journal* 2, 231–5.

Ruzek, S.B. (1978) *Women's Health Movement: Feminist Alternatives to Medical Control*. Praeger, New York.

Sabatier, P. (1991) 'Political science and public policy', *PS: Political Science and Politics* 24 (2), 144–6.

Scharlieb, M. (1907) 'Alcoholism in relation to women and children', in Kelynack, T.N. (ed.) *The Drink Problem in its Medico-Sociological Aspects.* Methuen, London.

Sclare, A.B. (1970) 'The female alcoholic', *British Journal of Addiction* 65 (2) 99–107.

Scottish Home and Health Department and Scottish Health Services Council (1965) *Alcoholics: Report on Health Services for their Treatment and Rehabilitation.* HMSO, Edinburgh.

Sedgwick, P. (1982) *Psycho Politics.* Pluto Press, London.

Seeley, J. (1962) 'Alcoholism is a disease: Implications for social policy', in Pittman, D. and Snyder, C. (eds) *Society, Culture and Drinking Patterns.* John Wiley, New York.

Shaw, S., Cartwright, A., Spratley, T. and Harwin, J. (1978) *Responding to Drinking Problems.* Croom Helm, London.

Shepherd, M. (1980) 'Mental Health as an integrant of primary medical care', *Journal of the Royal College of General Practitioners* 30, 657–64.

Shepherd, M., Cooper, B., Brown, A.C. *et al.* (1966) *Psychiatric Illness in General Practice.* Oxford University Press, London.

Single, E. (1997) 'The concept of harm reduction and its application to alcohol: the 6th Dorothy Black Lecture', *Drugs: Education, Prevention and Policy* 4 (1) 7–22.

Sippert, A. (1975) 'Treatment and rehabilitation: The development of national health services for the treatment and rehabilitation of alcoholics', in Caruana, S. (ed.) *Notes on Alcohol and Alcoholism.* Edsall, London.

Skog, O.J. (1981) 'Alcoholism and social policy: Are we on the right lines?', *British Journal of Addiction* 76, 315–21.

Skog, O.J. (1985) 'The collectivity of drinking cultures: A theory of the distribution of alcohol consumption', *British Journal of Addiction* 80, 83–99.

Smith, C.S. (1991) 'Networks of influence: the social sciences in the United Kingdom since the war', in Wagner, P., Weiss, C.H., Wittrock, B., Wollman, H. (eds) *Social Sciences and Modern States: National Experiences and Theoretical Crossroads.* Cambridge University Press, Cambridge.

Smith, R. (1987) *The National Politics of Alcohol Education: A Review.* Working Paper 66, School for Advanced Urban Studies, Bristol.

Society for the Study of Addiction (1999) *Tackling Alcohol Together.* Free Association Books, London.

Stallings, R.A. (1973) 'Patterns of belief in social movements: Classification from an analysis of environmental groups', *The Sociological Quarterly* 14 (Autumn), 465–80.

Standing Advisory Medical Committee (1973) *Alcoholism*. SAMC, London.

Stedward, G. (1987) 'Entry to the System: A Case Study of Women's Aid in Scotland', in Jordan, A.G. and Richardson, J.J. (eds) *Government and Pressure Groups in England*. Clarendon Press, Oxford.

Stimson, G.V. and Thom, B. (1997) 'Reducing drug and alcohol related harm', *Drugs: Education, Prevention and Policy* 4 (1), 3–6.

Stockwell, T., Bolt, E. and Hooper, J. (1986) 'Detoxification from alcohol at home managed by general practitioners', *British Medical Journal* 292, 733–6.

Stockwell, T., Bolt, R., Milner, I., Pugh, P., Young, R. and Young, I. (1990) 'Home detoxification for problem drinkers: acceptability to clients, relatives, general practitioners and outcome after 60 days', *British Journal of Addiction* 85, 61–70.

Stockwell, T. and Clement, S. (eds) (1987) *Helping the Problem Drinker: New Initiatives in Community Care*. Croom Helm, London.

Stockwell, T. and Clement, S. (1988) *Community Alcohol Teams: A Review of Studies Evaluating their Effectiveness with Special Reference to the Experience of other Community Teams*. DHSS, London.

Stockwell, T., Hawks, D., Lang, E. and Rydon, P. (1996) 'Unravelling the preventive paradox for acute alcohol problems', *Drug and Alcohol Review* 15, 7–15.

Strong, P.M. (1980) 'Doctors and dirty work – the case of alcoholism', *Sociology of Health and Illness* 2, 24–47.

Tether, P. (1987) 'Preventing alcohol related problems: the local dimension', in Stockwell, T. and Clement, S. (eds) *Helping the Problem Drinker New Initiatives in Community Care*. Croom Helm, London.

Tether, P. and Harrison, L. (1988) *Alcohol Policies, Responsibilities and Relationships in British Government*. ESRC Addiction Research Centre, University of Hull.

Thom, B., Franey, C., Foster, R., Keaney, F. and Salazar, C. (1994) *Alcohol Treatment Since 1983. A Review of the Research Literature*. Report to the Alcohol Education and Research Council. Centre for Research on Drugs and Health Behaviour, London.

Thom, B. and Tellez, C. (1986) 'A difficult business: detecting and managing alcohol problems in general practice', *British Journal of Addiction* 81, 405–18.

Thorley, A. (1979) Commentary, *British Journal of Addiction* 74, 129–32.

Tober, G. (1991) 'The background to the New Directions in the Study of Alcohol Group', in Davidson, R., Rollnick, S. and MacEwan, I. (eds) *Counselling Problem Drinkers*. Routledge, London.

Townsend, P. (1962) *Last Refuge. A Survey of Residential Institutions and Homes for the Aged in England and Wales*. Routledge, London.

Trench, S. (1969) *Bury Me in my Boots*. Hodder and Stoughton, London.

Trotter, T. (1804) *An Essay, Medical Philosophical and Chemical on Drunkenness*. London.

Tuck, M. (1980) *Alcoholism and Social Policy: Are We on the Right Lines?* Home Office Research Study No. 65 HMSO, London.

Turner, J. (1980) 'State purchase of the liquor trade in the First World War', *Historical Journal* 23, 589–615.

Vannicelli, M. and Nash, L. (1984) 'Effect of sex bias on women's studies on alcoholism', *Alcoholism: Clinical and Experimental Research* 9, 344–8.

Vogt, I. (1984) 'Defining alcohol problems as a repressive mechanism: its formative phase in imperial Germany and its strength today', *International Journal of the Addictions* 19 (5), 551–69.

Walker, C.E. (ed.) (1991) *Clinical Psychology: Historical and Research Foundations*. Plenum Press, New York.

Wallace, P., Cutler, S. and Haines, A. (1988) 'Randomised controlled trial of general practitioner intervention in patients with excessive alcohol consumption', *British Medical Journal* 297, 663–8.

Wallace, P. and Haines, A. (1985) 'Use of a questionnaire in general practice to increase the recognition of patients with excessive alcohol consumption', *British Medical Journal* 290, 1949–53.

Walt, G. (1994) *Health Policy: An Introduction to Process and Power*. Zed Books, London.

Waterson, J. (1996) 'Gender divisions and drinking problems', in Harrison, L. (ed.) *Alcohol Problems in the Community*. Routledge, London.

Webster, C. (1988) *Health Services Since the War, Volume I. Problems of Health Care The National Health Service before 1957*. HMSO, London.

Webster, C. (1996) *The Health Services Since the War Volume II. Government and Health Care: The British National Health Service 1958–1979*. The Stationery Office, London.

Webster, R. and Chappell, I. (1995) *Breaking into the System: A Guide for Alcohol Services on Partnership with the Police, Probation and Prison Service*. Alcohol Concern, London.

Weiss, C.H. (1986) 'The many meanings of research utilisation', in Bulmer, M. (ed.) *Social Science and Social Policy*. Allen and Unwin, London.

Weiss, C.H. (1991) 'Policy and Research: data, ideas or arguments', in Wagner, P., Weiss, C.H., Wittrock, B. and Wollman, H. (eds) *Social Sciences and Modern States: National Experiences and Theoretical Crossroads*. Cambridge University Press, Cambridge.

Wiener, C. (1981) *The Politics of Alcoholism: Building an Arena around a Social Problem*. Transaction Books, New Brunswick.

Wilkins, R.H. (1971) 'Care of the abnormal drinker in general practice', *Journal of the Royal College of General Practitioners* 21, 567–9.

Wilkins, R.H. (1974) *The Hidden Alcoholic in General Practice*. Elek Science, London.

Wilkins, R.H. and Hore, B. (1977) 'A general practitioner study of the estimated prevalence of alcoholism in the Greater Manchester Area', *British Journal of Addiction* 72, 198–200.

Williams, E.E. (1937) *Journal of the American Medical Association*, October, 1472–3 (queries and minor notes).

Williams, L. (1951) *The Sober Truth*. Backus, Leicester.

Williams, L. (1952) 'A review of 200 chronic alcoholics', *Lancet* 1, 787–9.

Williams, L. (1956) *Alcoholism: a Manual for Students and Practitioners*. Livingstone, Edinburgh.

Williams, G.P. and Brake, G.T. (1980) *Drink in Great Britain 1900–1979*. Edsall, London.

Wilson, P. (1980) *Drinking in England and Wales*. HMSO, London.

Wolfenden Committee (1978) *The Future of Voluntary Organizations*. Report of the Wolfenden Committee. Croom Helm, London.

World Health Organization (1951) *Report on the First Session of the Alcoholism Subcommittee*. Expert Committee on Mental Health, Technical Report Series No. 42, WHO, Geneva.

World Health Organization (1952) *Alcoholism Subcommittee Second Report*. Expert Committee on Mental Health, Technical Report Series No. 48, WHO, Geneva.

World Health Organization (1954) *Expert Committee on Alcohol First Report*. Expert Committee on Alcohol, Technical Report Series No. 84, WHO, Geneva.

World Health Organization (1955) *Alcohol and Alcoholism*. Report of an Expert Committee, Technical Report Series No. 94, WHO, Geneva.

World Health Organization (1967) *Services for the Prevention and Treatment of Dependence on Alcohol and Other Drugs*. Expert Committee on Mental Health, Technical Report Series No. 363, WHO, Geneva.

World Health Organization (1979) *International Classification of Diseases* (9th revision), WHO, Geneva.

World Health Organization (1980) *Problems Related to Alcohol Consumption*. Expert Committee on Mental Health, Technical Report Series No. 650, WHO, Geneva.

Younghusband, E. (1959) *Report of the Working Party on Social Workers in the Local Authority and Welfare Services*. HMSO, London.

Zacune, J. and Hensman, C. (1971) *Drugs, Alcohol and Tobacco in Britain: The Problems and the Response*. Heinemann Medical Books, London.

Index

Index compiled by Sue Carlton